JUST THE FACTS, MA'AM

a writer's guide to investigators
and investigation techniques

THE HOWDUNIT SERIES

JUST THE FACTS, MA'AM

a writer's guide to investigators and investigation techniques

Greg Fallis

WRITER'S DIGEST BOOKS
CINCINNATI, OHIO

Visit our Web site at www.writersdigest.com for information on more resources for writers.

To receive a free biweekly E-mail newsletter delivering tips and updates about writing and about Writer's Digest products, send an E-mail with "Subscribe Newsletter" in the body of the message to newsletter-request@writersdigest .com, or register directly at our Web site at www.writersdigest.com.

02 01 00 99 98   5 4 3 2 1

Library of Congress Cataloging-in-Publication Data

Fallis, Greg
    Just the facts, ma'am / by Greg Fallis.—1st. ed.
      p. cm.—(The Howdunit series)
    Includes bibliographical references and index.
    ISBN 0-89879-823-X (pbk.: alk. paper)
    1. Detective and mystery stories—Authorship. 2. Private investigators—handbooks, manuals, etc. 3. Criminal investigation—Handbooks, manuals, etc. I. Title. II. Series.
PN3377.5.D4F35   1998
808.3'872—dc21   98-38642
                                           CIP

Edited by Jack Heffron
Production edited by Bob Beckstead
Designed by Mary Barnes Clark
Cover illustration by Chris Spollen

Acknowledgment

My thanks to Jeanne F., Holly C., Lillian Dote and Jean L. The Irish have a saying (of course they do; they've a saying for everything): *Aithnítear cara i cruatan*, "In hardship a friend is recognized." These folks have been friends indeed—and that leads me to another Irish saying: *Sin a bhuil, tá sé in am deoch*, "That's all, it's time for a drink."

And thanks as well to Jack Heffron for his patience and support.

Table of Contents

PROLOGUE

We are writers. We may have other roles as well—teacher, bartender, computer programmer, mother—but down at the bone we are writers. We write for different reasons: Some of us feel compelled to write; some of us write to express ourselves; some write to touch others; some just want to make a buck without breaking a sweat. Our motives for writing are of less consequence than the fact that we take the risk of putting words on paper. What matters is that we write.

We are writers who have chosen to practice our craft within the constraints of a literary genre—mystery and detective fiction. Regardless of what some critics say, there is no shame in working within a genre. Good writing is hard work whether you're writing a scholarly treatise, a mainstream novel or a mystery. There are constraints and limitations in every discipline. Some painters choose to work in watercolors; some photographers elect to work in black and white; some cabinetmakers rely on Japanese hand tools. Like them we have *chosen* our field, not been consigned to it. We are mystery writers by choice.

As writers we have certain obligations to our readers. Above all, we owe them a good story. A good story requires effort, and we have an obligation to our readers to make that effort. Part of that effort is research.

Readers of mystery and detective fiction are a singularly persnickety lot. They demand honesty and accuracy, and they are quite vocal about it. If you give them work that is dishonest or inaccurate, they will let you know. But the fact that mystery readers are demanding isn't the only reason for doing research. We do research out of respect for ourselves and for our craft. We do research because we want to be good writers.

This book is intended to help you be honest and accurate in your writing. I will explain how and why investigators—both public and private—do some of the things they do. You should not accept everything in this book as gospel—as the *only* way investigators work. There is tremendous variety in how detectives do their work. This book will open a window for you to peek at their work. But at the heel of the hunt, *you* have to do the really hard work: You have to write.

O N E

THE SKILLED INVESTIGATOR

Just the facts, ma'am. This was the mantra of Joe Friday, the Bland Buddha of the LAPD. Week after week Sergeant Friday and his stone-faced sidekick, relying on this mantra, kept the neighborhoods of Los Angeles safe and secure (on television, at least). It was a minimalist approach to detective work—a cheap suit, a flat affect and stolid persistence. Tell me what I need to know and *only* what I need to know, nothing more, nothing less.

Just the facts, ma'am. It's a good line. But let's face it, it's not good detective work. A good investigator wants—*needs*—to know more than just the facts; the facts don't always tell the whole story. Good detectives understand this. So do good writers.

Good detectives have a lot in common with good writers. It's been said that all novels, down at the bone, are mysteries. Through plot and characterization writers try to explore elemental aspects of the human condition. Holden Caulfield, Hannibal Lecter, Little Lord Fauntleroy, Sam Spade—each of these characters is trying to make sense of an often confusing world, trying to find some common connecting link between the seemingly disparate patterns of life around him.

That's what good detectives do as well—try to create a logical and plausible narrative out of seemingly disparate facts. It's not an easy thing to do. In fact, it can be damned hard work. Ask any detective. Ask any writer.

Uncovering the Origins of Detectives

It's worthwhile to note that the word *detect* comes from the old Latin term *tegere*, which means "to cover." Combine the term with the negative prefix de- and you have a word meaning to uncover. To de-tect, therefore is to un-cover.

It makes a great deal of sense, doesn't it.

As a writer of detective fiction, you have to make your characters, and especially your protagonist, convincing. They have to bear at least some semblance to reality. In many ways it doesn't matter whether your protagonist is good or evil, male or female, white or black, gay or straight, upper class, lower class or working class. It does matter that your protagonist has at least some of the qualities of a good investigator.

In this chapter we'll look at the qualities and skills of a good detective. In later chapters we'll discuss how those qualities and skills are attained and how they are used.

The Qualities of a Good Investigator

Good detectives are just like everybody else—only more so. Fictional detectives are often depicted as somehow different, apart from ordinary folks. That's fine. People who willingly poke their noses into the most intimate and private aspects of the lives and affairs of other people *are* probably qualitatively different from "normal" folks. But good detectives are rarely otherworldly. To be a good detective—that is, to look into the hearts and minds of others, to understand and not shy away—you have to be very, very human.

Trying to delineate the attributes of a good investigator is like shoveling smoke. It's a task that's both elusive and illusive, and in many ways it's a waste of time. Good detectives often violate all the expectations. In general, though, the qualities of a good detective can be said to fall into four broad categories:

- physical
- social
- intellectual
- emotional

These aren't mutually exclusive categories; there are no clear boundaries between them. They bleed into each other.

Physical Qualities

Of all the attributes of a good detective, the physical qualities are the least important. Even in fiction and film, where protagonists almost universally meet the conventional standards of health and attractiveness, we find detectives who are obese, disabled, ugly or somehow incapacitated. The truth is you don't need to be a perfect physical specimen to do good detective work.

By and large, however, it helps for a good detective to be in reasonably good shape. During my own PI career I've had to climb trees, tote all manner of heavy objects, shimmy down a tiny crawl space into a cellar, climb into dumpsters, dig into landfills, rummage through the remains of a collapsed burnt building, tail a speed walker and occasionally work thirty-six hours or more without a break. None of that requires the strength of a weight lifter or the agility of a gymnast, but it does require a certain level of fitness.

Perhaps the most critical physical attribute of a good detective is stamina—the vitality to endure, to keep going through weariness, through boredom, through hunger, through pain. Not the pain of a gunshot wound—that's a TV injury—but the chronic knee or back pain that comes from spending hours outside on a cold, wet surveillance or combing through old files and records. Stamina is different from determination; stamina is what allows you to satisfy your determination.

It ain't sexy, but reality rarely is.

Social Qualities

Detectives are often portrayed in fiction as misanthropic loners, unable—or unwilling—to fit in and get along with the rest of society. That may make for an interesting character study, but it

Hard Work

I know a private detective who is an ex-police officer and a former member of a special forces unit in Vietnam. While carrying sixty-five pounds of equipment he's been chased through steamy jungles by people intent on killing him. Yet he insists the hardest work he's ever done in his entire life involved spending a twenty-hour period going through boxes of canceled checks, comparing them to old accounts payable records. There was no adrenaline rush to keep him going, no band of brothers to encourage and motivate him, no larger cause to inspire him—nothing but a long, dull job that needed to be done.

doesn't appear to have much basis in reality. The best detectives are those who have an intuitive understanding of social interaction. They're people who can fit in anywhere and get along with anybody. They may choose not to, but they can if they want. And when they choose not to get along, there's usually a good reason (there will be more on this later in this chapter and in chapter four "Interrogation and Interviewing").

Despite the advent of the computer, little traditional detective work is done in social isolation. All detective work, whether done by a police detective or private investigator, whether done on the street on in cyberspace, is grounded in the gathering of information. The vast majority of information gathering done by detectives involves social interaction—getting people to give them the information they need. Even when the desired information can be found in file drawers, dusty records or computer databases, social interaction can be crucial. The investigator may have to convince some recalcitrant clerk to give access to those file drawers and records. That takes good social skills.

When I say social skills I don't mean knowing which is the proper fork to use for the shrimp or the appropriate mode of address for speaking to a cardinal of the church (although that sort of knowledge is handy as well; you may find yourself in a situation in which your credibility depends on using the correct fork). I'm talking about the ability to quickly establish a rapport with others, to understand others, to communicate effectively and to move gracefully through almost any social situation.

Social skills, for a detective, include:

- an awareness of the social graces
- the ability to quickly establish a rapport
- good listening skills
- appropriate speaking skills
- understanding body language

Awareness of the Social Graces

You don't often see *social graces* and *detective* in the same sentence. For some reason, fictional detectives are often rude and offensive in their interactions with others. In the same way that good detectives are able to get along with just about anybody, they should also be able to move in many levels of society without attracting attention. That means they need to be aware of the social graces.

The social graces are those skills that allow a person to fit in with a certain culture. For example, dining etiquette at a biker picnic is radically different from the rules for dining alfresco at a benefit for the Museum of Modern Art. Acceptable behavior in an Episcopal church would be out of place among foot-washing Baptists. The social graces of one culture aren't any better or any worse than those of another culture; they're just different. Good detectives make an effort to be aware of the social graces of the cultures they're dealing with.

A good detective may not always follow the rules of a given situation but should be aware of them. Failure to comply with the social graces should be a conscious choice, not a result of ignorance. Martha Stewart would probably be a good detective; she always seems to know how to behave in any social circumstance.

Ability to Quickly Establish a Rapport

Although it's important for both police and private investigators (to understand the distinction between police and private investigators, see chapter two) to be able to quickly establish a rapport with just about anybody, this skill is more critical for PIs. Police agents have an advantage inherent in their official status. They can compel a certain level of cooperation. Private investigators can't. PIs may try to scam the naive and unsuspecting into *thinking* they have some legitimate authority, but legally they have no more authority than any other private citizen (more on this in chapter two).

Why do investigators need to be able to establish a rapport with a stranger, and to establish it quickly? Because people are at the heart of most criminal and civil investigation. People give you information; if they can't actually give it to you, they can give you access to it. And information is the investigator's stock in trade.

Unfortunately, few detectives—private or public—receive any worthwhile training in how to establish a rapport. The easiest way to build a harmonious relationship is simply to show an interest (preferably a genuine interest) in the other person. Men, by and large, aren't terribly good at this. An unfortunate proportion of men think establishing a rapport requires nothing more than a clap on the shoulder, a grin and the question, "Hey, how 'bout those Red Sox?"

Good Listening Skills

Among those of us who have done detective work, this is one of the biggest criticisms of fictional detectives. They just don't listen. Even worse, they constantly interrupt the people they're interviewing—with threats, with demands, with wisecracks, with more questions. Here is a universal truth of detective work: If you don't listen, you won't hear.

The fact is, people like to talk. Even people who are shy and retiring will, if encouraged and given a sympathetic ear, often chatter like magpies. And when people talk, they reveal information, even if they don't mean to. They can't help it. People have to be trained, either formally or through experience, to be guarded when they talk. Sadly, most people are accustomed to the fact that nobody is really paying attention when they talk, so when encouraged to talk freely, they often let things slip unintentionally.

Oddly enough, a lot of people also have to be trained to listen. Again, women tend to demonstrate better listening skills than men. A lot of male detectives have to be trained to overcome their socialization, to learn to listen instead of talking. It's not easy for them. But good detectives listen. That's how they get results.

I'll discuss these listening skills in more detail in the chapter on interrogation and interviewing.

Appropriate Speaking Skills

A good investigator has to be fluent in the language of social class. Bankers speak a form of English different from that of gas station attendants. A good detective has the ability to shift between languages, to speak like a banker to a banker and like a gas station attendant to a gas station attendant. Just as important, a good detective knows when to speak like a gas station attendant to a banker or a banker to a gas station attendant. Speaking in the language of the appropriate social class can help establish a rapport; speaking in the language of an inappropriate social class can intimidate. It isn't pretty and it isn't nice, but intimidation, used sparingly, can be an important tool for the investigator (see chapter four).

Understanding Body Language

We communicate to each other in a variety of nonverbal ways. Although this topic will be discussed in more detail in chapter four, it's important to remind the writer that a good investigator is necessarily a competent interpreter of body language. Too often mystery writers tend to focus on the more subtle and nuanced aspects of body language—the flutter of an eyelid, the minute twitch of the lip, the all-but-invisible dilation of a pupil. Let's face it, those things are difficult to see. We forget that gross body language (I mean large, not disgusting) can often give us the same information. When a suspect is jerking around like a gaffed tuna, we don't need a fluttering eyelid to tell us to pay attention.

Intellectual Qualities

Good detectives are smart. A person of average or below average intelligence can do much of what a good investigator can do, but a really good investigator has to be creative, has to be able to adapt to rapidly changing situations, has to be able to interpret subtle interpersonal cues. Detective work ain't rocket science, but it ain't no disco either. A good detective needs:

- street sense
- intense curiosity
- a fund of eclectic information
- analytic reasoning

We all have these qualities to some extent. Most of us have them to a degree much greater than we realize. Good investigators, like good writers, are simply more aware of these qualities and put them to use.

Street Sense

This is a term that's often mentioned but rarely defined. There's a good reason for that failure. Street sense is like art in that it's not only difficult to define, it's difficult to describe.

Having said that, let me define and describe street sense. In general, street sense is an intuitive understanding of the way the urban world works and how people move through it. It's an awareness based on an often subconscious process of observation. We're often not aware of our street sense until it issues some sort of warning. Street sense is what tells a good detective what is happening even when there are no overt, observable indications of it.

Street sense, like a lot of intuitive processes, can be cultivated. People's street sense gets sharper the more time they spend on the street. All it requires is acute attention to detail.

You can sharpen your street sense. How? By spending time out there. This should be a natural activity for writers. Get out in the world and pay attention. Take walks—they're good for you and they expose you to people. Pay attention to others—who they are, what they're doing, how they carry themselves. Try to explain their behavior. Go to a coffee shop or a tavern. Observe the way the customers interact with each other. Watch how they treat the staff. Try to identify the regulars. Go back to the same tavern or coffeehouse at different times of day and night. See if the customers are different. You might feel silly, but even that can be instructive; you'll notice how your own discomfort can spark the street sense of those around you.

Intense Curiosity

Every good detective I've met—and every good writer—is intensely curious. Each has a deep, abiding desire to know and

Street Sense

I recently had a friend visit me in New York City. It was his first time in New York. We spent an evening out catching up on old times and wandering around the city. As we passed through one of the seamier areas of the city, we encountered an older man who appeared to be wonderfully intoxicated. Not incoherently drunk, not angrily drunk, not offensively drunk; this man looked to be expansively drunk, cheerful, in love with life and the world and everybody in it. He stumbled a bit stepping off a curb, and my friend put a hand out to steady the man. The drunk greeted my friend as if they were old army buddies.

Of course, the man wasn't that drunk at all. He may have been entirely sober. He was just looking for a friendly, open, out-of-town face—somebody he could talk to, somebody he could lean on, somebody whose pocket he could pick. Following half a block behind was another man, a respectable-looking fellow. After our "intoxicated" acquaintance had picked my friend's pocket, the thief had stumbled into the respectable-looking fellow and handed off my friend's wallet.

My friend had enough street sense to be cautious, but not enough to fully understand what was going on. Everybody has some street sense, but in order to keep it sharp, you have to spend time on the street.

understand. To know and understand what? Anything and everything. How long does it take cement to set? When were eyeglasses invented? Why do people of different cultures have different notions of personal space?

Curiosity is a fine thing, but let's face it, intense curiosity is not always an attractive quality. Intensely curious people tend to ask nosy questions—rude, interfering, highly personal questions. Most folks don't understand that powerful need to know and may not appreciate the drive behind it.

Having an intense curiosity doesn't mean good detectives necessarily give in to it. In fact, most good detectives, especially private investigators, must learn to control their curiosity in regard to their cases. PIs understand there are occasionally questions that shouldn't be asked, answers that shouldn't be sought. Homicide investigators would sometimes prefer not to know what their key witness was doing on that corner at that hour of the night ("I'm sure you had a good reason to be there, and if you're called on to testify I have no doubt you'll be able to tell us what that good reason was"). Criminal defense investigators will rarely ask their clients if they are guilty of the crimes with which they are charged; instead they'll ask something vague ("What can you tell me about what happened? What can you tell me that will help your case?").

At times detectives can better serve their clients or the public by not seeking all the answers. This is an unnatural act for detectives—just as it is for writers—but at times it needs to be done.

A Fund of Eclectic Information

One product of an intense curiosity is the acquisition of a fund of eclectic information. By eclectic information I'm talking about those bits of knowledge you collect over the years, knowledge that rarely has any practical use. Who recorded the *Theme From Shaft*, for example, or which flowers to plant near the garden to keep the bugs away or how to patch a bicycle tire. Writers and detectives are probably the only people in the world who routinely have use for such information.

How is this eclectic information useful? It can give the investigator a way to worm into the good graces of another person, a person who has something—evidence or information—the investigator wants. Because people are so diverse and have such diverse interests, it's impossible to know what sort of information may be important. But good investigators are generalists; they know a little bit about everything.

Good detectives and good writers build on their funds of eclectic knowledge. They read a lot, and they read everything— science, historical novels, ingredient labels, anything with words in a row. They don't read simply to increase their funds of eclectic information; they read because they're curious. Good detectives also listen when other folks talk. Everybody, even the dullest person, has some worthwhile information to offer. And who knows, someday it may be critically important to be able to discuss the rules of bocce ball.

The Way to a Doctor's Heart . . .

You never know what sort of information will come in handy. One time I needed to interview an ER doctor in a small hospital in New Hampshire. He was busy when I arrived, treating a young girl who had hurt herself somehow. As I waited I listened to him talk to the girl. I was happy to hear he had a pleasant Southern accent. Having lived a chunk of my formative years in the Deep South, I was determined to use that connection to establish a quick rapport. As he was finishing with the girl I heard him call her "dawahlin'," which is how natives of New Orleans mispronounce 'darling.' New Orleans means food, and that means gumbo, and real gumbo needs filé, which is a powder made from ground sassafras root. I happened to know where to find possibly the only store in all of New Hampshire where a person could find both filé and Zatarain's Crab Boil.

As soon as I had a chance to talk to the doctor the first thing I did, after identifying myself, was to ask for an antacid tablet. I'd made up a big ole pot of crab and filé gumbo, I told him, and was suffering from it. The man smiled like he was meeting the illegitimate child of royalty. He might have talked to me anyway, but I'm convinced he told me more than he would have ordinarily told a private detective, and told it more enthusiastically. And I was happy to tell him where he could buy filé. Southern folk up in the land of Yankees need to stick together.

Analytic Reasoning

Detectives, both private and public, solve puzzles. That's the nature of investigative work: trying to figure out what happened (not necessarily why it happened, but just what the hell actually took place). Good detectives can take bits of information that appear unconnected and incompatible and somehow fit them together into a plausible and logical order. This requires an agile mind, a mind capable of seeing situations and facts from several different points of view, a mind able to interpret those situations and facts objectively.

Hippocrates wrote, a long, long time ago: "Overlook nothing. Combine contradictory observations." He was writing for ancient Greek physicians on the importance of meticulous observation for diagnosis, but the principle is the same. Not all puzzles can be solved, of course, but those that can be are best approached calmly and rationally.

Emotional Qualities

Detective work is emotionally demanding. Detectives usually only get involved in situations after somebody's life has gone all to hell.

The emotional qualities required of good detectives fall into two categories: those that are a function of the job (occupational demands) and those that are a result of the job (personal demands).

Occupational Demands

In order to remain effective and cope with the occupational demands, a good detective needs the following:

- a balanced professional distance
- tenacity
- a high tolerance for stress and ambiguity
- a strong sense of self

Balanced Professional Distance

Complete objectivity is impossible and probably emotionally unhealthy. It's inconceivable, for example, that a detective would feel entirely objective about a case involving the sexual murder of a child. This is true whether you're trying to convict the offender or defend him.

Still, it's imperative for a good detective to be able to evaluate data and information with as much objectivity as possible. You can't do the job in a satisfactory manner if you're outraged, disgusted, frightened or under the sway of any powerful emotion. This doesn't mean good detectives don't feel powerful emotions; it simply means they learn to control them, to put them into a box while they're on the job. That sort of emotional detachment probably isn't entirely healthy either, but it's the only way to be effective.

I was once supervising a new criminal defense investigator, accompanying her on her first major felony case. It probably wasn't the best case to inflict on a new PI. It was a rape case. The defendant was accused of four counts of rape—three counts against young boys, one against a young girl. The defendant, a member of a group of pedophiles called NAMBLA (North American Man/Boy Love Association), didn't think of the counts against the young boys as rape. To him they were incidents of seduction. And, indeed, there was plenty of evidence that the young boys were willing participants (as willing as twelve- and thirteen-year-old boys can be). The young girl, however, had been drugged and raped anally. The new investigator and I spent three months deeply immersed in a culture of pedophiles. Based on the evidence we discovered (evidence of police misconduct), three of the four charges against the defendant were dismissed. Fortunately, the fourth charge stuck and the defendant was convicted. But the new investigator never quite got over the ugliness of the case. A few months after the case ended she resigned and found more tolerable employment.

In order to do the work, a detective needs to be able to maintain a professional distance from some aspects of the work.

Tenacity

When you find your trail has led you to a brick wall, you have only three choices: You can give up and walk away (a perfectly reasonable choice), you can try to find some way to sneak around or over it (my personal favorite), or you can just keep pounding your head against the wall until you bust through. Of the three choices, the only one that is unacceptable to a good detective is the first.

Good detectives are stubborn. They don't give up easily. They continue to try long after any reasonable person would give up. Part of this, I suppose, is pride or arrogance—an unwillingness to admit defeat. Part of it is experience: You know that if you worry at a knot long enough it will probably come undone. Probably.

It's important, however, to be alert to the line between tenacity and foolish persistence. A good detective persists as long as there's a reasonable chance of success, then just a bit longer. And then maybe just a little bit longer than that. And then puts the problem aside. A good detective doesn't give up; he just puts the problem to the side and gets on with the next problem, the next case. The problem may continue to bother him for a while, maybe a long while, but he can't let it interfere with the next case.

High Tolerance for Stress and Ambiguity

Detective work is inherently stressful. As noted earlier, detectives only get involved when people are in trouble, when lives are falling apart. Good detectives, however, are generally islands of calm effectiveness in a sea of crisis, tension and anxiety. They appear to be less vulnerable to the effects of stress than are "normal" people.

Even when they feel the tension and anxiety, good detectives learn to act as though they aren't affected. It may be a pose, but it serves a purpose. If you act calm, other folks calm down. It makes them feel everything is under control. In fact, the entire combustible world may be about to burst into flame, but good detectives will act as though they are impervious to fire, and besides, a good blaze is exactly what they've been waiting for.

One major source of stress is ambiguity. Detectives are often involved in situations they don't fully understand and over which they have limited control. Many critical decisions have to be made with woefully inadequate information. These are constant threads in detective work.

Not only are detectives faced with ambiguity in their daily work, they are often denied the satisfaction of resolution. Here's one significant difference between real life and fiction: Real life doesn't have to make sense. In traditional mystery and detective fiction all, or most, of the threads come together into a coherent resolution. At the end we all nod and say, "Yes, of course, that's what happened." It's very gratifying.

In real life, however, an investigator may never really know what took place. This is especially frustrating considering good detectives also have intense curiosity. Good detectives want to know, but they must live with the knowledge that they probably never will.

Fifteen years ago I had a client charged with a singularly odd and violent murder. Initially I assumed he was guilty (it's usually a safe assumption; most of the folks who are accused of crimes are guilty of something), but as the investigation progressed I changed my mind. Perhaps he was innocent. Perhaps. There was, I thought, as much evidence of his innocence as his guilt. The jury felt the same way; there was enough reasonable doubt that they refused to convict him. It's been a decade and a half, and I still wonder if justice was served.

Strong Sense of Self

Good detectives have a good grasp on who they are. This is important because there are times when detectives have to present themselves as something other than what they are. Sometimes the job may demand you appear to be stupid, or racist, or perverse. And you may be required to appear that way in public. This is almost impossible to do—unless you have a strong sense of who you really are. Sometimes it's difficult to do even then.

Crossing the Line

One of the most difficult things I ever did as a private investigator was to cross a picket line. My father was a classic union-supporting Democrat (one who would vote for a yellow dog if it was on the Democratic ticket). Crossing a picket line was anathema to me, even though I would be crossing it for a good cause. I was, after all, working for the attorney of one of the strikers who had been assaulted by some replacement workers. I even had friends who worked at the plant and occasionally stood on the picket line.

As I drove through the picket line and into the factory gate, the strikers shouted at me. They called me scab, they shouted obscenities, they spit on my car. And there was nothing I could say or do. If I had stopped at the picket line to explain myself, I would have risked alienating the witnesses I was going to interview.

The only thing that kept me going through that picket line and into that gate was my sense of myself. I knew I was doing the right thing for the right reasons, even if nobody else knew it. But it was cold comfort.

Personal Demands

Here's an ugly fact: All detectives—police and private—earn their livings off the suffering of other people. It's difficult to face that level of pain and suffering on a daily basis. Investigative work is emotionally tough, and all those who engage in it pay a price.

How do they cope with this ugliness? Some drink too much, some become hard and cruel, many become control freaks and most develop some level of cynicism. And nearly all acquire a dark and wickedly sharp sense of humor. Detectives may be the funniest people I know, and yet you rarely hear much laughter around them.

You've Got to Be Fast . . .

I still recall the day I was waiting to interview a detective at a midsize police department in New England. As I sat there I couldn't help overhearing a couple of detectives doing riffs on a recent murder case. A young man had died after being shot in the very top of the head with a 9mm. One detective asked the other how it had happened.

"We think he was trying to duck."

"A 9mm? You got to be *fast* to duck a nine. A .38, now, you can get under those bad boys. But you got to be Carl Lewis to duck a nine."

"Could be he was trying for a head butt."

They did at least three minutes on this before one wandered away, and every minute was worth the price of admission to a comedy club. And yet nobody laughed. Nobody even cracked a smile.

I've always regretted not writing it all down the moment I got in my car. And I've waited for years for the chance to use it. Writing it down, though, takes some of the humor out of it. I guess you had to be there.

These are all techniques of distance, of pushing the ugliness away long enough to do the job. But the ugliness never really goes away, and everybody who deals with it regularly gets scarred. When the scars become too thick, feeling ceases. In a short story, Dashiell Hammett offers the following description of the manager of a detective agency: ". . . his gentle eyes behind gold spectacles and his mild smile, hiding the fact that fifty years of sleuthing had left him without any feelings at all on any subject."

This, in my opinion, is the greatest danger of detective work. It isn't getting beat up or shot at; it's losing your humanity. And it's so easy to do. The habit of packing away emotions that interfere with the job can bleed over into detectives' personal lives, leaving them feeling nothing but a vague sense of loathing—for the frailities of other people and, sometimes, for themselves.

Conclusion

Just the facts, ma'am. We've discussed the qualities of a good detective. These qualities are shared by most public and private detectives (in the following chapter we'll look at the distinctions between the two). But none of this is written in stone. Detectives are a diverse lot, and not all good detectives share the same qualities.

Of the four qualities of a good detective (physical, social, intellectual and emotional), I suspect the most important are the social qualities. What is the main implication of this? Given that the majority of detectives are men, it means the best detectives are those who are, dare I say it, in touch with their feminine sides. I hate to indulge in generalizations, but the fact is that men are socialized in such a way that their social skills are impaired. One of the most remarkable feats of detective work I've ever seen was performed by a woman I took to a party. The party mainly included my friends, most of whom she'd never met and none of whom she knew well. By the end of the party she knew more personal information about my friends than I did. And she did it just by being genuinely interested in them, making them feel at ease and listening to what they had to say.

Was Joe Friday a good detective? He certainly had some of the characteristics of one. True, his style was distinguished more by a certain bovine persistence than by cleverness. True, nobody is going to suggest Joe Friday was in touch with his feminine side. But he got the job done, and in the end that's the true mark of a good detective. However, Joe Friday was a television detective. All television detectives, even the most ridiculous ones, somehow get the job done. Real life is infinitely more complicated.

In real life, just the facts just ain't enough.

INVESTIGATORS—PUBLIC AND PRIVATE

Police detectives and private investigators—surely these are the staple character types found in detective fiction (I'm purposely omitting amateur sleuths because, well, they're amateurs and not professional investigators). Inspector Alleyn, Sam Spade, Edward X. Delaney, Kinsey Millhone. We all know them.

But what distinguishes a police investigator from a private investigator? How are they different? In what ways are they similar to each other? It's alarming how many beginning writers, and even some seasoned writers, remain ignorant of the distinctions between the two.

In the United States we have what amounts to dual investigative systems, one that serves the public good and one that serves private need. Sometimes these systems cooperate, sometimes they compete. Sometimes the goals of these two systems complement each other; sometimes they are in conflict.

The system that serves the public good, obviously, includes a wide variety of policing agencies, from your local police department to the Federal Bureau of Investigation. The services of the public investigative system, in theory, are available to everybody.

They're free. The police cannot directly charge the public for their work.

The system that serves private needs includes private security companies, private investigative agencies, bail recovery agents (bounty hunters), process servers, loan default agents (also known as repo men) and a wide variety of other areas of expertise. Their services are generally for sale to the highest bidder.

Although the two branches have some things in common (for example, they often recruit their employees from the same pool; over half of the licensed private investigators have law enforcement experience), they are also radically different. Each approaches investigative work differently, and they differ in three key ways:

- clientele

- autonomy

- functions

In this chapter we will examine both policing agencies and the private security industry, concentrating on their investigative aspects.

Public Investigators

We have a tendency, when we think of public investigators, to picture municipal police detectives. In truth, public investigators are a much more diverse group. Still, all public investigators have some things in common.

Clientele

Public investigators work, obviously, for the public—for you and me and every other citizen. In fact, even noncitizens have the right to call on the services of public investigators. In theory we are all guaranteed equal access and equal protection under the law.

Reality, however, demonstrates that the theory isn't always applied. Research consistently shows that some people receive preferential treatment. For example, when the victim of a crime is white and at least upper middle class, police investigators tend to give better service. Why? Those are the folks who generally run the government (at the local level, at the state level and at the federal level). It's the people who have the power who usually get the best treatment.

Autonomy

The important implication of the preceding paragraph is the following fact: Public investigators cannot refuse a case. They don't have a great deal to say in regard to what cases they investigate. If a crime has been committed, the police have an obligation to investigate it. Every crime, under all circumstances, regardless of the offender or the victim.

Again, that's the theory. The truth, as always, is more complex. There are two reasons the theory crashes when held up to real life. We've already discussed one: Not all "clients" are treated the same. While public investigators may have a duty to investigate all crimes equally, we know certain groups of people will receive better service. We know that a murdered Latina prostitute will not get the same quality of investigation that a Park Avenue matron will receive. It's ugly, but it's reality.

The second reason not all crimes are treated equally is what criminologists refer to as the Myth of Full Enforcement. The fact is the police not only *don't* enforce all laws equally all the time, they *can't* enforce all laws equally all the time. There are too many laws, too many violations of those laws and too few police officers. Even if we wanted full enforcement, it would be impossible. And, let's tell the truth here, we don't really want full enforcement. What most folks really want is to see the laws that are important to them to be enforced against those identified as bad guys. It's not very consistent of us, but there it is.

Functions

In general, public policing agencies have three primary functions:

1. order maintenance

2. crime prevention

3. criminal investigation

It is the third function we see most often in detective fiction and that is the focus of this book. Still, a good mystery writer ought to be aware of all the policing functions.

Order Maintenance

Although it receives the least amount of attention, order maintenance is the most common police function. This has less to do with enforcing the law than it does with keeping the peace and maintaining order on the streets. This includes advising loiterers to move on, keeping an eye on those kids on the corner, warning a street dancer to turn down his portable stereo. Order maintenance refers to the things police officers do to discourage disruptive, though not necessarily illegal, activity. Order maintenance allows us to feel safer on the streets.

Crime Prevention

Crime prevention is somewhat more formal. It involves policing activities designed specifically to deter criminal activity. This includes such routine activities as patrol (motor, foot, bicycle, boat), which acts as a reminder of police presence.

Police in larger cities also often give seminars designed to help small-business owners prepare for shoplifters and burglars. In most towns the police assign officers to give lectures to schoolchildren, warning them not to take drugs or get into the cars of strangers.

Criminal Investigation

Criminal investigation is what takes place when order maintenance and crime prevention fail. It is the reactive phase of policing. A crime has been committed. The police are charged with the responsibility of discovering who committed it and uncovering enough evidence to prove that person's guilt. Obviously, this is the meat and potatoes of mystery and detective fiction. Or at least the meat. We'll look at different facets of investigation in more detail in later chapters.

The roles and functions of public investigators vary according to jurisdiction. Jurisdiction refers to the area over which an individual policing agency has authority. This can be a geographic area (for example, your local police department has authority over crimes committed within the incorporated limits of your city; your county sheriff has jurisdiction throughout the county and over county buildings). Jurisdiction can also refer to a specific area of the law (the Internal Revenue Service has jurisdiction only over violations of federal tax codes).

There are four basic levels of public policing jurisdiction:

- federal
- state
- county (or parish or borough)
- municipal

Each jurisdiction, and each agency within each jurisdiction, has its own strategic and tactical area of responsibility. We'll take a quick look at each.

Federal Agencies

Federal policing agencies operate at the national level and are responsible for investigating and preventing federal crimes. Federal crimes are those that transcend state interests or borders. Federal crimes can include everything from killing a bald eagle (an endangered species and a national symbol) to killing a president.

There are over sixty federal agencies having policing or investigative powers and functions. Some, such as the Federal Bureau of Investigation, are well known and have thousands of agents. Others, such as the U.S. Supreme Court Police Force or the National Gallery of Art Protection Service, operate in relative obscurity and employ only a few officers. A list of the various federal agencies and their distinctive jurisdictions would cover many pages. The vast majority of federal law enforcement, however, is carried out by the ten agencies within the four departments listed below.

1. Department of Justice
    - Federal Bureau of Investigation. The FBI is the principal investigative arm of the Department of Justice. The FBI has investigative jurisdiction over violations of more than two hundred categories of federal crimes, ranging from bank robbery (banks are protected by federal laws) to kidnapping to the killing of protected species. The bureau is also authorized to investigate matters in which prosecution isn't contemplated; for example, the FBI conducts background security checks on nominees to sensitive government positions.

- Drug Enforcement Administration. The DEA is the agency that enforces the laws as they pertain to the manufacture, distribution and dispensing of controlled substances. These agents manage a national drug intelligence system; they coordinate investigations with other federal, state and local law enforcement agencies; they cooperate with international law enforcement agencies and maintain offices in approximately forty-five foreign countries.
- Immigration and Naturalization Service. Among their various duties, INS agents are responsible for deterring illegal entry into the United States, as well as apprehending or removing those aliens who have entered or remain in the United States illegally, or whose presence is deemed not to be "in the public interest." The INS has the further responsibility of investigating those who knowingly offer employment to illegal aliens. Finally, this agency is required to investigate aliens who receive public benefits to which they are not entitled.
- U.S. Marshal's Service. The Marshal's Service deals with matters pertaining to federal courts. They are responsible for providing protection for the federal judiciary, transporting federal prisoners, protecting endangered federal witnesses (this is the agency that handles the Federal Witness Protection Program), pursuing and arresting federal fugitives (in the movie *The Fugitive*, the people pursuing Dr. Richard Kimball were federal marshals) and managing assets seized from criminal enterprises.

2. Department of the Treasury
   - Customs Service. The mission of the Customs Service is to ensure that all goods entering and exiting the United States do so in accordance with U.S. laws and regulations. This includes the introduction of prohibited items and products (such as certain plants and animals, certain drugs), the extraction of certain technologies (software cryptography, certain technologies with military applications) and the assessment and collection of revenues (duties, taxes and fees on imported merchandise).

- Bureau of Alcohol, Tobacco and Firearms. The duties of the BATF have changed over time. Although these investigators remain responsible for enforcing the federal laws relating to alcohol and tobacco (mainly ensuring the appropriate taxes are paid), their primary focus is on firearms, explosives and arson. BATF agents led the ill-fated assault on the Branch Davidian compound in Waco. They also led the investigation of the Unabomber and the bombings at the World Trade Center in New York and the federal building in Oklahoma City.
- Secret Service (see the sidebar on page 27).
- Internal Revenue Service. The IRS is the largest agency in the Department of the Treasury, with 102,000 employees and a budget of $7.8 billion in 1997. Obviously, IRS investigators have jurisdiction over violations of the tax laws.

3. United States Postal Service. The Postal Inspection Service of the USPS is responsible for enforcing postal laws and protecting the mail. Investigators handle cases of mail fraud and illegal use of the mail (the dissemination of illegal products such as child pornography). They are also responsible for maintaining security of post office property and personnel.

4. General Services Administration. The U.S. Federal Protection Police (USFPS) of the Office of Federal Protective Service Management are responsible for providing traditional policing services to all the federal communities controlled by the GSA. All those federal buildings and all the people inside them are under the jurisdiction of the USFPS. When somebody in the Bureau of Land Management is suspected of using government funds to pay for her vacation travel or when an official in the Bureau of Standards and Measurement is suspected of getting kickbacks, the USFPS is responsible for investigating. Its uniformed police are responsible for protecting the million federal employees and three million visitors to federal buildings, as well as the billions of dollars in U.S. assets (computers, copying machines, etc.) housed therein.

For the most part, the jurisdiction of federal agencies involves areas of law rather than areas of geography. The primary exception to this involves American Indian Tribal Police, who are responsible for the prevention and investigation of most crimes committed within the borders of individual tribal reservations. There are over two hundred various tribal agencies involved in some aspect of criminal justice (including over sixty direct law enforcement agencies). Most of these are concentrated in the Southwest, primarily in Arizona and New Mexico.

State Agencies

State policing agencies fall into two general categories: highway patrol and state police. These two categories reflect the diversity of policing duties state agencies are required to fulfill.

As the name indicates, the services of highway patrol agencies are concentrated on traffic-related activities. For the most part highway patrol officers are uniformed and engage in some form of patrol. Because their jurisdiction is limited, their investigative duties are also limited; generally they only investigate traffic accidents. These are the folks behind the radar guns, the ones who pull over truckers for speeding or freight violations, the ones who scrape the remains of drunk drivers off the highway. They're the ones in the goofy hats.

By contrast, state police are intensely involved in investigative work. Generally, the state police operate an individual state's crime laboratory (this service is especially helpful to smaller towns that cannot afford the equipment, staff or training required to conduct complex forensic examinations). State police are also commonly responsible for investigating state crimes, such as state tax evasion and legislative corruption.

County Agencies

County policing agencies fall under the control of a sheriff. The office of sheriff is unique. The term is derived from the old Norman office of "shire reeve." A reeve was an official appointed by the king and charged with control and enforcement of a specific aspect of the king's property. A deer reeve, for example, watched over the king's deer and guarded against poachers. The

Secret Service

When most people think of the Secret Service they envision the special agents who protect the president—those sober-looking men in sunglasses with radio wires dangling from their ears and wearing responsible-looking suits over Uzi machine pistols. In fact, protecting the president was not part of their original mandate. While presidential protection is the primary concern of the modern Secret Service, it is not the agency's sole policing function.

The Secret Service, established in 1865, is one of the oldest federal law enforcement agencies (only the U.S. Marshal's Service, established in 1789, is older). The Secretary of the Treasury wanted a specialized policing force to combat the growing problem of currency counterfeiting. He broached the idea with President Lincoln, who thought it was a grand idea. Ironically, that very night Lincoln was assassinated. Despite the assassination of Lincoln, the Secret Service did not acquire the task of protecting the president until 1881, after President Garfield was assassinated. Special agents of the Secret Service, however, aren't simply bodyguards; they're also investigators. It's their duty to look into any threats made toward the people they're assigned to protect. That means going into the field and gathering intelligence on every nutcase who sends the president hate mail.

In addition to physically protecting the president (and the vice-president, and former presidents, and presidential candidates, and visiting foreign dignitaries *and* all of their families), the Secret Service remains responsible for investigating counterfeit currency and forgery (the agents investigate instances of forged government checks, bonds and even postage stamps). As the nature of currency changed over time, the Secret Service found itself in charge of investigating other illegal forms of financial exchange. This is called access device fraud. An access device is anything that can be used to electronically initiate a transfer of funds, such as credit cards or telephone cards. It is the Secret Service's authority over access devices that makes it the federal agency responsible for federal computer crime. The 1989 crackdown on computer hackers (Operation Sun Devil) was a Secret Service operation.

If that's not enough, the Secret Service also has a Uniformed Division charged with maintaining security at the White House and foreign embassies. They also guard the precious metals in the vaults of the Treasury Department and valuable historical documents (such as the Constitution and the Declaration of Independence).

---

shire reeve was the reeve for an entire shire, or English county. The shire reeve also collected taxes for the king. You'll recall the Sheriff of Nottingham, Robin Hood's nemesis—just another law enforcement officer doing his job.

The office of sheriff operates within every aspect of the criminal justice system. The sheriff is a law enforcement officer, an officer of the court and a corrections officer. As law enforcement officers, the sheriff and sheriff's deputies are responsible for policing the county (at least those areas not covered by municipal police). This includes the usual police functions of crime prevention, investigation and order maintenance. As an officer of the court, the sheriff is responsible for providing protection for the courts and judicial officers. Officers who provide courtroom security are called bailiffs. In addition, sheriff's deputies are often responsible for serving warrants, subpoenas and other legal documents issued by the court. As a corrections officer, the sheriff is responsible for managing the county jail and transporting prisoners to and from court, as well as escorting them to prison after conviction.

If the various duties of the office weren't complicated enough, in most states the office of sheriff is an elected position. In many rural counties the sheriff is the most powerful political figure. A sheriff, in the course of his duties, must therefore be cognizant of the political realities in the county. This sometimes means that the policies of the sheriff reflect the needs and wants of his political backers. The potential for corruption is great.

This is a personal opinion: The political, jurisidictional and investigative complexities involved in sheriff departments seem a perfect setting for detective fiction. There is simply so much happening in the sheriff's bailiwick—criminal investigation, political intrigue, jail crises (which can include everything from jail

Jail Versus Prison

Although this topic doesn't really pertain to investigation, it needs to be addressed. Too many writers (and other folks, including reporters and politicians) confuse jails and prisons. Jails are county or municipal facilities; prisons are state facilities. Jails generally hold two distinct groups of inmates: those awaiting trial (for both felonies and misdemeanors) and those who have been convicted of misdemeanors (which are punishable by a sentence of one year or less). Prison, on the other hand, only holds those convicted of felonies (punishable by a sentence of more than one year). On occasion prisons are used to hold safe-keepers—people awaiting trial who require a great level of security (perhaps an escape risk, perhaps a suicide risk, perhaps a person at risk from the local populace). Some states also have a sort of bastard offense—an aggravated misdemeanor—which is punishable by a sentence of two years. These sentences are generally served in prison.

breaks to hunger strikes to suicide attempts to escapes). I am surprised so few writers have taken advantage of this setting.

Municipal Agencies

Municipal or city police are the men and women we normally think of when we hear the term "cop." These are the folks we see every day on the streets, the ones cruising neighborhoods in the patrol cars, the people with badges who try to solve the routine, everyday crimes—murder, robbery, rape, assault. Municipal police officers and detectives are the most common law enforcement officers, a fact accurately reflected in detective fiction.

Municipal police have a limited geographic jurisdiction. They are charged with preventing and investigating crime that takes place within the municipal city limits.

Here is an odd fact: The average police officer works in a large city, yet the average police department is a small-town police department. There are far more small-town police departments than there are big-city departments, yet big-city departments employ more officers than all the small towns combined.

For example, New York City, where this book was written, has the largest police force in the United States, with nearly forty thousand officers serving in seventy-six precincts covering five boroughs. The police department of Cincinnati, Ohio, where this book was published, has a police department of less than one thousand sworn officers serving in five districts. Yet both the NYPD and CPD are considered large departments. Approximately 75 percent of all municipal police departments in the United States have fewer than twenty-five sworn officers.

Jurisdictional Disputes

Since all the various policing agencies share the same general goals, it would be logical to assume they cooperate with each other. And, in many cases, they do. However, the cooperation is often halfhearted or given grudgingly.

The fact is that there is competition between various jurisdictions and between agencies at the same jurisdictional level. Municipal police sneer at highway patrol officers, state police investigators look down on county sheriff's deputies, BATF agents feud with DEA agents—and everybody hates the FBI.

The fact is all public policing agencies are, at heart, bureaucracies, and the primary unwritten function of any bureaucracy is to protect its territory (and, if possible, to expand into another bureaucracy's territory). Balzac said a bureaucracy is a giant mechanism operated by pygmies. The result of bureaucratic and jurisdictional disputes is, of course, inefficiency. Police bureaucracies are no different. Unfortunately, disputes between law enforcement agencies can have fatal results.

Interagency resentment, lack of cooperation, hoarding of information—these factors have allowed serial killers time to kill more victims, allowed hate groups time to bomb more churches and civil rights organizations, allowed serial rapists the opportunity to commit more rapes. The same bureaucratic defensive thinking also puts the lives of law enforcement officers at risk. Perhaps the most celebrated instance of this took place in 1975, when an undercover team of DEA agents spent weeks setting up a drug sting only to discover at the last moment that their customers were undercover customs agents operating their own drug sting. Think about the situation for a moment: two groups of nervous, heavily armed federal agents, each prepared to draw and fire, meeting in a warehouse at night. A firefight was averted only because one customs agent recognized one of the DEA agents from an earlier undercover operation.

A plan to consolidate the DEA and the BATF into the FBI has been under consideration for years. It would save money, it would improve communication, it would reduce redundant operations and it would probably save lives. The DEA and the BATF have consistently resisted the plan. No surprise.

Private Investigators

Here is a startling fact: The private security industry is both larger and better funded than the public police. According to data provided by the federal government there are approximately seven hundred thousand full-time, sworn police officers in the United States. The number of private security personnel is estimated to be approximately twice that number. It has been estimated that in New York City private security personnel outnumber public police officers by twenty to one.

Obviously, the private security industry is a burgeoning field of enterprise and offers a wide range of services, of which only one is covered in this book: private investigation.

Before we look at the distinctions between public and private investigators in regard to clientele, autonomy and function, it's important to understand an even more fundamental difference between police investigators and private investigators. Private detectives are just common citizens. They have no special powers, no exceptional legal authority, no exemptions from the law. The only real legal difference between private detectives and regular folks is that PIs can charge money for conducting investigations. Any private citizen can do virtually everything a PI can do (or could if they had the connections, the contacts, the training and the willingness to do it). You don't have to be licensed, for example, to conduct a surveillance. But if you get burned and the police show up to find out why you've been sitting in a car outside the day care center for five hours, having a PI license can be exceedingly helpful. The main thing a PI license does for you is give you an aura of legitimacy.

Categories of Private Security Services

- Proprietary/in-house security. These are the security guards who are employed by and for a specific business or building rather than by a private security agency. Many bank guards, for example, are employed by the bank rather than by an agency.

- Uniformed guard and patrol services. These are the security personnel who work for the private security agencies. They operate as a private adjunct to the public police.

- Alarm services. These people sell, install and maintain home and business alarms. They often work in conjunction with a uniformed guard service, which supplies the response to any tripped alarms.

- Armored car services. These are private agencies that transport currency and precious metals.

- Manufacturers and distributors of security equipment. Somebody has to supply the accoutrements of the industry—the uniforms, the flashing lights, the nightsticks, the motion detectors.

- Security consultants and engineers. These are the people who look at a facility and determine what security devices and personnel are needed.

- Private investigative services. These are the people you may be writing about.

- Miscellaneous security services. These include guard dogs, drug testing, polygraph examination, personal protection, and computer and data security.

In addition, the conduct of the police is regulated in a number of ways (ranging from the U.S. Constitution to internal departmental regulations). No similar universal constraints are placed on private detectives. In fact, of the fifty states, only thirty-five have statewide agencies that license and oversee the conduct of private detectives. Another twelve states, as well as Washington, DC, license PIs at either the city or county level. Three states don't license private investigators at all.

If that's not confusing enough, here's another odd fact: Some states license only individuals, some states license only agencies, some states license both. Nor are the licensing criteria uniform across states. For example, New York requires an individual seeking a PI license to first work under the supervision of a licensed PI for two years and to pass a written test. In New Hampshire, on the other hand, an individual need only be bonded and pass a minimal background check in order to be approved for a private detective license.

This concerns you as a writer. If your protagonist is a private detective, you'll need to know the licensing policies of that character's community. It will require a bit of research, but the effort will result in a character with more depth. Where do you find this information? As you might expect, it varies from state to state and changes over time. The sidebar on page 34 will give you an idea of where to start your research.

Clientele

Here we find the most striking difference between public and private investigators. The police detective exists to serve the public good. The private detective exists to serve the needs and wishes of the client. Contrary to popular belief, the police aren't advocates for the victim of a crime; they are advocates of public order. By fulfilling their roles and functions, police detectives serve the society at large. Private detectives, on the other hand, are generally advocates for their clients. As individuals they may be concerned about the public good, but their job is to represent their clients.

Who are those clients? Research shows that nearly two-thirds of PI clients aren't individuals, but business concerns—primarily law firms, insurance agencies, manufacturing companies and retail businesses.

A great many private detectives prefer working for businesses over individuals. Why? For the same reason Willie Sutton gave when he was asked why he robbed banks: That's where the money is.

- A business tends to produce more casework. An individual might offer a more interesting case, or one that might be more personally rewarding, but once that case is over it's over. Businesses offer PIs a steady income.

Private Detective Licensing

Alabama	License issued at local or county level
Alaska	License issued at local or county level
Arizona	State license issued by Arizona Department of Public Safety
Arkansas	State license issued by Arkansas State Police
California	State license issued by Bureau of Security and Investigative Services
Colorado	No license required
Connecticut	State license issued by Conn. State Police
Delaware	State license issued by Del. State Police
Florida	State license issued by Fla. Dept. of State
Georgia	State license issued by Georgia Board of Private Detectives
Hawaii	State license issued by Department of Commerce and Consumer Affairs
Idaho	License issued at local or county level
Illinois	State license issued by Department of Professional Regulation
Indiana	State license issued by Indiana Department of Professional Licensing
Iowa	State license issued by Ia. Dept. of Public Safety
Kansas	State license issued by Kansas Bureau of Investigation
Kentucky	License issued at local or county level
Louisiana	State license issued by Louisana Board of PI Examiners; licensing also at local and parish levels
Maine	State license issued by Maine State Police
Maryland	State license issued by Md. State Police
Massachusetts	State license issued by Mass. State Police
Michigan	State license issued by Mich. State Police
Minnesota	State license issued by Minn. Board of Private Detective and Protective Agent Services
Mississippi	No license required
Missouri	License issued at local or county level
Montana	State license issued by Department of Commerce, Licensing Bureau
Nebraska	State license issued by Neb. Sec. of State

Nevada	State license issued by Office of the Attorney General
New Hampshire	State license issued by N.H. State Police
New Jersey	State license issued by N.J. State Police
New Mexico	State license issued by New Mexico Regulation and Licensing Dept.
New York	State license issued by State Department of Licensing Services
North Carolina	State license issued by North Carolina Private Protection Services
North Dakota	State license issued by North Dakota Private Investigator Board
Ohio	State license issued by Division of Consumer Finance
Oklahoma	License issued at local or county level
Oregon	License issued at local or county level (state licensing is under legislative consideration)
Pennsylvania	License issued at local or county level
Rhode Island	License issued at local or county level, overseen by Div. of Licensing (State Police)
South Carolina	State license issued by S.C. State Police
South Dakota	License issued at local or county level
Tennessee	State license issued by Tennessee Department of Commerce
Texas	State license issued by Texas Department of Public Safety
Utah	State license issued by Utah Department of Public Safety
Vermont	State license issued by Ver. Sec. of State
Virginia	State license issued by Department of Criminal Justice Services
Washington	State license issued by Department of State, Licensing Division
Washington, DC	License issued by Washington, DC, Metropolitan Police Department
West Virginia	State license issued by W.Va. Sec. of State
Wisconsin	State license issued by Wisconsin Department of Regulation and Licensing
Wyoming	License issued at local or county level

Humanitarian Private Detectives

There are a number of private investigators who use their occupation primarily to serve the public good. A number of PIs specialize in locating lost or kidnapped children. Others attempt to secure the release of men and women convicted of crimes they did not commit. Some use their skills to track down deadbeat dads, or combat consumer fraud, or uncover corporate environmental violations. There is even a Florida investigator who, like the Jim Carrey movie character Ace Ventura, maintains a sideline tracking down lost or stolen pets.

The work of these dedicated PIs is admirable. It should be noted, however, that serving the public good rarely pays well. The vast majority of these specialists have another source of income.

- Businesses tend to pay higher fees.
- A business tends to pay bills on time and with less fuss, which is an attractive quality in a client.

There are other, less important, reasons real-life private investigators tend to prefer businesses as clients. You don't have to advertise, you don't have to spend as much time actively seeking casework, and you don't have to deal as often with upset clients. When a business hires a PI it's an economic decision. When individuals hire a PI it's because some aspect of their life is in crisis. Nobody hires a PI for amusement. We'll look at this a little closer when we discuss PI functions.

Finally, it's important to remember that private investigators have to pay their rent and buy groceries just like everybody else. The failure to recognize that a PI needs to earn a living may be the single most egregious error committed by mystery writers. Unlike a police detective, who is guaranteed to receive a salary every two weeks regardless of the results of the investigation, a private detective has to produce consistent results *that satisfy the client* to stay in business.

Autonomy

In law school students are told, "Lawyers are not a bus." That sounds rather like a Zen koan, but it actually makes sense.

Buses are common carriers; they are required to accept any passenger who can pay the fare. Lawyers are not buses; they are not required to accept all clients who can pay the fees.

This quirky analogy can also be used for police and private detectives. Police detectives are like a bus. As noted earlier, the police cannot refuse to provide their services; they are available to all. Private detectives, on the other hand, are not a bus. They have the absolute right to decline certain cases or refuse to work for certain clients. The services of police detectives are offered to the public for free (if we disregard the fact that their salaries come from our taxes). The services of a PI are generally for sale.

In addition, the behavior of police investigators is constrained by the U.S. Constitution. They can only conduct searches and seizures of property and individuals under certain conditions. They are prohibited from asking certain types of questions after a suspect is arrested. Private investigators, contrarily, are private citizens and under no such constitutional stricture. We'll look at specific examples of this in other chapters.

Functions

Private investigators fulfill two primary functions:

- commercial function
- advocative function

The distinguishing feature between these two functions is the nature of the clientele.

Commercial Function

In general, private detectives serving a commercial function act to promote and protect the interests of corporations. These investigators gather information that businesses can use to their financial, political or social advantage.

Historically, private investigators and all facets of the private security industry (and the public police, for that matter) have always acted in the service of powerful commercial interests. Modern insurance investigators share the same fundamental mission as the "slugging detectives" of the Ford Motor Company in the 1930s to 1940s and the strike-breaking Pinkertons of the 1870s to 1890s: the protection of the corporate interests of the powerful.

Obviously, the types of information sought by business clients are diverse, as are the uses for the information. Here are a few examples of the types of cases PIs will undertake in their commercial function:

- background checks (of prospective employees or potential business partners)
- industrial investigations (ranging from investigations of assembly line sabotage to uncovering the secrets of business rivals)
- insurance work (for insurance companies rather than for plaintiffs)
- criminal prosecution (such as for theft or embezzlement)
- missing persons cases (including skip-tracing, locating bail absconders and process service for corporations involved in legal matters)

The information obtained in such investigation serves a variety of commercial ends, including the mitigation of liability, fraud reduction, deterrence of theft (both internal and external), protection of corporate property and the location of debtors.

Advocative Function

Private investigators serving an advocative function conduct investigations in the interest of individuals (although they may also work for collectives of individuals).

Group Clients

There are several examples in which PIs work for collectives. The Citizens Action Committee in the small town of Griswold, Iowa, hired a private investigator to conduct an investigation into allegations of police brutality. The investigation resulted in the resignation of the police chief and the firing of one officer. This sort of group advocacy, however, is less common than advocacy for an individual.

This is the traditional role of the private detective in fiction and the popular entertainment media—the lone man or woman standing up against powerful, malignant forces in defense of the innocent and the powerless.

While the popular media portrayal is obviously exaggerated, there is some basis in reality for it. Take the work done by Rhode Island PI Frank Fitzpatrick. Fitzpatrick's client claimed to have been sexually molested in Fall River, Massachusetts, by his parish priest some twenty-five to thirty years before. Despite resistance from the Catholic Church, Fitzpatrick located the priest, James Porter, who had left the priesthood in 1974 and moved to Minnesota. In the course of his investigation, Fitzpatrick discovered many other victims. In December of 1993 Porter pleaded guilty to forty-one counts of sexual assault.

As advocates, private investigators serve an amazing variety of client needs:

- They act for individuals in contention with other individuals (such as in divorce, infidelity and child custody matters).

- They act as paid intermediaries between an innocent public and a shadowy and seemingly inscrutable world (such as in locating missing children, spouses or other persons).

- They serve as defenders of civil rights for unsavory and unpopular clients (in criminal defense and civil rights cases).

- They intercede on behalf of persons in conflict with—or lost within—the bureaucratic labyrinth (locating debtors, tracking witnesses).

- They act for persons in conflict with corporate interests (such as in personal injury cases).

Private detectives as advocates tend to be more personally invested in their cases. You're working for a person, not a faceless corporate entity. And while PIs working as advocates generally make less money, they tend to be more dedicated to and happier with their work.

These two functions aren't mutually exclusive. Individual private investigators may, and often do, engage in both. For example, a PI's caseload may include both a criminal defense case (advocative) and a copyright infringement case (commercial). Indeed, although some case categories are restricted to one function—such as criminal defense, which by its very nature must be advocative—other case categories are more ambiguous. In personal injury cases, for example, a PI may be working either for the injured party (advocative) or for the company being sued (commercial).

Conclusion

The distinctions between public and private investigators are important, and it's critical that the writer of mystery and detective fiction understand them. But it's also important to remember that all detectives, public and private, share something in common. It is their job to gather information. It is *not* their job to assess the value of the information. Public investigators give their information to prosecutors, who determine what to do with it. Private detectives give their information to their clients, who decide what to do with it.

This distance from the product of their labor contributes to the cynicism that writers so often attribute to detectives. It helps shape their views of the world. If you want to create a convincing detective in your writing, you need to understand the things real-life detectives take for granted.

T H R E E

CRIME SCENE INVESTIGATION

The scene of the crime. The phrase itself has a certain dramatic grittiness. It carries a frisson of excitement that writers are understandably eager to exploit. Crime scenes, however, are fraught with danger—for the investigator and the writer. It's easy to make a mistake when dealing with crime scenes. And in both real life and fiction, if you make a mistake at the crime scene, that mistake may come back to haunt the rest of your work.

Evidence is the point on which criminal trials are balanced. The more evidence pointing toward a defendant's guilt, the more likely there is to be a conviction (although, as any trial lawyer will tell you, there are no guarantees). The more exculpatory evidence produced, the more likely the defendant will walk.

There are two basic types of evidence: verbal evidence and physical evidence. Verbal evidence is what folks say about what took place. We'll look at verbal evidence in the next chapter. Physical evidence, as the name indicates, pertains to stuff—the physical indications of a crime. Broken windows, fingerprints, burn patterns, bits of cloth, dead bodies, the bugs attracted to dead bodies. Crime scenes are mostly about physical evidence.

Physical evidence is generally considered to be the most important type of evidence. Why? Because physical evidence is morally neutral. It doesn't lie. In fact, physical evidence cannot lie. A broken window is a broken window. A fingerprint is a fingerprint. A bullet hole is a bullet hole.

While physical evidence doesn't lie, it is open to interpretation. Different people may have different opinions on, say, a blood spatter pattern—how it got there, who it belongs to, from what direction or height it came. But its physical existence can't be questioned. It's there—manifest truth, just waiting to be understood.

Police and private detectives both have a keen interest in the physical evidence found at crime scenes. However, they are often looking at different things for different reasons. Police detectives, of course, have a single, simple focus: They want to catch the person responsible for the crime. Private detectives, on the other hand, have a much more complicated view in regard to crime scenes. We're going to look at crime scenes from both perspectives. We'll concentrate mainly on murder scenes, since that's the crime most commonly found in detective fiction.

The Crime Scene—Police Detective's Perspective

An undisturbed crime scene (which sounds like an oxymoron) offers the police a tremendous opportunity. By closely examining a crime scene, a good detective can often obtain a fairly accurate idea of what took place; that is, the progression of the crime. Evidence at the crime scene may even offer suggestions as to why the crime took place. It might even point to who is responsible. A crime scene, after all, is the residue of criminal behavior, and behavior reflects personality.

The first forty-eight to seventy-two hours are the most critical in solving a homicide. It's easier to find and talk to witnesses, and their memories are generally more accurate soon after the crime. A 1994 study found that in two-thirds of solved murder cases, police take a suspect into custody within twenty-four hours. If the case has not been solved within forty-eight hours, the chances of it ever being solved fall drastically.

Because those first hours are so critical in clearing a homicide case, a staggering amount of work is undertaken. Everybody works overtime. All the resources of the state are put into play. This is especially true in smaller cities and towns in which homicides are still uncommon.

What Does a Police Detective Do at a Crime Scene?

The police have four priorities at a crime scene:

- Secure the crime scene.
- Conduct the initial examination of the crime scene.
- Locate and interview witnesses to the crime.
- Collect physical evidence.

These aren't necessarily listed in order of priority—although I suspect every detective would agree that the first imperative is to secure the scene. Often two or more of these activities are taking place at the same time.

Securing the Crime Scene

In quantum physics it is an accepted truth that you can't measure a subatomic particle's speed or direction without subtly altering it; the very act of measurement changes the thing being measured. In an odd way, the same is true of a crime scene. The very act of examination damages the scene.

Crime scenes are terribly fragile. A crime scene begins to deteriorate the moment a person enters it. The more people who enter it, the more damage is done and the greater the potential for an irrevocable error. It has been said that a victim is only murdered once; a crime scene can be murdered a thousand times.

Consider the number of people who routinely enter a murder scene: the detectives, the uniformed officers who first respond to the scene, the person who discovers the body, the watch commanders, the forensic team, the emergency medical team (when there is still some hope for survival), the folks from the morgue. Dozens of people, each of whom might bring in or take out trace evidence, any of whom might make a fatal error for the best of reasons.

Most of the damage done to a crime scene is done inadvertently, perhaps as a result of poor training or simple ignorance.

Cold Case Squad

In the 1980s a lot of large cities experienced a tremendous rise in their homicide rates (the rates have gone down in recent years). The rise in unsolved homicides was largely a result of drug-related murders, which are notoriously difficult to clear. In 1991 only 54 percent of the homicides in Washington, DC, were solved. Obviously, having a fifty-fifty chance of getting away with murder only encouraged drug dealers to resolve their turf and financial disputes with violence.

In Washington, DC, a special squad of highly experienced police detectives and FBI agents was formed to investigate "cold cases," murder cases that were at least one year old and had little chance of being solved. The Cold Case Squad (CCS) did not respond to any fresh crime scenes or any of the other duties of regular homicide detectives. They were allowed to focus all their energies on their cases. By reviewing the case files, reinterviewing all the witnesses, and reexamining all the evidence, the CCS has not only closed old cases, but developed spin-off cases (a witness in one cold case may have information about another case involving the same suspect, or may have observed another homicide in the same neighborhood).

Whereas time usually works against most investigators, the CCS has discovered that time can work in its favor. Over time the relationships between witnesses and suspects may change, especially in drug-related murders. People who were once friends and lovers may now be enemies. Also, the initial fear factor will change. A witness who was afraid to identify a suspect at the time of the crime may be less fearful at present. Finally, a number of witnesses to drug-related homicides may have fallen afoul of the law themselves in the time since the original crime; they may be willing to offer a statement in exchange for favorable treatment on their own cases. Finally, as time goes by and the offender continues to get away with the killing, the odds increase that he'll begin to brag about the crime, which produces still more new witnesses.

Since its inception, the Cold Case Squad has cleared more than 150 previously unsolved homicides.

Some of it is done with good intentions. Why the damage is done is irrelevant. The fact is, mucking about at the crime scene reduces the odds of an arrest and, if an arrest is made, of a conviction.

The primary rule of a crime scene is touch nothing. There are only two clear exceptions to this rule. The first is if the victim is still living. Obviously, it is more important to treat the victim than to preserve the crime scene (although homicide detectives will grumble if a perfectly good crime scene gets messed up and then the victim dies anyway). The second exception to the touch nothing rule is that any weapons found at the scene that are in reach of suspects/witnesses/bystanders must be immediately seized. If weapons aren't seized, somebody will pick them up. Maybe to give to the police, maybe to hide from the police, maybe to use against the police, or maybe just because some enterprising young lad sees a chance to get himself a free weapon, but weapons left lying around a crime scene will be picked up.

Indoor Versus Outdoor Crime Scenes

When a police detective is notified of a crime, one of the first questions asked is whether the crime took place inside or outside. Why? Because the location of the body plays a significant factor in solving the crime. Homicides that take place inside a building—a private home, a public building, a restaurant—have a greater likelihood of being cleared (homicide detectives, by the way, "clear" cases rather than "solve" them. A great many detectives feel uncomfortable with the term "solve"; it stinks of television).

Indoor Crime Scenes

Detectives like to have the victims' bodies inside buildings. There are a number of reasons for this. First, a crime scene in a building is much easier to secure than one on a street. The very fact that a building has walls and a roof keeps out curious onlookers and nosy members of the news media and limits the number of people who can come in and mess up the scene.

Second, trace evidence in a building is easier to obtain and to attribute to specific individuals. If a detective finds a cigarette butt in a house, it can usually be traced to a specific person, proving that person was in that building. A butt on the street could belong to anybody.

Third, buildings are full of smooth surfaces that catch fin-gerprints: walls, light switches, doorknobs, doorways, windows, desks, silverware. Detectives, and juries, love fingerprints.

Fourth, a building itself offers an amazing amount of infor-mation. It often narrows the range of potential suspects. Who has access to the building? Who owns the building? Who has keys? Why is the body in the building? Did the victim belong in the building, or was she brought there after the killing? Who is nor-mally in the building at the approximate time the crime was committed?

Fifth, bullets don't travel as far inside. Walls (as well as victims) get in the way. It's much easier to collect spent rounds inside a building.

Sixth, a building is out of the weather. This is an important consideration for detectives when the weather is foul. Of course, if the body is in a late stage of decomposition, a building will contain and intensify the odor. Nobody enjoys being inside a small room with a decomposing body. And the weather, obvi-ously, has an effect on the state of the body's deterioration. But those are usually secondary considerations; the fact is, detectives like to stay warm and dry. The attraction to inside homicide scenes, of course, does not apply on nice days in the spring or on hot days in the summer if the building is not air-conditioned.

Outdoor Crime Scenes

Outdoor crime scenes generally come in two basic varieties: a street (or alley) and a park/wooded area. Neither scene is popu-lar with detectives; however, a body found in a park or wooded area is generally considered the worst of all possible crime scenes. A body in the woods often means it was killed someplace else and dumped there. That severely limits the amount of available evidence.

Obviously, an outdoor crime seen is far more difficult to secure than a crime scene inside a building. By the time a street crime scene has been taped off, a tremendous amount of traffic—both foot and vehicle—may have passed through. Even when taping off a street to prohibit people from polluting the scene, the police can't erect walls to keep prying eyes from observing the course of the investigation. Bystanders can compromise an

Disposing of the Body

Every major city has a favorite, almost traditional, dumping spot for those awkward, unwanted bodies. In New York it's the meadowlands—the fens and marshes just over the river in New Jersey; in South Florida it's the swamps around the Everglades; in Baltimore it's a park on the west side of town; in New Orleans it's the bayou. Each of these places has some common features: They are easily accessed, they are rarely visited at night, and the terrain is such that a body might lie there for a long time without being discovered—or might never be discovered at all.

It's not just bodies that are dumped in these spots. All manner of inconvenient materials are illegally dumped there: hazardous waste, old tires, broken appliances and furniture.

The local dumping ground is usually common knowledge among law enforcement personnel (as well as among the more violent criminal element). As a writer, it might be worth the effort to discover (or create) the dumping area where your story is located.

investigation by discussing details of the scene that the police would prefer to keep quiet.

Unlike a crime scene in a building, an outdoor crime scene can make the collection of trace evidence difficult, or even pointless. It's often difficult to determine what is evidence and what is litter. How does an investigator determine if a broken beer bottle next to a body in an alley is significant? It might have been dropped there by anybody at any time. A detective may waste hours or days tracking down false leads.

It's also far easier for bullets to disappear when fired outside. There are fewer walls to stop them, and those walls are much farther apart. Plus there are fewer appropriate places to search for fingerprints at a street crime scene, and a great many more possible people who could have left the prints. All that makes it more difficult to collect evidence.

Crime scenes on a street also lack the personal grounding of a crime scene inside a building. Nobody owns a street, anybody can reasonably pass down a street, and there is simply far less personal evidence on the street.

On the other hand, one of the street's disadvantages also offers one significant advantage: The lack of walls lets evidence escape, but it allows witnesses to observe. Streets are public places. People are using them all the time. A murder inside a building is private; a murder on a street is accessible to an audience. The odds of finding a witness are much greater when the crime occurs in a public place.

Conducting the Initial Examination of the Crime Scene

One of the most common scenes we see in detective fiction is the arrival of the detective at the scene of the crime. And what does the detective do? She rushes over to examine the body. The body, after all, is the star of the crime scene; few detective and mystery novels are without a body.

In real life, most homicide detectives ignore the body at first. Why? Two reasons. First, there is an inverse relationship between the likelihood that physical evidence will be overlooked or disturbed and its proximity to the body. That's a fancy way of saying the farther the evidence is from the body, the more likely somebody will muck about with it—and ruin it as evidence.

The second reason is that there is no need to hurry to the body. Another of the universal truths of detective work is this fact: The body ain't going nowhere. With the possible exception of certain police districts in Transylvania, dead bodies rarely wander off. They're pretty much immobile. In Newtonian terms: A body at rest tends to remain at rest. The body can wait. What can't wait is the other evidence scattered around the crime scene.

So most detectives begin their examination of the murder scene by making a slow, gradually shrinking orbit around the area, finishing at the body. They look in the dark corners, in the trash, behind doors, in other rooms.

And they take notes about what they observe. Lots of notes. Paper and ink are cheap, and a carefully recorded observation will serve the detective well long after her memory of the incident and the crime scene has faded.

Here is another universal truth: A thing worth doing is worth doing twice. After the initial examination of the area, detectives have the area photographed. Notes are good, photographs are good, but notes *and* photographs are best. Film may not be as cheap as pen and paper, but good detectives are liberal in their spending of film. Photographs are taken of everything. If the crime scene is inside a building, photographs are even taken of rooms that don't appear to have been involved in the crime. Photographs are taken of the outside of the building.

Once the notes have been made and the photographs taken, a detective sketches and diagrams the critical components of the crime scene (a corollary of the universal truth mentioned earlier: Anything worth doing twice is worth doing three times). Exact measurements are taken. Measurements must be triangulated. In other words, the location of the object being diagrammed must be measured from two fixed points (see illustration on page 50). The fixed points must be objects that cannot be moved: It does no good to state an object was 5'3" from a lamp and 2'9" from the right corner of a television; if those objects are moved, the diagram is worthless. Why is this important? A detective's notes might report that a knife was on the floor "near the victim's left hand." A photograph might show that the knife was, indeed, in the proximity of the victim's hand. But a diagram with measurements will prove the knife was six inches from the victim's hand. That degree of precision may not matter, but a good detective takes no chances.

A detective knows she has one best chance to process a crime scene. After that, the crime scene may be too contaminated to be useful. One way to avoid a serious snafu is for the detective to follow an established procedure. Most major police departments have a report format their detectives are expected to follow. These report formats generally cover the same twenty-one information points. In effect, these information points actually outline the pattern of a homicide investigation. By carefully following each point of the report format, a detective ensures a thorough investigation will be conducted. Below are the twenty-one points most police agencies follow for a death scene investigation:

1. Case number.

2. Pedigree of the deceased. This includes (when possible) full name, date of birth, age, race, sex, present address, marital status, next of kin and employment information. It should

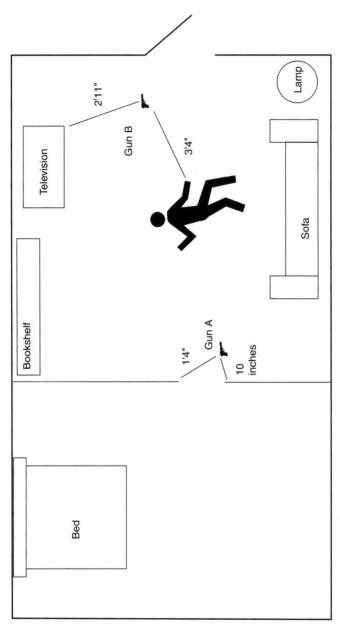

Guns A and B are both measured by triangulation. However, only gun A has been properly diagrammed. Gun B has been measured from objects that can be moved (the television and the body). Gun A has been measured from fixed points (the north and south sides of the bedroom door). While it might be important to measure the distances of both guns from the body, the diagram above makes it impossible to accurately fix the location of gun B.

also include a physical description of the deceased, including approximate weight, height, hair color, complexion, birthmarks, moles (or warts or tumors), physical deformities and body modifications (tattoos, piercings, scarring, etc.).

3. Information on who reported/discovered the deceased.

4. Time the investigator responded to the scene, and who was present when the detective arrived.

5. A general description of the location. For example: a single-family dwelling, an apartment complex of X number of units, a wooded area at the southeast corner of the park.

6. A general description of the overall scene of the death. Is there any sign of a struggle? Any indication of a forced entry? Any incongruities (for example, the windows open in the winter)? The detective should also include associated indications of time of death (see the sidebar on page 53).

7. A specific description of the location and position of the body. For example: Subject was found in the (location) lying on his (back, left side, etc.) on a (nature of surface, such as a tile floor, gravel driveway). The subject's feet were (direction) and head was (direction). All of this, of course, will be documented by a sketch and photographs as well.

8. A description of the subject's clothing. Not merely the color and fabric (and, as is increasingly common, brand names), but also if the clothing was disturbed and a description of any "defects" in the clothing, such as stains, tears or cuts. Also include descriptions of any items found inside the subject's clothing.

9. Postmortem changes. This includes body temperature (note the instrument used in addition to the time and part of the body from which the reading was taken), livor mortis (the areas involved and blanchability), rigor mortis (degree and location where it is actualized) and state of decomposition (including any insect life—see the sidebar on forensic entomology on page 57). Good detectives also comment on the weather conditions.

10. Injuries to the body of the deceased. Bruises, cuts and wounds are documented.

11. Jewelry and other valuables. This is done for two reasons.

The first is accuracy. The second is to prevent any later claim by the family of the deceased that items of value were stolen by the police.

12. Method of identification. At least two means of ID should be obtained. For example: Subject was visually identified by his wife at the scene and was compared to the photo on the driver's license found in the deceased's right rear pocket.

13. Notification of next of kin. The time, date and location where notification was made, to whom it was made and by whom it was made.

14. Items possibly related to the cause, manner or determination of death. Some police departments provide forms for a wide variety of types of death—by gunshot, by hanging, by blunt object, by edged or sharp object, by gas and so forth.

15. Witness statements.

16. Criminal history. This includes any record of arrest, prior convictions, prison or jail sentences, or intelligence on suspected criminal activity (good criminals don't get caught, but may still come to the attention of law enforcement).

17. Information regarding the subject's medical history. This should include current and prior medical conditions (noting the source of the information), any medications the subject was taking (or should have been taking) and any history of psychiatric conditions or treatment. If the cause of death is not readily apparent, all medications should be seized. Items such as poisons, chemicals, cleaning agents and pesticides that appear out of place should be seized.

18. Transportation of subject to the morgue. The time the body was transported and by whom it was transported. It's also important to note any evidentiary preparations made prior to transportation; for example, the subject's hands were placed in new, clean paper bags secured at the wrist with masking tape prior to removal from the scene.

19. Pronouncement of death. Who officially pronounced the subject dead and the time at which the pronouncement was made.

20. Special requests for forensic examination. Although it is presumed the medical examiner and forensic teams will

conduct all the appropriate forensic tests, a detective may sometimes request specific tests to be performed on the body or on evidence seized at the scene. For example: Test the barrel of the shotgun for the presence of vaginal fluid.

21. Other notifications. There are occasions in which a detective will notify parties who have no direct relationship to the subject or the incident, but who may nonetheless have an interest in the matter. For example, a murder involving a member of the police force or the attempted burglary of the headquarters of a national political party.

Aids in Determining Time of Death

In addition to the standard indicators of time of death (rigor mortis, livor mortis, body temperature, etc.), there are a number of associated indicators. The detective should note the following:

- Mail in the mailbox. Check for the earliest dated piece of mail. If several days of mail have accumulated, the detective should check with the postal carrier assigned to that route.

- Newspapers. Has the morning paper been collected? What time is it normally delivered? How many papers have piled up on the lawn?

- Appliances. Are the lights on? Is the heating element of the coffeemaker on? How much coffee is in the pot? Is the television on? If so, in what room? A television turned on in the bedroom may suggest something different than a television in the living room. Is there a television guide? If so, to what day/page is it opened?

- Food. Is there any food out or dirty dishes in the sink? If so, does the evidence correspond to the victim's last meal as determined by the medical examiner?

Locating and Interviewing Witnesses to the Crime

We see this on television all the time: The detective on the homicide scene turns to a uniformed officer and says, "Canvass the neighborhood. Find me a witness." It's one of the few times television gets it right. A witness—any witness—is valuable. A good witness is precious.

What makes a good eyewitness? Remember that there are two basic audiences a witness needs to impress: the detectives and the prosecutors. The detective is primarily concerned with catching the offender, so is mainly interested in the ability of the witness to recall the event accurately. The prosecutor, however, has to convince a jury that the witness is reliable. A prosecutor wants a witness who is disinterested (not uninterested, but without any stake in the outcome), who is clean both socially and physically (socially in that the witness has no criminal record, physically because people tend to believe a clean person more than a dirty person) and who is respectable (a concept that, like pornography, is difficult to define, but most folks generally recognize it when they see it).

It's important to remember that eyewitness testimony is not the most reliable form of evidence. Folks who actually witness a crime often have a faulty and confused understanding of what took place. Still, juries and detectives love eyewitnesses.

Collecting Physical Evidence

Physical evidence aids the investigator in three ways: (1) It can help establish the facts of the crime; (2) it can associate a suspect with the crime scene; and (3) it can help trace or locate a suspect. Obviously, detectives love physical evidence.

The collection, analysis and interpretation of physical evidence is known as criminalistics. It's a field that draws on a wide variety of sciences and disciplines. Among them are chemistry, anatomy, zoology, physics, archeology and entomology.

The collection of physical evidence can be a routine process, or it can be a highly technical procedure involving specialized training and technology. Not only are there a variety of technical problems involved (for example, taking fingerprints off a light switch involves a different technique than taking one from a sheet of paper), but there are also several legal considerations that must be taken into account.

It would be impossible to provide in this book a detailed description of the methods for collecting physical evidence. Indeed, there are a large number of textbooks and professional

Even the Best Witnesses . . .

While living in Washington, DC (in what sociologists like to call a transitional neighborhood, meaning it was a bad neighborhood on its way to becoming a moderately bad neighborhood, with the promise of someday becoming a good neighborhood), I had the back luck to witness a stabbing on a busy street. This is what I saw: some pushing and shoving, people shouting and jumping back, one young Latino clutching his side and stepping backward, several people—at least some of whom were Latin—running away, the guy who'd been stabbed sitting down and his shirt turning red. Did I see a knife? I think so, but I'm not sure. Could I describe it? Not a chance. Did I see the person who did the stabbing? Yes, I must have, but my attention was on the guy who got stabbed. Could I identify the person who did the stabbing? No, absolutely not. Could I even describe that person? Medium height, dark clothes. The stabber was almost certainly Latino, but I couldn't swear to it.

Now, I'm a trained observer. I have been a private detective, a counselor in the psychiatric/security unit of a prison and a medic in the military. I have far more experience than most folks at paying attention to detail. I am far more accustomed to chaos and crisis situations. I am not disturbed by the sight of blood and gore. Yet I was almost worthless as a witness. Imagine how difficult it is for the average citizen.

journals devoted to the subject. If, as a writer, you need to describe the process of collecting a specific type of evidence, I recommend you consult one of the texts listed in the bibliography (or, for those of you with access to the Internet, the list of forensic Web sites).

Rather than do an inadequate job of describing the evidence collection process, I'll provide a brief overview of the types of things detectives look for. In general, police detectives at a crime scene are looking for the following:

- what's there
- what's there that shouldn't be
- what isn't there but ought to be

These are heavily contextual observations; the circumstance determines their significance. Here's an example: In an apartment you find the body of a man and a purse. Does the purse have any meaning? It depends entirely on the context. If the apartment was rented by the man, the purse may be significant. Why is the purse there? Has a woman been at the apartment? Who is the woman, and where has she gone? Perhaps the man had stolen the purse. Why? To support a drug habit? Are we looking at a drug-related murder? Maybe the man is a cross-dresser. Could that be related to the murder?

If the apartment was rented by a woman, the purse could still be significant. How likely is it that a woman has only one purse? Where are the other purses? Where, for that matter, is the woman? Is the woman tenant another victim? Or a suspect?

As a writer you have the luxury of being in total control over the crime scene. You get to decide what's there, what's there that shouldn't be and what isn't there but ought to be. You have command over the context.

The Crime Scene—Private Detective's Perspective

In fiction we often find both police and private investigators poring over the evidence at crime scenes. In real life, however, PIs are rarely present at an active crime scene. It's not because PIs aren't welcome (although, in fact, they aren't); it's because private investigators usually don't even get involved in a case until days, weeks, even months after a suspect has been arrested and charged. Private detectives engaged in criminal work almost always work for a defense attorney. After the suspect has been arrested and charged, after he has hired a lawyer (or had one appointed)—that's when a PI gets involved. And by that time the crime scene is almost certainly ruined.

In seven years of criminal defense work, there was only one occasion in which I knew about a major crime scene before the police. A woman who was out on bail for a drug charge shot a man after he had sexually abused her with a shotgun. She fled the scene and called her lawyer, who in turn called me. We met the client in a safe place and listened to her story. We certainly

Bugs on the Body

As an example of the esoteric nature of collecting physical evidence, consider the problem of bugs on a body. Dead bodies attract bugs. Forensic entomologists can often learn a great deal from examining the bugs found on, and in, dead bodies—the approximate time of death, how long human remains have been undetected, whether the body has been moved after death, perhaps even the location of the murder.

But in order to do that, the bugs need to be properly collected. How does a detective collect bugs as evidence? With a net and tweezers, of course.

It is actually more important to collect larvae and pupae than adult insects. Larvae are those white, wingless, wormy-looking things crawling about feeding off the body (the larvae of flies are called maggots, a term you're probably familiar with). Pupae, on the other hand, don't move at all. They look more like seeds or bits of soft rice. The detective needs to get a cross section of sizes of pupae and larvae, but must be sure to include the largest examples of each. If possible, the detective should collect adult insects as well. If unable to catch them, then extra larvae and pupae should be collected and kept alive in order that they may be raised by the lab. It's easier to determine the species of adult insects.

The larvae and pupae should be put in a container filled with 70 to 80 percent isopropyl alcohol (higher concentrations aren't recommended because they make the insects brittle). Each evidence container should hold only those larvae and pupae collected on a particular part of the body, and should be labeled accordingly—for example, "groin area" or "eye socket." If a large number of insects are placed in a single container, the alcohol should be changed a few hours later. The bodies of insects contain a large proportion of water, which will dilute the alcohol to a point where it will be ineffective as an agent to prevent decay.

Larvae and pupae placed in alcohol will, of course, die. If some are being collected to be raised to adulthood for identification, obviously the detective should not place them in alcohol. Instead they should be put in a container filled with wet cotton balls (to prevent them from drying out). The lid of the container should be replaced with a coffee filter, which allows them to breathe. Again, each container should only contain insects from a particular part of the body.

---

had valid reasons to visit the crime scene, the most important of which would be to verify that a crime scene *existed*. The only thing we knew for certain was that our client said she'd shot somebody.

After consideration, we decided simply to notify the police and let them determine if a crime had been committed. The risk of being accused by the police of tampering with evidence outweighed any possible advantage we could gain by being first on the scene. Besides, crime scenes are best left to the experts. We called the police and told them we thought a crime may have been committed. Shortly thereafter the police confirmed a dead body had indeed been found at the scene, and we made arrangements to accompany the client when she turned herself in. We weren't able to see the actual crime scene until several days later.

A private detective's interest in the crime scene is entirely different from that of a police detective. The police investigator wants to discover who committed the crime; the criminal defense investigator wants to represent the interests of the defendant. The former is searching for truth (or should be); the latter is defending the constitutional rights of an accused person (or should be). Having such disparate motives, it's not surprising police and private detectives look at a crime scene through different lenses.

In general, a private detective's interest in a crime scene can be expressed in two questions:

- What did the police do wrong?
- What did the police miss?

As you can see, the focus of the defense crime scene investigation is directed more toward the police than the offender. Why? Because the state has the burden of proof. To get a conviction, the state has to prove a crime was committed and that it was committed by the defendant. The evidence offered as proof must be gathered legally and according to proper evidence collection techniques. It is the job of the defense team (lawyer and investigator) to make sure the police follow the rules of law and evidence collection. How is this done? By trying to answer the questions I just mentioned.

What Did the Police Do Wrong?

Trying to ferret out mistakes made by the police may seem a mean-spirited and sleazy goal for an investigation. The police, after all, are only trying to do their job, trying to catch the bad guys. Sometimes—maybe through an excess of enthusiasm, maybe out of ignorance—they'll make mistakes. Hey, they're only human. Why can't we cut them some slack?

Those are good arguments and that's a good question. Here's the answer: We can't cut the police any slack because a person's liberty is at stake. It's easy to forget that every defendant who steps into a courtroom is technically innocent. The whole purpose of the trial is to determine if that person is guilty. Mistakes made by the police must be spotted and exposed to reduce the chance of an innocent person being wrongly convicted. Our sympathies may lie with the victims and their families, but as cold as it sounds the victim is not at the center of the trial process—the accused is. And the rights of the accused must, regardless of how offensive it may be, take precedence.

Convicted, but Innocent

We hate to admit this, but every year innocent people are wrongly convicted of crimes. A study of over two hundred wrongful convictions revealed that over 10 percent were due to either carelessness or negligence on the part of members of the criminal justice system. Scary? Absolutely, but not as scary as this fact: 15 percent of the wrongful convictions were due to *intentional* police misconduct.

One of the functions of a criminal defense investigator is to review all the physical evidence to determine if it was properly collected. For example, let's assume the police collected some bloody clothes—shirt, pants, socks. Were these items packaged in plastic? If so, that's an error; bloody cloth sealed in plastic will rot (bloody clothes must be placed in paper bags). Were the items packaged separately or together? If together, then the items will contaminate each other. Did the items come into contact with anything else before being packaged and sealed? If so, they may have been contaminated.

How does the private detective determine if the police made mistakes at the crime scene? By looking at everything—police reports, lab reports, all the film shot at the crime scene (by the police, by news media, by bystanders). By talking to everybody—lab folks, witnesses on the scene, police officers (who likely will refuse to talk informally). By comparing what was done to what should have been done. By taking nothing for granted and by questioning everything.

I once worked a perjury case, a charge you rarely encounter in real life. The perjury charge actually grew out of a failed murder prosecution. The police suspected the defendant had shot and killed a man during an argument. Their theory was the defendant had arrived late to a party at an apartment complex. Just after he'd parked his car and before he'd made his way to the apartment where the party was being held, according to the police theory, the defendant encountered the victim—a man with whom he'd had a long-standing feud. The police believed the two argued and the argument ended in the shooting.

The only problem with the police theory was that they couldn't prove it. They had no witnesses to the shooting. They had several people who were aware of the bad blood between the two. They had the owner of the apartment, who had received a telephone call from the defendant saying he was on his way to the party. They had several other partygoers who heard the victim, who had learned the defendant was coming to the party, say he was going to meet the defendant in the parking lot and "kick the shit out of him." They had the defendant's live-in girlfriend, who had reluctantly told the police her boyfriend had left for the party (she'd asked him not to go because she knew the victim was going to be there, and refused to go with him when he insisted on going). The girlfriend stated the defendant left for the party but returned about forty-five minutes later saying he'd changed his mind. The police had, in other words, a circumstantial case—but no real proof.

The defendant was taken before a grand jury where he stated under oath that he didn't shoot the victim, that he'd left his apartment intending to attend the party but changed his mind and just drove around for a while. He testified he'd never gone anywhere near the apartment complex where the murder took place. However, another grand jury witness stated she had attended the party and had stepped outside for a breath of fresh air. She testified that while she was outside she saw the defendant drive into the apartment parking lot and park his car. She returned to the party without seeing anything else.

The defendant was charged with perjury—lying under oath that he'd never been near the apartment complex where the murder occurred. My job was to investigate the witness who claimed to have seen the defendant there.

After reading the statement the woman had given to the police detective, I went to her home to interview her. She, of course, refused to speak with me. I then began to interview the other people at the party, asking them about the witness and her relationship with the victim and the defendant. Although everybody at the party agreed the witness had been there, nobody could say whether she'd left the party briefly for fresh air as she'd claimed in her testimony.

I also began a background check of the witness. The background check revealed she had been arrested several times on minor charges but had never been convicted. In fact, in all but the first couple of cases the charges against her were dropped. The woman's friends had a ready explanation for this; they said she was sleeping with a cop.

You hear that sort of story fairly often from folks who are routinely involved in petty crime, usually about somebody who has been lucky in her criminal career. It's rarely true, but some folks would rather believe a person has a Get Out of Jail Free card than to say that person was just lucky. I doubted the story was true, but I checked it out all the same.

To my surprise, it appeared the story might be true. I wasn't able to confirm that the witness had a sexual relationship with the police officer, but I gathered enough information to establish they had some sort of relationship. It took a lot of talking, a lot of smiling and a great deal of effort, but I eventually learned the name of the cop. It was the same detective who had taken her statement in the perjury case. In fact, this same detective had been in charge of the defendant's homicide investigation. This detective, I discovered, was what is known as a blue flamer—an eager detective who clears a lot of cases and is being groomed for promotion. A lot of his cases had been initiated by information provided by a confidential informant.

Given the witness's history of having criminal charges dismissed and the detective's history of clearing cases based on a confidential informant, it seemed likely she was his regular CI. They may or may not have been sleeping together, but clearly they were involved with each other. It appeared possible—maybe even probable—that the detective, unable to get the defendant on a homicide charge, decided to cook up the perjury charge.

If the witness had, in fact, seen the defendant arrive at the party, the police made a mistake by having her give a statement to a detective with whom she had a relationship. It damaged both his and her credibility. In addition, the police made a mistake having the detective who had failed to get a homicide indictment also be in charge of the perjury investigation. It smacked of personal spite.

Did the defendant kill the victim? I don't know. Did he perjure himself when he claimed he never went to the apartment complex? I don't know. Did the witness and the detective concoct the story in order to get the defendant? I don't know. What I do know is that the police made several mistakes. And when those mistakes were pointed out to the county attorney, the perjury charge was withdrawn.

What Did the Police Miss?

The police, as we've pointed out, are only human. Like all of us, they're sometimes prone to overlook things. Maybe because they're in a hurry, maybe because they've jumped to what seemed an obvious conclusion. The reasons they might overlook something aren't relevant. The fact is they do, and a good criminal defense investigator takes advantage of that fact.

It's difficult to categorize the things that police detectives might miss, but they generally fall into three broad areas. The police sometimes miss:

- asking the right question
- looking for other explanations
- looking at other suspects

It's easiest to demonstrate these with examples.

Asking the Right Question

One night in a small New England village somebody stole a bulldozer from a landfill and used it to level the police station. Nobody was hurt; it was a small police force with only a single officer on duty at night. That officer was out on patrol when the station was destroyed. Based on the report of a witness, a local man known to be an alcoholic was arrested and charged with the crime.

Although nobody saw the actual destruction of the station, the witness claimed to have seen the defendant—who was obviously intoxicated—messing with the bulldozer. The defendant was known to bear a grudge against the police in that village, and several folks had heard him utter vague threats against the police. The defendant claimed to have been in an alcoholic blackout at the time of the crime, but admitted to his defense team that it was possible he did it.

There was a strong circumstantial case against the defendant. There was no evidence to suggest the defendant might be innocent. But the police overlooked a basic element of the crime: authorization. They had to prove the defendant wasn't authorized to destroy the police station. It's not illegal to destroy a building; it's only illegal if the building doesn't belong to you or you haven't been authorized to destroy it.

A little research showed the property on which the police station stood wasn't owned by the village. It was actually owned by a private citizen who had intended to donate the property to the town but hadn't followed through with the paperwork. In addition, the station was built with materials donated by other private citizens.

On the day of the trial, the prosecution couldn't produce the owner of the property or the police station. There was nobody who could testify the defendant wasn't authorized to destroy the building. Nobody could show a crime had been committed.

Now, it's hard to fault the police for failing to ask about such an obvious fact. But those of us on the defense team asked the right question. If the police had taken the same care we had, they might have obtained a conviction.

Looking for Other Explanations

There was a young man known on the streets, and by the police, as a small-time dealer in soft drugs (marijuana and hashish). The police had arrested the man in the past but had failed to get a conviction. An informant (another low-level drug dealer who had been arrested and was looking to cut a deal) told the police that this man was storing drugs in the cellar of his rented row house. Based on that information, the police got a search warrant, entered the cellar and, hey, they found a small brick of hashish stored in a locker.

At first glance it looked like a fairly solid circumstantial case. The defendant claimed the drugs weren't his and he had no idea how the drugs got into the locker, but defendants always claim that.

I got involved in the case several months after the defendant had been arrested. One of the last tasks I undertook in the investigation was to visit the row house where the drugs were found. The unit had been rerented, but I managed to convince the new tenant to let me nose around in the cellar (it's amazing how many people actually *want* to play a role in an investigation—as long as the investigation doesn't have anything to do with them).

The cellar, I discovered, was shared by the tenants of the other units in the row house. Each tenant had a separate door leading into the cellar. In addition, there was an outside bulkhead door, the lock on which was broken (at least it was broken when I saw the scene; it wasn't mentioned in the police reports). Anybody could have entered that cellar. The police hadn't attempted to find out what was behind the other doors in the cellar; they simply found the drugs in the locker and stopped looking.

It's possible—even likely—that the defendant put the drugs in the locker. But because the police didn't check to see who else had access to the cellar—and the locker—they were unable to establish beyond a reasonable doubt who put the drugs in that locker.

Looking at Other Suspects

Rather than cast a wide net and see who *might* have committed a crime, police detectives tend to focus on a few likely suspects and then start to build a case against them. This makes sense, of course. It's certainly the most time-efficient way of solving crimes.

However, it's not always the best way.

One afternoon several years ago a man entered a small-town bank, walked up to one of the tellers and politely told her to fill a pillowcase with money. He showed her a handgun and she complied, emptying not only her cash drawers but those of the other tellers. As the man backed out of the bank he wet his pants.

This was a small branch of a small bank in a small town; it didn't even have surveillance cameras. However, the tellers all gave the police a similar description—a man approximately thirty years of age, of average height and weight, with a ruddy complexion and a wide nose. Despite a search of the area, the man was not caught.

A couple weeks later one of the tellers was working the drive-through window. A man who looked suspiciously like the robber drove through and cashed a check. The teller wrote down his license number and immediately called the police. The police responded quickly, chased down the suspect's car and forced him off the side of the road. They surrounded the car, pulled the suspect out at gunpoint and put him face down on the ground. The man wet his pants.

At a lineup, each of the tellers present during the robbery identified the man as the robber. He certainly fit the physical description they'd given earlier. The police began their investigation. They discovered the man had no alibi[1] for the day and time of the crime. He'd been laid off from his job—a well-paid, skilled craftsman position—a few months earlier. The family had been having trouble paying its bills. The man was charged with the crime and placed in jail pending trial.

A few weeks later, the bank was robbed yet again. By the same polite man with the same pillowcase, according to the frightened tellers. When they notified the police, the tellers demanded to know why the suspect had been released from jail. He hadn't; he was still sitting in his cell, working on his San Quentin tan (which is what correctional officers call the distinctive prison pallor of a person who has been inside for a long period of time).

---

[1] The term "alibi" is often read by many people as "lie." In fact, an alibi is simply a declaration that a person was elsewhere at the time of a given event. The word itself is Latin for "elsewhere."

Despite all the circumstantial evidence to the contrary, the tellers had identified the wrong man and the police had arrested the wrong man.

How Can You Defend Those People?

In the discussion of crime scenes from the private detective's perspective, we've managed to avoid mentioning an ugly truth. We've talked about the police making mistakes and the police missing evidence. What we haven't talked about is the fact that despite their mistakes, the police are almost always right about the defendant. Most of the people charged with crimes are, in fact, guilty.

Most. That's the key term. Most are guilty; some aren't. One study offered a conservative estimate that 0.5 percent of all the people arrested for violent crime are factually innocent. I suspect the percentage is higher—probably closer to 2.5 percent and maybe as high as 5 percent. But for the moment let's accept the most conservative estimate. Now consider there were over 9.5 million arrests made for violent crimes in 1995. Even using the most conservative estimate, that means nearly half a million innocent folks were arrested. Not all of them went to trial, of course. But in each of those half million cases, the police believed they were arresting the right person.

That's why the police have to be held to the same high standard of proof in every case. That's why a professional criminal defense investigator can't choose only to defend innocent clients. It's unpleasant to defend a client you know to be guilty. But if the police aren't forced to prove their case every single time, even when the client is blatantly guilty, then it's easier for the occasional innocent person to wind up in prison.

Conclusion

The crime scene is a staple of mystery and detective fiction. It's important for the writer to establish the correct ambience and tone when describing the crime scene, and much of that tone must depend on how the characters behave at the scene.

Police detectives see a crime scene as the best, first link to catching the criminal. For them the scene is hot, active and alive with potential. Good detectives are protective of their scenes, aware that every foot that passes through the scene degrades it. And they see it as *their* scene; they own it and are resentful of those who carelessly disturb it.

Private detectives, on the other hand, usually see cold crime scenes and examine them coldly. They pick through the bones of the scenes looking for some means to attack the cases against their clients. The PIs look for mistakes.

As a writer you have the right to present the crime scene any way you choose. But it's important that you know the truth before you embellish or alter it. There's no reason you can't have a PI discussing evidence at an active crime scene with a police detective, so long as you're aware it doesn't happen that way in real life.

F O U R

INTERROGATION AND INTERVIEWING

Gathering information is the meat and potatoes of detective work. Information generates evidence. As noted in the previous chapter, there are two basic types of evidence: physical evidence and verbal evidence. We've looked briefly at physical evidence; now we turn our attention to verbal evidence.

As I stated before, physical evidence is generally considered to be the most important type of evidence. One reason for this is that physical evidence, while open to interpretation, is inanimate. It's just stuff. It doesn't have motives; it can't intend to deceive. A fingerprint is a fingerprint is a fingerprint. We can debate who the print belongs to, or how it got there, or even whether it was properly collected, but the fingerprint itself is just a thing.

Collecting physical evidence certainly requires some skill, but it's technical skill. Almost anybody can be trained to collect physical evidence. Collecting a fingerprint from a body that's been in the water for a week requires a different set of skills than collecting one from a living person, but once you've learned a new technique it's only a matter of practice.

Collecting verbal evidence is a lot trickier because people are more complex. People mislead, obfuscate, make mistakes,

The Truth About Lying

Let's spend just a brief moment on lying. Lying is an equal opportunity activity. Guilty people lie. Innocent people lie. Crooks lie. Police lie. Presidents lie. Rock singers lie. Parents lie. Children most definitely lie. Movie stars lie. Priests and nuns and ministers and rabbis and mullahs lie. If Santa tells you he was at the North Pole when the crime was committed, you'd better put a detective in a parka and send him to check the alibi. Among the universal truths of detective work is this: Everybody lies.

Guilty people lie because they have reason not to tell the truth. Innocent people lie because they're embarrassed, or because they think the police won't believe the truth, or to protect a friend, or for any of a thousand other reasons.

get confused. Sometimes they just flat-out lie through their teeth.

There are two primary methods of obtaining verbal evidence: interrogation and interviewing. They share a common goal: getting the subject to reveal information. Sometimes it's information the subject has and is reluctant to reveal. Sometimes it's information the subject has and isn't aware of it. Sometimes it's information the subject has and is just waiting for the opportunity to deliver. Interrogation and interviewing are generally used under different circumstances. In addition, they are grounded in radically different psychologies.

In general, people suspected of a crime are interrogated; witnesses (and potential witnesses) are interviewed. Interrogation relies on power and authority; interviewing is a form of verbal seduction. Interrogation is often high intensity; interviewing is usually more laid back. Interrogation is New York; interviewing is Los Angeles.

Interrogation

Most of what the general public knows about interrogation is based on what they've seen on television and in the movies. That's about like getting your information on cosmetics and

Verbal Evidence Versus Testimony

It's important not to confuse verbal evidence with testimony. Verbal evidence is what an investigator gathers during the investigation. It's what people say. Testimony is what is said under oath. Testimony is a person's sworn word.

An interesting sidenote: The term "testimony" comes from the Latin word *testis*, the same word that forms the root of "testicle." When Roman soldiers swore an oath to tell the truth, they placed their hands not over their hearts but over their testicles. Needless to say, women were neither allowed nor capable of giving testimony.

makeup by watching circus clowns. The underlying concept is there, but it's not portrayed very accurately.

In general, interrogation is a style of obtaining information based on the authority of the questioner to compel the subject to cooperate. This is why interrogation is generally the province of police detectives. They have the inherent authority of the badge, an authority that's derived from their monopoly on the power to use lethal force and to detain and arrest (although only the latter plays a part in interrogation).

This is not to suggest that interrogation can't be subtle. It most definitely can. A good interrogator is a master of manipulation and a wonder to behold. A good interrogator could get the archbishop of Canterbury to admit he used to drop slugs into the offering plate when he was a boy.

At the heel of the hunt, interrogation is about control—control of the setting of the interrogation, control of information, control of access to the subject by other people and control of the subject himself.

Control of the Setting

All police stations have at least one interrogation room. It usually has a nickname—the box, the bowl, the shack (all cops seem to have a penchant for nicknames, though I haven't a clue why that's so). Most interrogation rooms look essentially alike: stark, bleak, bare rooms furnished with purely functional institutional-style furniture—a table and a few uncomfortable chairs.

There may be other incidental features—a two-way mirror, a videotape recorder, a voice tape recorder—but the heart and soul of an interrogation room is that it looks heartless and soulless.

This is no accident. Interrogation rooms aren't spartan and austere merely because of budgetary constraints. By controlling the setting the detective sets the mood, and the proper mood for an interrogation is isolation and despair. A good interrogation room is designed to eliminate even the slightest hint that the subject has any connection to an outside world. Preferably no windows, no intercom and certainly no telephone. The table is usually set as far from the door as possible, and the subject usually sits at the farthest end of the table, as far from freedom as possible. Even the light switch and thermostat are often controlled by keys, so if a subject is left alone in the room he has no control over the environment.

The more isolated the subject feels, the more vulnerable and exposed he feels; the more uncomfortable he his, the more likely it is that he'll talk. And that's the point.

Control of Information

Not only do police detectives isolate the subject physically, they also control his access to information. This includes information about what is going on outside the interrogation room, who else is present in the police station (other witnesses, other suspects, friends or family of the subject) and, most importantly, the nature of the evidence in the case. The reason for this is to deprive the subject of any source of emotional strength and to keep him off balance.

As a rule, only the information that may induce a subject to talk is allowed. There are, of course, a few legal exceptions. For example, the police are required to inform a subject if his lawyer arrived.

The control of information also includes the control of *mis*-information. The courts have given police detectives a great deal of latitude with the truth when interrogating a subject. The police can, and do, lie: "We have a witness who saw you do the shooting." "Your picture was taken by a surveillance camera." "The lab found blood on your sneakers." "We found where you stashed the gun." Again, the reason for this is obvious. If the subject believes the evidence is going to show he did it, he's more likely to talk.

But lying to a subject is risky. The risk isn't that the courts might overturn any conviction that comes from the lie; the risk is that the subject will discover the lie. If you tell the subject you know where he stashed the gun, but the subject knows he didn't stash it at all but that he sold it to a buddy, then your credibility is shot. He knows you don't know what you're talking about. And he's far more likely to keep silent.

Control of Access to Other People

One of the biggest impediments to a successful interrogation is other people, such as additional suspects, friends, family or a lawyer. Especially a lawyer. The reason for this is obvious: An outsider is likely to give the subject good advice, such as, "Keep quiet."

As always, there are exceptions. Detectives may allow the subject to catch a glimpse of another suspect, hinting that the other person is in the process of giving a statement incriminating the subject. This may convince the subject that he should try to cut as good a deal for himself as possible. Similarly, the detective may allow the subject to see a minister. Ministers are almost as good at getting people to confess as detectives.

Control of the Subject

Above all a good interrogator controls the subject physically. By this I mean the detective controls the subject's body and his ability to meet his bodily needs. The subject's movement is restricted: He sits, while the detectives stand and move around and tower menacingly over him. The subject's speech is controlled: The interrogators can shout, whisper, bellow, murmur, even sing, but the subject is generally only allowed to speak politely or to cry. Anything the subject wants—a cigarette, a cup of coffee, an aspirin, a sandwich—must come from the interrogator. All of the subject's physical needs—to go to the bathroom, to sleep, to eat— are granted or denied by the interrogator at the interrogator's wish. The subject is dependent on and under the control of the interrogator. This fact is impressed on the subject both overtly and subtly (see the sidebar on confessions on page 74).

Once control is established, it can be relaxed—at the discretion of the detective. Small considerations normally taken for granted, such as going to the toilet or smoking a cigarette, suddenly seem like gifts, like acts of kindness and thoughtfulness. For which the subject is very grateful. How can he express his gratitude? By talking, by giving the interrogator the information she wants to hear.

We all know the good cop/bad cop routine. It's become such a universal part of popular culture that young people in Iran and Indonesia know the routine. It's become something of a cliché. Because it works. It worked fifty years ago; it works today. And it will continue to work in the future.

In the end, an interrogation is a poker game between the subject and the interrogator. A good interrogator stacks the deck as best she can. But the subject always has access to a wild card, a joker that, played properly, will bring any interrogation to a crashing halt. The subject can refuse to answer any questions and demand a lawyer.

Sounds simple, doesn't it. Certainly we all know our Miranda rights by now. We've heard them in the movies and on television often enough. We know we have the right to remain silent and that anything we say can be used against us in court. We know we have the right to a lawyer and that if we can't afford a lawyer one will be appointed to us. For free. We know that if we've committed a crime the very last thing we ought to do is talk about it with the police. We all *know* this.

That's why much of what the detective does in an interrogation—controlling the setting, the information and the access to others—is done in an attempt to keep the subject from playing that wild card. And hey, it usually works. Research shows that nearly 85 percent of people suspected of a crime waive their right to counsel and they answer the questions of the police.

Why? Because the police are clever. They know they must stop questioning a suspect as soon as he demands they stop and requests they fetch him a lawyer. But they also know that unless a suspect makes that demand and requests it in just the right way, they can get around it. A subject who says, "I think I ought to talk to a lawyer," is, according to the law, not actually asking for a lawyer. Similarly a subject who says, "Maybe I shouldn't answer any questions until I talk to a lawyer," isn't specifically refusing to answer questions *or* asking for a lawyer. He's just making comments and observations, which can legally be

Voluntary Confessions?

How far can an interrogator legally go to get a confession? Pretty far. A confession, in order to be admissible in court, must be voluntary. But what does "voluntary" mean? There is no single, clear answer. According to the law (*People v. Breidenbach*, 875 P.2d 879 Colo. 1994), a court should consider the "totality of the circumstances" under which the confession was given. This includes:

- whether the suspect was in custody or was free to leave—and was *aware* of his situation
- whether the suspect had been given the Miranda warnings *prior* to any interrogation, and whether the defendant *understood* and waived his rights
- whether the suspect had the chance to talk to a lawyer or anyone else prior to the interrogation
- whether the suspect was subjected to any overt or implied threat or promise
- the method and/or style used by the interrogator to question the suspect, and the length of time and place of the interrogation
- the suspect's mental and physical condition immediately prior to and during the interrogation, as well as his educational background, employment status and prior experience with law enforcement and the criminal justice system

That's the law. In practice, it's not quite so clear. Consider the case of *Wisconsin v. Konshak*. Konshak, a single male parent with two children, was suspected of being involved in a crime. One afternoon while his children were at a park with a neighbor, the police came to Konshak's home and asked him to accompany them to the police station. He agreed. He wrote a note to the neighbor asking her to care for the children until he returned. At the police station Konshak was read his rights, then interrogated—from 3:30 P.M. until nearly 10:30 P.M. During that time he was not allowed to contact his children; the detectives merely informed him that the kids were being "cared for." Konshak later claimed the interrogating officer told him she would try to get him home to his children, but only if he told her what she wanted to hear and confessed. The detective denied this claim. The police later acknowledged Konshak had been previously diagnosed as suffering from depression. Konshak confessed.

The court later declared Konshak's confession had been voluntary. He had, after all, been given his Miranda warnings. According to the detectives in the case, Konshak had not complained of being tired (despite the seven-hour interrogation). He had been offered and had accepted coffee and cigarettes. He was allowed to use the rest room. Nor did the court believe his assertion that the interrogating detective had coerced him with promises that she would try to get him home to his children if he confessed. According to the court, the "totality of the circumstances" did not support Konshak's argument that his confession was involuntary.

---

ignored. In fact, they can be used against the subject.

"You want a lawyer? OK, it's up to you. But once the lawyers get involved I can't do anything to help you. Go ahead, get yourself some young public defender right out of law school. But I'm telling you, the DA is looking at First Degree here. Myself, I don't think you meant to kill the guy, but hey, if you don't want to give me your side of the story. . . ."

This is where good interrogators become diabolically clever. Once the subject is isolated and controlled, a good interrogator offers the subject the thinnest possibility of hope. Salvation. Or at least a way out of the mess he's in. And all the subject needs to do to find this salvation is talk.

It's a cold business, interrogation.

Interviewing

An interview is a much less intimidating method of obtaining information. Interviews aren't as concerned with control and domination. Where an interrogation is designed to induce the subject to make some sort of admission, interviewing is designed to gather a broader spectrum of information. Interviewing is no less manipulative than interrogation; it's merely less coercive.

Unlike an interrogation, which usually takes place in the controlled setting of a police station, an interview might take place just about anywhere—a subject's home, your office, a bar, a crime scene, a park bench. Since the interviewer doesn't have the same level of control as an interrogator, he must find other ways to induce the subject to talk.

Many private detectives feel police officers (and former police officers turned private investigators) make lousy interviewers: They're simply too accustomed to relying on their authority to get the information they want; they're never forced to find other ways to get people to talk.

Interviewing, at its best, is a form of verbal seduction. You cannot compel the subject to talk; you have to somehow get the subject to *want* to talk. The subject may have to be enticed, coaxed, charmed, wheedled, flattered, cajoled.

An interview is like jazz—improvisational, spontaneous. But don't confuse informality with casualness. As in jazz, the spontaneity must be grounded on a rock-solid base of skills. These include:

- interpersonal skills
- preinterview preparation
- standard interviewing techniques

Most of these skills can be learned. Others are more intuitive; you either have them or you don't.

As writers, some of you will have conducted journalistic interviews. The skills are largely the same. The difference is primarily in the subject on whom the skills will be used. A great many people want to be interviewed for journalistic reasons; very few people want to be interviewed by private detectives.

Interpersonal Skills

A good interviewer needs to be able to get along well with a wide variety of people in an equally wide variety of settings. A good interviewer is a person who can fit in wherever he is—at a horse show, in a biker bar, in an executive's office, in a trailer park. This doesn't mean the interviewer will be at home in all those situations, just that he or she will be able to blend in and not attract much attention.

The interpersonal skills needed to be a good interviewer include:

- courtesy

- adaptability

- self-confidence

These aren't exceptional skills or talents. However, a good interviewer hones them until they become second nature.

Courtesy

Perhaps the most egregious error made in detective fiction is the portrayal of the wisecracking detective. It makes for good dialogue, but it's generally bad detective work. Detectives, as I said earlier, are among the funniest people I know, but they rarely share their humor with outsiders. While there are certainly occasions when it's a good policy to get the subject smiling, wisecracks directed toward an interview subject tend only to alienate the subject. It's rude.

One of the things that made me an effective private detective was the fact that I was raised by a Southern mother. She instilled in me an outmoded notion of courtesy and civility that has proved invaluable. In truth, my courtesy isn't real courtesy at all; it's just good training. If you hand a weapon to anybody who has completed military basic training, that person will check to see if the weapon is loaded. More than a considered act of safety, it's a habit born of training. That's the way my courtesy works. If I see a person approach a door, I hurry to open it—not because I'm polite but because it's a habit born of training.

Courtesy, though, is more than helping folks with their coats or holding the elevator for a hurrying passenger. The very core of courtesy is putting other people at ease, making them feel comfortable. To do that, you have to pay attention to them. Most people have a fairly good intuitive feel for human nature. Unfortunately, many of us are too busy paying attention to our own needs and wants. Good interviewers pay attention to their subjects.

A person who feels comfortable and at ease is more likely to talk openly and freely. Personally, I think you should be courteous even when you're *not* trying to weasel information out of somebody. But when you need to get information from somebody, you'd be foolish not to show her common courtesy.

There are, of course, circumstances under which a good interviewer is rude. The trick is to know *when* to be rude, and then to be rude on purpose. Casual, unthinking discourtesy doesn't take any talent at all.

Think about rudeness for a moment. Rudeness often suggests power. Bosses are rude to their employees. Civil servants are rude to their customers. Police officers are rude to citizens. Why? Partly just because they can get away with it. They can be rude to you and there's really not a damned thing you can do about it. You want your driver's license renewed? Then take a number and get in line and I'll get to you when I get to you. We all recognize that people who are rude to us often have some sort of power over us.

Private detectives use that knowledge. Many times I've started an interview with a witness who has some limited criminal liability in a case—maybe a codefendant in a crime, maybe a witness with a criminal record—and then realized fairly early in the interview there was no point in being polite. Then I get rude. I let them think I don't need their statement and I'm talking to them to give them a chance to help themselves. "You don't want to talk to me? Fine. You got nothing to say I haven't already heard. There's a shit storm coming and I just wanted to give you a chance to get out of the way. If you're too stupid to take advantage of that, I could care less."

The witness becomes confused. The detective is supposed to *want* her statement. Maybe, she thinks, she should start talking, if only to keep out of trouble.

The important thing is for the detective to make a conscious decision to be rude and to be rude only when it's the best or quickest way to get the information.

Adaptability

The psychology graduate student who conducts experiments on lab rats is something of a cliché. But consider this: If it's difficult to predict how a rat will behave, it's far more difficult to predict how a human will behave. Humans, after all, are more complex than rats. Most humans, anyway.

An interview is a process. Despite the preinterview preparation (which we'll discuss later), it's difficult to know how a subject will respond to any given point of that process. A good interviewer pays close attention to the subject of the interview—is the subject nervous, uncomfortable, angry—and adapts as the interview progresses.

Self-Confidence

A quiet self-confidence is critical to the interviewer. Since interviews are often a free-form process, it's important for the interviewer to believe he can handle any situation that arises within the interview. Self-confidence communicates itself to the subject. So does self-doubt.

Preinterview Preparation

Even before a word is spoken, a good interviewer has been at work. It is important to know as much as possible before the interview begins. Knowledge is power. These are some of the things a good interviewer considers before the interview begins:

- Purpose of the interview. Why is this person being interviewed? What sort of information can this person be expected to have? What sort of information is being sought? Interviews are fluid enough that it is easy to go off on a tangent and forget to ask important questions. Several years ago I interviewed a really old man—so old he had served in the Army tank corps under Black Jack Pershing during World War I. This old guy had so many great stories to tell that I kept getting sidetracked. I had to keep reminding myself why I was there, and even then I found myself asking questions about Paris in 1918.

- A general overture tactic. How should this person be approached. Obviously, a bartender will be approached differently than a doctor will be, an older doctor might be approached differently than a younger one, and a woman doctor might be approached differently than a male doctor. It's a good idea to prepare an overture to the subject, but remain adaptable and be prepared to scrap your planned approach and try something different.

- Review of all the available information. Although we sometimes refer to "cold" interviews—those for which the interviewer simply can't prepare in advance—the fact is a good interviewer *always* knows something about the subject before the interview. It might only be how the subject is dressed, but even that can be revealing. A cold interview over the telephone is probably the most difficult generic type of interview, but even in those situations a good interviewer will learn something in advance: Is it a home phone or a business phone? What is the address where the phone is located? Does the subject have an accent or speak in a dialect?

- Interview location. Unlike an interrogator, an interviewer may not have any control over the location of the interview. Still, a good interviewer will take the location of the interview into consideration. Will it be at the subject's house? At her place of work? At the interviewer's office? At a bar? Each location has advantages and disadvantages. I once unwisely sent an adult law student to interview a witness in a bar. The subject had a few drinks and talked freely. Unfortunately, the law student did the same. Her notes were unreadable and her recollection of the interview was pretty vague. A good interviewer considers the advantages and disadvantages of the location before the interview begins.

The better prepared you are for the interview, the easier and more productive the interview will be.

Having said that, I would add a caveat: *Don't overprepare.* While a good interviewer is prepared for the interview, too much preparation can lead to tunnel vision. Some interviewers even write questions in advance, a practice I think leads to a mechanical interview. It makes it too easy to focus on your questions rather than on the subject's answers. Still, different people work in different ways, and some excellent investigators prepare all their questions in advance.

Preinterview preparation won't guarantee a good interview any more than a good interview can guarantee you'll get good facts. But being properly prepared will certainly increase the chances of getting a good interview.

Standard Interviewing Techniques

Anybody can learn standard interviewing techniques, just like anybody can learn to be a plumber or bricklayer. Like any other craft, once you are familiar with the basic skills you can begin to modify them to suit your own style and personality.

Here are some of the things a good interviewer needs to know:

- the appropriate types of questions to ask
- the appropriate vernacular to use
- when to use silence
- when to use embarrassment
- when to be rude
- how to trigger memory

This is not a comprehensive list of things an interviewer needs to know. I'm not sure a comprehensive list is even possible. There are simply too many variables involved. But a good interviewer masters these basics and uses them to mold a personal style.

Appropriate Types of Questions

Interview questions come in two basic categories: closed and open-ended. A closed question is intended to elicit very specific information. It can be answered with a single word. Yes or no. Left or right. North, east, south or west. Closed questions are precise, quick to answer and easily understood. They are good for obtaining fundamental facts. Unfortunately, closed questions only give the interviewer a limited amount of information and don't allow any nuance.

Open-ended questions are more sweeping in nature. They are intended to elicit more detailed and nuanced answers. "What did you see?" is an open-ended question. An open-ended question makes more demands on the subject, requires more time to answer and includes the risk of obtaining a lot of useless, irrelevant information.

In general, it's best to begin an interview with open-ended questions to elicit as much information as possible. Once the interviewer has a grasp on the basic facts, it's possible to gradually narrow the questions to closed questions. Begin with questions like "What did you see?" and finish with questions like "Was the desk lamp turned on or off?"

There are also forms of questions a good interviewer avoids, including these:

- Leading questions. These can contaminate the answer by giving the subject information she might not have had previously. "He was carrying a .45 caliber pistol, wasn't he?" "He had a tattoo of a dolphin on his shoulder, didn't he?"

- Double-barreled questions. These questions, actually two questions in one, confuse the subject. "Did he have an accent or any scars?" "Were you wearing your glasses, or was the lighting sufficient?"
- Presumptive questions. These questions presume information that hasn't been offered. "What's his favorite brand of scotch?" "What church do you attend?"
- Damning questions. These are questions that have no acceptable answer. A classic example is, "Do you still beat your wife?" Any response damns the subject.

The form of the question will often determine the value of the response. A good interviewer deliberately molds the questions to get the best possible information.

Appropriate Vernacular

It's important for the interviewer to be aware of the level of the conversation. A good interviewer generally tries to speak at the same social level as the subject. This doesn't mean the interviewer should try to speak like the subject. Nothing sounds quite so absurd as a middle-class suburban white guy trying to walk and talk like a black inner-city gangster. However, it's possible (and generally helpful) to match the social level of your speech to the social level of the subject. When talking to a truck driver, talk at the truck driver's level. When talking to an Episcopalian minister, talk at the minister's level.

When matching your speech to the social level of the interview subject, it has to sound natural and unaffected. People aren't stupid—well, some are. But even stupid people can often tell when a person is trying to sound like someone they're not.

On the other hand, there are times when it's advisable to deliberately talk at a different social level from that of the subject. Formal English can sometimes be more intimidating to a truck driver than a handgun. Conversely, street language may elicit more information from an Episcopalian minister than will standard English. The important thing is to know when the switch is appropriate.

When to Use Silence

We live in a culture that insists on filling every waking moment with noise. Conversation, television, radio. Even our cars and vending machines talk to us. We have grown uncomfortable with silence.

A good interviewer uses that. Silence during an interview almost always works to the interviewer's advantage. It might be that the subject is giving serious consideration to his answer, which is good. Or it might be that the subject is trying to avoid an answer, which is also good. If the subject is trying to avoid answering, the answer is probably important. Given our cultural discomfort with silence, the subject will often try to fill the gap in the conversation. In doing so, something worthwhile may be revealed. The more awkward the silence, the more likely something interesting will come out.

When to Use Embarrassment

Most people are made uncomfortable by another's embarrassment. When we see somebody who has made a fool of himself, we often try to make him feel better. At some point in their careers all interviewers make embarrassing mistakes. Their first instinct is to cover up, to rid themselves of the shame. A really good interviewer will use his own embarrassment to get the subject's sympathy. In that situation the interviewer will use his own weakness as a strength. Instead of letting his embarrassment ruin an interview, a good interviewer will turn it to his advantage and use it to control the subject.

Although it is much more difficult, a good interviewer will also use a subject's embarrassment to advantage. It's a little like social judo. Judo is the martial art that's based on turning the attacker's power against him.

When to Be Rude

Earlier I stressed the importance of courtesy and gave a brief example of when to be rude. Controlled incivility is useful to shock the interview subject, to throw her off balance or to show that the interviewer means business. It's much more difficult to learn to be rude effectively than it is to learn to be polite. Discourtesy requires a delicate touch; it can more easily offend the subject and ruin any hope of a successful interview. But on certain occasions, under certain circumstances, it can be an effective technique.

Embarrassment—An Effective Investigative Tool

Once I needed to interview a young couple about an attempted murder. They were reluctant to get involved, and when I appeared at their door they grudgingly let me in. The couple had a toddler of indeterminate gender careening around the room in diapers. After a few minutes it was obvious the couple weren't going to talk to me about the incident, but they were too polite to tell me to leave. In an attempt to ingratiate myself, I picked up the toddler as it wandered by me and dandled it on my knee as I talked. The child was an enthusiastic dandlee and squealed in delight. The parents, however, weren't impressed. Just as I was about to give up, the child got a surprised look on its face and had a prodigious bowel movement. It strained the capacity of the diaper, and a bit dribbled onto my pants. The parents, of course, were terribly embarrassed. As was I. But it proved to be just the wedge I needed to get the couple to talk.

How to Trigger Memory

Another of the universal truths of detective work is this: People forget. They forget simple things—where they put their glasses. They forget trivial things—the author of that novel about the medical examiner. They forget really important things—anniversaries, appointments, where they put the car keys. A good interviewer needs to be able to spark memories, to get people to remember things they think they've forgotten.

There are several methods for triggering memory. Among the most effective are the following:

- Build on a specific reference point.
- Relate the incident in reverse chronological order.
- Relate the incident from a different perspective.

Some of these techniques require more time and effort than others. If one doesn't work, try another.

Build on a Specific Reference Point. Few people will claim a totally clear memory of any event. However, in every event there are usually several small incidents or moments that the subject recalls clearly. It might be anything—cutting a cake, a joke somebody told, a specific conversation. Those are reference points. Solid reference points are fairly easy to establish. They come naturally during an interview. The subject will often state something like, "We were playing Frisbee when we heard the first shot," or, "Martha had just started dinner when . . ."

Once the reference point is established, use questions to build on it: Who were you playing Frisbee with? Who was facing in the direction of the shots? What were you doing immediately before you played Frisbee? Did you see anybody in the area? Who first commented on the shots? What did that person say? What happened next?

Establish the reference point. Build on it. Develop a flow from one reference point to the next.

Relate the Incident in Reverse Chronological Order. Time, according to Aristotle, is the measure of change with respect to before and after. What he meant is that people tend to think of time in a linear way. That's how we relate events when discussing them with other people. First incident A happened, then incident B, followed by incidents C and D. Our memory of all these incidents may not be equally clear. We're pretty solid on D because it happened more recently than A. Despite that, we generally begin our descriptions of events with incident A, often the incident we remember least well.

Sometimes it helps to start at the end and go backward. Incident D happened. What happened just before? Incident C, and that happened right after incident B. The novelty of imagining the events in reverse order, combined with our clearer knowledge of more recent events, can often spark more and better memories.

Relate the Incident From a Different Perspective. A person naturally tends to relate an event from a personal perspective. This is what *I* saw. This is *my* memory of the event. Sometimes a lodged memory can be jarred loose by having the subject relate the event from a different perspective. Say to the subject, "Imagine you are a ghost standing in the corner of the room during the incident. What would you have seen?" It's remarkable how a different version of the event can emerge.

False Memories

It appears to be remarkably easy to implant a false memory, especially in younger people. Dr. Elizabeth Loftus, the preeminent scholar of the topic of witness memory, illustrated the point by having one of her researchers make up a fictional account of an incident in which a young boy got lost in a shopping mall and was helped by a kindly older man. Even though the incident never happened, it was related to a four-teen-year-old boy as a true story, one that had allegedly happened to that boy when he was five. Within two days the fourteen-year-old could remember how frightened he had been while he was lost, how fearful he was that he would never see his family again. He could clearly recall the man who had found him and helped him, even recalling the man's flannel shirt and the fact that he was bald and wore glasses. He could recall how upset his mother had been after they were reunited. Even after being told the event never happened, the young boy clung to his memories.

When trying to trigger a memory, it's critical that the interviewer not actually *plant* a new memory. Memory, especially that of children, is fragile and can be molded by an incompetent or unscrupulous interviewer.

Some Basic Interviewing Tips

The most common interviewing mistake is the failure of the interviewer to establish a rapport with the subject. I'm not suggesting that the interviewer and the subject need to like, care for or respect each other; I'm saying that there needs to be some sort of bond between them. I've seen some videotapes of experts interviewing sexual sadists. A more despicable lot of men would be hard to find, and yet the interviewers are uniformly considerate with them. Not friendly, necessarily, nor sympathetic, but considerate. These are good interviewers (otherwise I wouldn't be seeing the videotapes); they've managed somehow to establish a bond with people most of the population would prefer to see die slowly.

The following are a few interviewing tips I found particularly helpful during my career as a criminal defense investigator.

Suppress Your Personal Opinions

What the detective believes and feels is entirely beside the point. The detective's job is to get information, not establish her opinion or correct the subject's flawed view of the world. It doesn't matter if you are an animal rights activist and your subject is a fox hunter. What matters is the information you are seeking. I've had to interview child molesters, rapists, ardent racists—people I find reprehensible. But each of them had (or might have had) information I needed. It was more important to get the information than to spare my tender feelings.

Never Judge the Subject

You may think the subject's religious beliefs are nothing more than offensive superstitions. You may find the subject's sexual practices disgusting. You may loathe the subject's stance on reproductive rights. You're absolutely allowed to disapprove of the subject's attitudes, opinions and behavior.

What you should not allow yourself to do is disapprove of the subject himself. Everybody is sensitive to the feeling of being judged. A subject who feels personally condemned is almost certainly not going to give you the information you want.

Don't Think of the Next Question

This is a common interviewing mistake. The investigator is so busy thinking of her next question that she's not listening to the subject's answer to the question just asked. People catch on quickly to whether you're paying attention to them. They're properly insulted if they discover you're not listening. In effect, you're saying their answers aren't worth listening to.

Never Tell a Lie That Isn't True

I realize this sounds strange. But there are times in an interview when the interviewer may be less than truthful. For me, this took place most often during the early part of the questioning, while I was attempting to establish a rapport with the subject. I sometimes found myself inventing characteristics that were similar to the subject's. Did the subject have a domineering husband? My father was domineering. Does the subject suffer from migraine headaches? I've had terrible cluster headaches for years. Is the subject wearing a Green Bay Packers football jersey? I admit to being a cheesehead.

Each of those statements about myself was a lie. But when I said them, they actually seemed true. It didn't matter that I really don't care for football and hadn't seen a Packers game on television since Paul Hornung played; I *was* a Packer's fan. It didn't matter that my father really was a gentle, considerate man; I *felt* the oppression of a domineering father.

I don't know how detectives develop this trait; I don't even know if it is something that can be developed. It's probably a sign of some incipient personality disorder, but when I say such things, they seem entirely true to me. And that's important, because most people can sense counterfeit emotion.

Conclusion

Interrogation and interviewing are primary skills for detectives. Aside from a few folks who specialize in surveillance or highly technical fields, no detective—police or private—can survive long without some degree of expertise in these skills. As a writer you should be aware of the reality. Whether the behavior of your characters conforms to reality or not is entirely an artistic decision, but you should be able to make an informed decision.

One of the things I find most disconcerting about many detective stories is the way the protagonist treats the people he is trying to get information from. It's great fun to write dialogue for a wisecracking detective, but a real investigator who spoke that way to witnesses, cops, supervisors and clients would be out of business in a New York minute. Too often that sort of dialogue is just a cheap way to show the detective is clever and a loner.

Even worse, in my opinion, are the detectives who, when confronted by a group of thugs, insult them. These scenes almost always end the same way; the thugs knock the detective around. And who can blame them?

What offends me most about this common hard-boiled scene is that getting beat up and hurt is just bad business. Even if we disregard the physical pain, we should remember that getting hurt costs money. Not only are there medical bills, but it's also hard to work when you're in pain. And for private detectives if you don't work, you don't get paid.

Remember, for real-life detectives it's not about proving that they're tough; it's about getting the job done.

F I V E

SURVEILLANCE

This is one of the tasks most often associated with private detectives. The trench-coated private eye leaning against the lamppost and burning a butt is a stock image in American popular culture. Of course, it's a dreadful way to conduct a covert surveillance, but the image is more about style than substance.

When we speak of surveillance, we're generally talking about stationary surveillance. Mobile surveillance is commonly called tailing (and will be discussed in the next chapter). It's a small distinction, but one worth noting. Small distinctions are important to writers and detectives alike.

Surveillance refers to the act of watching, preferably without being observed. While there are certain circumstances when a police detective or a private investigator will conduct an overt surveillance, most surveillance is done covertly.

Surveillance is a quiet craft, although you wouldn't know it from the way it's portrayed in the entertainment media. In the movies surveillance is often shown as a sort of pajama party. Somebody is always slipping out to get food. There is some giggling, some deep and meaningful personal discussion, the occasional spat. There are almost always two characters involved, and always in the same room or car—there isn't much cinematic tension in a person sitting quietly and alone.

Unfortunately, many writers seem to take their cues on surveillance from the movies. Folks, it just ain't that way. At least not if it's done properly. In this chapter we'll take a look at how to do it properly. We'll also discuss some of the common errors and problems that take place in the field. It's important for the writer to remember that the field has no respect for the textbook.

There isn't much difference between the surveillance techniques used by police detectives and private investigators. Each group has some advantages over the other, which I'll point out as they arise.

Overt Surveillance

Overt surveillance is the least common form of surveillance. It's a violation of all the standard rules of surveillance (which is generally the act of seeing without being seen). In overt surveillance the investigator takes pains to make certain the subject is aware he is being watched. This is done simply by being obvious. By standing in the open, by smiling and nodding and waving at the subject. Maybe even by wearing a trenchcoat and leaning against the lamppost while burning a butt.

Overt surveillance is conducted for two reasons:

- to make an announcement
- to make the subject nervous

Although overt surveillance is rarely used, it is used more by police detectives than by private investigators.

When used as an announcement, overt surveillance is meant to intimidate the subject. The detective is gloating, informing the subject, "You're nailed. I own you. There is nothing you can do, no way you can avoid the inevitable. It's only a matter of time until I arrest your butt."

Overt surveillance is also used to make the subject nervous. Sometimes it is used as a bluff, a last-ditch attempt to force the subject's hand. If nothing else works, perhaps the police can rely on their coercive power to make the subject jittery and apprehensive enough to make a mistake.

The police, of course, have the corner on the legal coercion market, but there are occasions (most commonly in domestic matters) when private detectives use overt surveillance. When it is used, it is used for the same reasons: to either make the subject uncomfortable and nervous or to announce that the game is over.

The problem with overt surveillance is that it is harassment. Harassment is illegal, for both police and private detectives. Overt surveillance is stalking (though stalking laws often require some form of threat). The very fact that it is illegal is, sometimes, part of the intimidation. The detective is announcing that not even the law can keep him from getting to you.

Overt surveillance can be unnerving to the subject. That's the point.

Covert Surveillance

This is the most common form of surveillance. The reason is obvious: People don't behave normally (whatever that means) if they know they're being watched.

Why conduct a covert surveillance? Police detectives generally have only two reasons: They either want to catch somebody committing a crime (or prevent them from committing that crime), or they want to learn the contacts of a known criminal (knowing who visits a drug dealer, for example, is valuable information). Private detectives, on the other hand, may just want to see if somebody is doing something she shouldn't be doing (an "injured" worker chopping wood, for example, or a spouse engaging in illicit sex), or may simply be trying to learn who the subject meets (or who visits a certain building).

The focus of covert surveillance can be:

- a person
- a location

In essence the focus depends on the object of suspicion. Most commonly the object is a person—an errant spouse, a suspected criminal, a distrusted employee. However, sometimes the focus is a location. For example, the police may surveil a suspected crack house or a private investigator may try to locate a bail jumper by staking out his mother's house.

Obviously a person is far more difficult to surveil than a location. People are mobile, they're quirky and unpredictable. On the other hand, people are usually more interesting to watch. Surveillance of a location offers the detective a variety of advantages. The more familiar a detective is with the surroundings, the better. Of course, familiarity breeds contempt; surveillance of a location is generally duller, and it's easier to make a mental mistake.

Getting Gotti

Surveillance of a location can be a pure nightmare. Consider the difficulties faced by the FBI in maintaining a surveillance on the Ravenite Social Club on Mulberry Street in New York City's Little Italy. This small, unassuming little building was the headquarters of Mafia don John Gotti.

In theory it should not have been difficult to maintain a surveillance of the club. It was, after all, a small building with a clearly visible entrance on a fairly well-lighted street. However, the street is quite narrow and, although it's located in Little Italy, the club is located away from the more crowded restaurant section. The narrow street makes it difficult for the subject to slip away unnoticed; however, it also makes it difficult for surveillance to go unnoticed. The area has the feel of a small neighborhood, where people are wary of strangers. And, of course, the fact that the folks who frequented the club (Mafia soldati) were constantly on guard didn't help. Yet because they prepared properly, the FBI managed to maintain surveillance on the club for a long time.

There are basically three aspects to covert surveillance: preparation, the surveillance itself and breaking off the surveillance. Proper preparation will make it easier to conduct the surveillance and to break it off at the appropriate time (which, essentially, is before you get caught).

Surveillance Preparation

A successful surveillance is predicated on proper preparation (if you'll forgive the alliteration). Preparation should always be the detective's first concern. As a writer, you have an active imagination. In preparing for a surveillance of any length, use that imagination to speculate on all the things that might possibly go wrong. You won't think of them all, but this exercise will help you think of many.

There are four main steps a good detective takes to prepare for a surveillance:

- Scout the area.

- Wear the appropriate clothes.

- Bring the proper equipment.

- Bring the necessary amenities.

It's certainly possible to conduct a successful surveillance operation without good preparation, just as it's possible to write a best-selling novel in one draft. It can be done; it's just not very likely.

Scout the Area

Scouting permits a good detective to become intimately familiar with the site of the surveillance. It allows the detective to locate several alternate spotting sites and to determine which will be best under what conditions. For example, one location might be best in the morning when the sun is low, and another might be best at night when the surveillance will be dependent on the street lighting and a clear line of sight.

Scouting also gives the detective the opportunity to consider the traffic patterns in the area, both foot and motor. It's possible that the success of the surveillance will depend on a detective's foreknowledge of the times of day when the streets and sidewalks are busiest or quietest.

Another advantage of scouting is that it allows the detective the chance to become familiar with the various entrances and exits to the area. There is no point in concentrating on the front door of an apartment building if you know the underground garage opens onto a side street.

Finally, scouting is important when a surveillance is expected to last any length of time. Smart detectives will become acquainted with the entire neighborhood—the stores, the gas stations, the markets, the places that have public toilet facilities. It may not be necessary to know about these places, but you never know.

Wear the Appropriate Clothes

It's important to wear the appropriate clothing for several reasons. First, it's necessary for the investigator to blend in with the surroundings. If the surveillance is being conducted by the docks and the detective is dressed in a sport coat and tie, he's going to get burned (caught, that is) rather quickly. Similarly, an investigator wearing an aloha shirt and Ray-Bans will attract attention if surveilling a tavern frequented by Wall Street bond traders. A surveillance is supposed to be inconspicuous.

A second reason the appropriate clothes are important is the investigator's personal comfort. It goes without saying that a detective should dress warm in the winter and cool in the summer, but consider the fact that detectives don't always have the luxury of moving around a lot when conducting a surveillance. You get both hotter in the summer and colder in the winter when you can't move around. And moving around too much on surveillance attracts attention.

Bring the Proper Equipment

Binoculars, monoculars, night vision (or starlight) scopes, still cameras (with the appropriate film and lenses), video cameras, voice-activated tape recorders, transmitters and receivers, audio amplification devices—these are all tools that might be used by police and private detectives during surveillance (we'll look at these devices in a later chapter). A good detective generally carries more than he thinks will be needed. And batteries, batteries, batteries. Nothing will make you feel sillier than to be sitting in a car surrounded by tens of thousands of dollars of high-tech surveillance equipment, only to discover that you can't use the one device you need because you don't have fresh double-A batteries.

Bring the Necessary Amenities

What is "necessary"? Necessity is determined by the situation. Sunscreen might be necessary. Or bug spray. Or a cotton sweater. Some items, however, should always be in the detective's vehicle when on surveillance:

- A small medical kit (including aspirin, bandages, eyedrops, tweezers, ointment) for all those bites, scrapes, nicks, cramps and headaches that plague humankind.

- Paper towels. Stuff gets spilled, messes are made, things drip. It's not pleasant working in a messy environment. A few clean rags are also nice for those situations that are too tough for paper towels.

- Tape (both duct tape and Scotch tape). Tape is a remarkably versatile tool. I've used Scotch tape to affix seven photographs of the legitimate inhabitants of a four-apartment unit to my window visors (I needed to be able to distinguish between folks who belonged in that unit and those who didn't). And when breaking off surveillance for the night, I've often put a small bit of duct tape on the tread of a vehicle's rear tire; when my replacement arrived early in the morning, he could determine if the car had been used after I'd left. I've used duct tape for everything from temporarily patching a fiberglass canoe to taping plastic bags over my feet to keep them warm in the winter.

- Plastic bags. Large self-sealing ones are best. These are handy for holding greasy radio frequency vehicle-tracking transmitters after they've been removed from the target car (covered in a later chapter), for holding everything from trail mix to polaroid photographs and, of course, for keeping your feet warm when it gets really cold in the car.

- Survival tool. This is a terrific all-purpose folding device. It functions as pliers and wire cutters, has one or more knife blades, a screwdriver blade, a Phillips blade and a saw-edged blade. I used to carry a small tool kit; this one device allowed me to pitch the whole thing.

- String. It isn't used often, but when you need string nothing else will do. I've used string to replace a broken shoelace, to tie an ink pen I kept losing to the door handle and, yes, to tie around my finger as a reminder to do something.

- Flashlights—a large four- or five-cell light and a pocket light. The big lights not only cast a high-powered beam, they can also double as effective clubs. Be sure to have extra batteries for both flashlights.

It's also wise to bring along extra pens or pencils, some breath mints and as many extra batteries as you can manage. Good detectives don't bring books or magazines; they're supposed to be paying attention to the subject, not catching up on their reading. I know some detectives who listen to audio books, but I've always found them distracting.

One category of amenity needs to be discussed: food and drink. A good detective gives this matter careful thought. It's important to find a balance between feeding the body and disposing of the waste (and I'm not talking about the wrapper on your Hi-Energy bar). From experience I recommend trail mix and a large thermos filled with ice chips. Trail mix can be a nice source of needed energy, it doesn't run through your intestinal system in a hurry, and a little of it can last a long time. Ice chips will quench your thirst without filling your bladder.

Food and drink are less of an issue for police detectives than for private investigators. Police detectives are rarely engaged in solo surveillance. They generally have the luxury of breaking away from the surveillance long enough to take care of those pesky bodily needs. Private investigators, on the other hand, may dislike solo surveillance but are more likely to find themselves conducting one. It's largely a matter of economics; a private client may not be willing to foot the cost of two, three or four agents conducting a surveillance. Police detectives also face budgetary constraints, but when a surveillance is approved it is generally accepted that several officers will be involved.

Surveillance Techniques

When you consider it, the actual act of surveillance is absurdly simple. One simply watches and pays attention. Anybody with decent vision (or vision correctable by eyeglasses) who can manage to remain awake can theoretically engage in surveillance. The techniques are basically the same whether the surveillance is being conducted by one person or by a team (although it's almost always easier and more effective with a team).

Of course, surveillance isn't simple at all. There are a great many things that have to be taken into account when conducting a surveillance. Among them are:

- mode of surveillance
- surveillance location(s)
- concealment

Oh, What a Relief . . .

Bladders and bowels. They have to be discussed. Nature can be stalled for a time but cannot be denied. At some point in a long surveillance the detective will almost certainly find it necessary to urinate and perhaps defecate. This may be one of the few areas of investigative work in which men have a true advantage over women. Men, after all, can urinate into a milk carton (I suppose a determined woman could also, but certainly not as easily).

If conducting a surveillance on foot, the detective can usually find some public or commercial building with a toilet—a gas station, a store, a hotel. If not, well, there are no rules covering this. Find a private spot and take care of business (again, easier for male detectives). I suppose it's possible to wear those adult diapers. I've never tried this, so I can't offer any advice.

The situation is somewhat improved when conducting a surveillance from a vehicle. Some surveillance vans have the luxury of built-in toilets, but a great deal of surveillance is conducted from a car. Although men have the advantage of being better equipped for this situation, don't imagine it's an easy process. I also highly recommend milk cartons for this procedure; most bottles have too small an opening—and this is not a project that is forgiving of mistakes.

In regard to how women investigators deal with this situation, I'm afraid I'm clueless.

Good detectives give some thought to each of these aspects of surveillance, both in preparation for and periodically during the surveillance.

Mode of Surveillance

There are three primary modes of surveillance:

- from a parked vehicle
- on foot
- from a building

Each mode has its advantages and disadvantages. Sometimes

Roughing It

The different expectations of private detectives versus police detectives in regard to food and creature comforts during surveillance were made clear to me several years ago. I was one of two PIs hired on a subcontract by a small investigative firm to maintain a surveillance of a doctor's office. The other subcontractor was a former police officer turned PI. This man arrived with a small cooler in his car. In the cooler he had three or four Dagwood-size sandwiches, a bag of tortilla chips, a container of jalapeño cheese dip and a six-pack of Jolt cola (a highly caffeinated soda; he correctly thought the caffeine would help keep him alert, but he didn't realize caffeine increases the need to urinate). You'd have thought he was going to watch the Super Bowl, not conduct a surveillance.

detectives, especially police detectives, will employ more than one mode during a surveillance. For example, one investigator may be surveilling the subject (or location) from a parked van while a second ghosts about the area on foot.

Of the three modes of surveillance I have a preference for surveillance on foot. It's more physically demanding, but I generally feel more involved in the case when I'm on foot. Being on foot also gives me a greater illusion of freedom (although, in fact, I'm still anchored to the target person or location).

Surveillance From a Parked Vehicle

Although I have no data on this, I suspect the majority of surveillances are conducted from parked vehicles. This has the distinct advantage of leaving the investigator instantly prepared to tail the subject should she leave. In addition, vehicles are large and can hold a great deal of equipment. Vehicles also provide the investigator with a certain level of concealment (especially if the vehicle is specifically designed for surveillance work). Finally, a vehicle offers some protection from the elements. Nothing is more miserable than conducting a surveillance on foot and being caught in a sudden downpour.

Vehicles, however, can't fully protect the investigator from the heat and cold because the heater or air conditioner can't be operated during the surveillance. A parked vehicle with either the air conditioner or heater running attracts far too much attention.

Perhaps the primary disadvantage of surveillance from a vehicle is that vehicles limit the locations from which investigators can conduct the surveillance. Vehicles are pretty much restricted to streets and parking lots.

Police detectives and a great many private investigators have access to vehicles (usually small vans) specially modified for surveillance. These are nondescript vehicles, usually having at least one one-way window with a reflective surface. Surveillance vehicles have several advantages, including storage room for a tremendous amount of surveillance equipment (some of which will be discussed in the chapter on investigative technology). In addition, surveillance vans often have small refrigerators or coolers for food and drink. Finally, surveillance vans possess that bit of technology most prized by experienced investigators—a toilet.

Surveillance on Foot

Foot surveillance is often used in conjunction with the other modes of surveillance. It has the distinct advantage of mobility. A detective on foot generally has a much larger selection of spotting locations—those places where investigators set up to conduct the surveillance. Also, moving around helps the detective to remain alert. An investigator on foot is much less likely to fall asleep on the job (although there have been times I've considered that a disadvantage).

There are two primary disadvantages to foot surveillance. First, the detective isn't immediately prepared to tail the subject if she should suddenly succumb to the urge to go for a drive. Second, it radically reduces the amount of equipment available to the detective. Certainly a detective engaged in foot surveillance can wear a small fanny pouch without attracting too much attention, but it's risky to tote around a small knapsack. Any carrying case large enough to haul around a useful variety of gear is going to be both too heavy and too conspicuous.

Surveillance From a Building

Under certain circumstances, surveillance will be conducted from a building. Obviously, this mode of surveillance is more likely to be used when the focus of attention is a location rather than a person. The location may be a public building, such as a bar or restaurant, or a private one, such as an office or apartment.

Buildings have two great advantages, the first being the ability to hold huge amounts of equipment. Tripods, for example, which allow the investigator to use long lenses, powerful telescopes and more sophisticated electronic equipment. The second advantage is personal convenience, such as running water, a refrigerator and a toilet.

Surveillance Location(s)

As I noted earlier when discussing preparation, it's important for the detective to select one or more surveillance sites. Obviously, when conducting a surveillance from a building this is only a factor once; you make whatever arrangements are necessary and you move in. However, surveillances on foot and, to a lesser extent, those conducted from a parked vehicle, require more than one surveillance location.

The advantages of multiple surveillance locations are twofold. First, a person or a vehicle that never moves from a location is likely to attract attention. People in the area (neighbors, shop owners, etc.) will begin to grow suspicious and may even notify the police. Second, moving around helps prevent the investigator from becoming bored and distracted.

If possible, good detectives scout primary and secondary sites in advance and become familiar with them. The primary site may change as the conditions of the surveillance change.

Concealment

Obviously, the point of covert surveillance is to see without being seen. That makes it necessary for the detective to blend into the environment. How this is done depends on the environment. While engaged in a foot surveillance I've dressed in dirty overalls and field jacket and sat on a stoop with drunks; a pint of vodka made me welcome, although I sipped from a bottle of water wrapped in a paper bag. I've dressed in poet's black and sat for hours with café writers in coffee shops. I've worn T-shirts and shorts and hung around a basketball court outside a gym (my ankle conspicuously taped up so nobody would ask me to play).

Surveillance from a parked vehicle, of course, offers a sort of built-in concealment. As noted earlier, most police departments and large private investigative firms maintain a surveillance van, but as long as the investigator doesn't drive a flashy car, a personal vehicle works just fine. When operating from my car, I liked to recline the seat until I could just see above the dashboard. I'd pull a baseball cap over my eyes and sink into a sort of meditative state. I was rarely noticed, but even on those few occasions when people did pay attention, they usually thought I was napping and left me alone.

I'll discuss the matter of concealment again in the chapter on tailing.

Breaking Off

When does a detective break off a surveillance? Obviously, surveillance should be terminated if the detective gets burned (discovered). Other than that, there are no hard-and-fast rules. It's a situational decision, a judgment call. Still, there are some general guidelines. Surveillance should (or could) be terminated

- If the detective thinks he *might* have been burned. This is not the time to take a chance.

- If the detective attracts any sort of attention. I had a friend who was keeping an eye on a person attending one of those Renaissance fairs (where a lot of folks dress up in medieval costume). He was drifting along in the crowd, doing his job quietly and efficiently, when he was accosted by a group of women street buskers. He suddenly found himself part of their act, standing in the middle of a circle of onlookers while these women sang a bawdy song mocking his manhood.

- When the risk gets too high. Again, *any* sort of risk—the risk of falling asleep, the risk of getting burned, the risk of getting mugged.

- About an hour after a detective who's working alone is *absolutely* certain the subject is in for the night. Ninety minutes is better.

Remember the O'Hara Rule: Tomorrow is another day. It's frustrating to be forced by circumstances to break off a surveillance, especially when you think you might be getting good information. Still, it's almost always better to break off and try again later than to get burned and blow the whole surveillance.

Mental Preparation:
The Zen of Surveillance

Surveillance can be the most dreary and tedious form of drudgery imaginable. It may sound sexy in theory, but in practice it can be like having your mind injected with novocaine. The detective may have to spend hours watching the outside of a building, waiting for the door to open or for the subject to walk by a window.

And yet, the detective has to remain alert. He can't be distracted by the weather, by passersby, by insects, by music, by aches or pains or by his bodily needs. After all, something could happen at any time.

This is without a doubt the single most difficult aspect of surveillance. It's the facet of surveillance that is the downfall of a great many detectives. All the other considerations may be bothersome, but they can be dealt with through foresight and preparation. But how does one manage to remain separate but involved? How does one stay detached but remain alert?

Not only is this difficult to do, it's difficult to explain. I suspect all good detectives have their own techniques, and I suspect each of them would find it hard to describe them. I'll try to explain how I did it, although it's much easier to do than to describe.

I sort of detached my brain from my body. It's easier to do when surveilling from a parked vehicle than when on foot. I'd get settled and comfortable, then sort of let my body drift away until it no longer seemed connected to me. Shut down all unnecessary systems. Become just a brain in a lump of meat. I was able to remain aware of what was going on around me, very alert— almost hyperalert—yet somehow unaffected by it all.

On foot the experience wasn't quite so pronounced, but it still kicked in. After all, a lot of our behavior is controlled at a subconscious level. We don't have to pay attention to walking. We don't have to think about adjusting our caps. We just do it. When conducting a surveillance on foot, I simply assign more functions to that lizard part of my brain and let my mind focus on the subject. Hours can fly by.

I realize this sounds absurd. But it worked for me, and I learned not to examine it too closely. And I never discussed it with any other detectives.

Conclusion

As a writer of detective and mystery fiction, you need to understand both the mechanics of surveillance and the odd Zen quality of waiting without anticipation, being aware without being involved. Surveillance is one of those package deals; a good detective needs to be good at both aspects. It's pointless to master the mechanics of surveillance unless you can also induce in yourself the proper mind-set to do the work. Conversely, the ability to sit quietly alert is worthless unless you know *where* to sit, *when* to sit there and *when* to get up and leave.

This is one of the few areas in which fiction and film occasionally get the detective game right. It's while on surveillance that detectives become the most philosophical. You start by thinking how much your knees hurt and suddenly find yourself pondering the intricate workings of the universe, and you've no idea how the one thought led to the other but you *know* they're inextricably linked together.

Surveillance is also an area that fiction and film get entirely wrong. Although there are times when conducting a surveillance with a partner that you'll find yourselves sitting together in a car having a clever or a heartfelt conversation, those times don't last long. The whole point of having two folks on surveillance, after all, is usually to cover more territory—and that means you spend most of the time apart.

I'd advise all of you to go out and conduct a surveillance. Pick out a bar or coffeehouse, one not in your own neighborhood. Spend eight to twelve hours hanging around outside. Create a scenario for yourself to explain why you need to keep an eye on this place (you're a writer, you can do this). Find out for yourself how to blend into the area, find your own spotting locations, figure out how to relieve those pesky bodily needs, and try to remain alert without wearing out your brain.

You may not enjoy it, but it will help you understand the process, and that's got to add something to your writing.

TAILING

Tailing is surveillance on the move. Take the difficulties of maintaining a stationary surveillance and multiply them by—pick any number you want. Tailing is infinitely more complex than stationary surveillance. Tailing is to stationary surveillance what combat is to target practice. The entire universe opens itself up to potential chaos.

The craft of tailing requires a remarkable synthesis of skills and knowledge. It calls on the detective's understanding of individual psychology, of social behavior, of traffic laws and herd instinct. It tests the detective's skills in driving, in concentration, in dealing with ambiguity and confusion. It demands the detective engage in a delicate balancing act—recklessness against prudence, confidence against cockiness, patience against the necessity of action. In my opinion tailing is the most frustrating, exciting, anxiety-producing and rewarding of the detective's many chores.

There is only one firm rule to tailing: Don't get caught. Beyond that, all we have are general guidelines. Although tailing is best done as a team, it can be done solo. Most of the guidelines we'll discuss apply to both team and solo tailing. It is far more common for private detectives to find themselves engaged in a solo tail. Again, it's a matter of resources.

Solo tailing is much more of a reactive skill. The subject acts; the detective reacts. While there are times when it becomes necessary for the detective to try to predict the subject's behavior—when you lose sight of the subject, for example—it's always a last resort. Teamwork allows the detective more discretion and reduces the risk involved in predicting the subject's behavior.

Tailing generally falls into two categories:

- on foot
- by motor vehicle

Of course, tailing can also involve other modes of transportation: boats, aircraft, horseback, snowmobile, bicycles, golf carts, snowboards. Anywhere people go, there is a detective willing to follow. We'll focus, however, on the most common methods of tailing—by foot and motor vehicle.

It's not uncommon for these two methods to be combined; for example, a detective may follow the subject from his home as he drives to the beach, then follow him on foot at the beach.

Tailing on Foot

In major cities, the majority of people travel on foot in conjunction with public transportation. As I write this I live in the borough of Manhattan in New York City; I only know one person here who owns a car, and she keeps it in New Jersey. But whether a detective lives in New York City, Columbus, Ohio, or Sioux City, Iowa, it's likely she'll have to conduct a tail on foot. People don't live in their cars, after all. They may drive to the mall, to the market and to work, but once there they have to get out and walk.

Preparation

It's amazingly easy to lose track of somebody—even somebody you know well—in a crowd. It happens all the time. I can't count the number of times I've been shopping with a woman friend, got distracted for just a moment and she would disappear. Right there in a store, an enclosed space with only a single public entrance, and she would just vanish. Imagine how easy it is to lose track of a stranger.

As with so many other things, preparation is the key to tailing on foot. A smart detective will study the subject as much as possible before initiating the tail.

What should be studied? There's not much point in studying features such as the subject's ear shape or eye color (although I've seen both described as essential features in some mystery novels). If you're close enough to the subject that you can distinguish his ear shape, you've probably already made a mistake.

Watch the Watch

There are occasions when the subject is suspicious and considers that he might be tailed (a member of an organized crime gang, for example, or a husband who is cheating on his wife). If so, the subject may attempt to elude the tail by disguising himself. After all, it's as easy for the subject to change his appearance as it is for the detective (check the section on concealment).

In these cases it's necessary for the investigator to study certain identifying features more closely. There are some items that a clever detective can key in on. For example, even when a male subject brings along a change of clothing to throw off a possible tail, he rarely brings a different belt or pair of shoes. And almost nobody, male or female, bothers to change watches.

For the most part, detectives concentrate on gross physical characteristics: the shape of the subject's head, the slope of the shoulders, the length of the arms and legs. These are things that can be recognized half a block away.

Just as important as the subject's physical features are the following:

- clothing and accessories
- walk, including his gait and stride
- posture
- idiosyncratic movements

Obviously, each of these characteristics can be changed or modified if the subject chooses, but if the surveillance and tail are done correctly the subject shouldn't have any reason to change them.

Clothing and Accessories

These are the most obvious features of a subject's appearance, and usually it makes perfect sense to focus on them. Unfortunately, we live in an age of uniformity. In every city in the United States (and, for the most part, in the world), you'll find the same stores selling the same clothes. A black T-shirt sold at the Gap in Los Angeles is exactly the same as one sold in the Gap in Columbus, Ohio. There are certain neighborhoods where every third person is wearing a Tommy Hilfiger jacket or carrying a Lands' End knapsack. This means, of course, that the clothing your subject wears is likely similar or identical to that of hundreds of other people on the street.

The good news, however, is that this uniformity can work in the investigator's favor. It makes it easier for a detective to blend into the surroundings (more on this later).

Walking Patterns

A lot of people have distinctive walking patterns. Some bounce, some swagger, some waddle. Some walk quickly, some stroll leisurely, some walk with a precise military bearing. Some take long strides, others take quick little steps.

For example, when I was young I had a pronounced bounce when I walked. I paid no attention to it until I found myself in military basic training. An absurd amount of time in basic training is spent in learning how to march, and a drill instructor's dream is even columns and rows of soldiers moving in perfect unison at a uniform pace. The sight of my lone bald head bouncing up and down during drill training regularly sent my DI into an incoherent fury. I no longer walk with a bounce.

The older a person is, the more likely he is to have a distinct walk. Every small ache and minor injury adds a little something to that person's walk. People grow into their ways of walking.

A person's walk may also change according to her pace. A person may walk differently at a shopping mall (where the pace tends to be more leisurely) than in a downtown shopping area (where people tend to be much more brisk).

Posture

Posture can also be highly revealing and distinctive. Some folks carry themselves loosely, as if they have fewer bones than the rest of us. Others have rigid, inflexible, almost brittle postures.

Many of the same factors that influence a person's walk affect his posture—all those small hurts and pains that accumulate over the years. I once had to tail a man who had been a photographer for years. He habitually carried his camera bag on one shoulder; even when he didn't have the bag, he still seemed to be leaning against its weight. He was an absolute delight to tail.

Idiosyncratic Movements

Most people have a series of odd gestures that are unique to them. A habit of brushing hair out of one's face, for example, or a nervous rolling of the neck muscles. Anybody who has seen the Akira Kurosawa movie *Yojimbo* is familiar with the distinctive shoulder twitch used by the actor Toshiro Mifune. Good detectives pay attention to these gestures and rely on them.

Concealment

Just as clothing, walk, posture and idiosyncratic movements allow the detective to maintain surveillance on the subject, the detective's own clothing, walk, posture and personal idiosyncrasies work against her. Good detectives are almost never flashy or obvious; they prefer to blend in with their surroundings. This is certainly one area in which Sergeant Joe Friday would excel— nobody would look twice at the Bland Buddha of the LAPD.

It is also a good idea for the investigator to be able to quickly change her appearance. That way the subject, especially a suspicious subject, does not become familiar with the investigator's appearance. It is even acceptable to occasionally violate the rule of being as invisible as possible. Sometimes it can be effective to wear an article of clothing that draws attention to the article of clothing itself. The subject sees the article of clothing, not the person wearing it. Of course, immediately after the subject notices the article of clothing, it should be discarded or covered. Personally, I avoid this tactic, but I've known other investigators who swear by it.

As with so many aspects of detective work, there are no hard-and-fast rules in regard to concealment for foot surveillance. However, in regard to clothing and other accoutrements, generally good detectives

- Wear layers. This allows the detective to quickly change her appearance, which decreases the likelihood of being spotted.

- Avoid bright colors. Bright colors attract attention. The exception to this, as mentioned above, is when the brightly colored article is just one layer. In that case a brightly colored article can actually be useful. As noted, when a person first notices a person in a brightly colored T-shirt, for example, the attention is more on the T-shirt than on the person wearing it. If the subject glances at an investigator in a brightly colored article of clothing, and the investigator then removes (or covers) that article, it can create a radical change in appearance.

- Wear comfortable, breathable shoes. Detectives quickly learn to be kind to their feet.

- Wear clothing in which they feel at ease. Of course, good detectives are capable of being comfortable in a wide variety of clothing styles. The more at ease the detective is, the less likely she will attract attention. This is an area in which private detectives generally excel over police detectives; too often police detectives wear every item of clothing as if it were a uniform.

- Dress appropriately for the location. Don't wear high heels, or dark socks and wing-tip shoes to the beach. Of course, this isn't always possible since the detective rarely knows in advance where the subject is heading.

- Avoid new clothing, clothing with slogans or anything that *might* attract attention.

- Wear glasses or sunglasses, which are a quick way to slightly alter one's appearance. Even if they don't wear corrective lenses, detectives can buy frames with clear glass at most good eyewear stores.

- Don caps and hats. Men often feel funny wearing hats, and hats are very visible and can attract attention. However, most men feel relatively comfortable in baseball caps (and, of course, they can be removed to change the detective's appearance). Other hats are trickier. A male detective might be able to wear a beret without causing comment in New York City or Seattle, but it might not be a wise choice in Boise or Kansas City.

- Tie back long hair, which can sometimes make radical changes in their appearance.

Good detectives learn to subordinate their own personal sense of style and comfort. The only consideration should be the job.

Tactics

Tailing, whether on foot or in a vehicle, is best done by a team of investigators. Three is best; two is fine. A single detective, when necessary—and it's often necessary—will do. As with surveillance, police detectives are more likely to engage in team tailing; private detectives are more likely to engage in solo tails. The tactics discussed here apply whether the detective is conducting a solo tail or is part of a team.

Tactics in tailing on foot all revolve around maintaining visual contact with the subject. There are two factors that need to be addressed in regard to maintaining visual contact: interval and direction.

Direction is easy. With a solo tail, the subject will almost always be in front of the detective—off to one side, perhaps, but still in front. I've heard of detectives who claim to use small mirrors (attached to their glasses or to the bills of their caps), which allow them to tail a subject from in front. I've never tried this and I've never seen it actually done. Frankly, it sounds loopy to me. I'd think the mirrors would be too small to provide much in the way of visual contact, or would attract attention from passersby.

Interval is a far more complicated matter. What is meant by "interval"? In the military we were always admonished to "watch your interval" when moving down a trail. That meant maintaining an appropriate distance from the man in front of you—close enough to keep an eye on him but far enough away to be safe if—when—something unexpected happened. The same is true for tailing.

Just how far away from the subject should the detective be? Far enough away to avoid attracting attention, but close enough not to lose the subject when he does something unexpected. And if there is a universal truth in tailing, it is that the subject will *always* do something unexpected. I have seen subjects suddenly dart across a street. I've seen them stop unexpectedly in the middle of a crosswalk. I've seen them stop in front of shop windows and reapply makeup. I had one subject who hesitated in front of a building, then suddenly reversed direction and walked directly toward me. I ignored him and continued several yards in the same direction before stopping in front of a store window. As I glanced back toward my subject, I was surprised to see him coming toward me again. I continued to study whatever was in the store window, waiting to see his reflection in the glass. After a moment I glanced back in his direction again. This time he was walking away from me. I stayed in front of the window for another moment, glanced at my watch (and took a quiet peek in his direction). Again, he was walking in my direction. I finally realized the subject was just pacing back and forth in front of the building, waiting for somebody.

Obviously, the appropriate tailing interval can vary radically from situation to situation. Forty feet in some circumstances is too far away; in other circumstances it is too close. Usually the investigator should be closer in a crowd, farther away in a less frequented area.

When You Got to Go . . .

Certainly the best people to tail on foot are those who are busy, hurrying from place to place, intent on their purposes. It may be tiring for the detectives to keep up, but at least the subjects are too focused to pay any attention to the world around them.

I think the worst experience I've had tailing on foot was a case involving a man who experienced diarrhea after a greasy lunch. You'd think that people who are worried about their bowels would have more immediate concerns than being tailed, and so they do. But my one experience of tailing a man with diarrhea taught me that people with diarrhea pay close attention to their surroundings. They're always looking around, trying to find the nearest rest room. It's probably true that unless I was wearing a sign that said "Men's Room," it's unlikely the subject would have noticed me. But the very fact that he kept stopping, turning and looking around anxiously was terribly disconcerting.

Maintaining visual contact doesn't mean the detective must always be looking directly at the subject. In fact, it's a good idea *not* to look directly at the subject—at least not very often. However, if the subject does something that attracts general public attention (spills a drink or knocks over a grocery store display of Cheez Whiz, for example), then a good detective will turn and watch. A determined refusal *not* to look directly at the subject when everybody else is can actually attract attention to the detective.

A lot of good detectives are more than a little superstitious; they tend to believe that looking too closely at the subject will somehow communicate itself to the subject. Instead, good detectives tend to rely on:

- reflective surfaces
- peripheral vision
- placement

These techniques allow the detective to keep an eye on the subject without having to maintain continuous direct visual contact.

Reflective Surfaces

Every city, every mall, every public space is jammed with reflective surfaces. Markets and shops often have convex mirrors designed to allow clerks and loss prevention staff to be aware of shoplifters. Many buildings are now made of reflective glass. Windows cast reflections. Each of these allows the detective to keep track of the subject without having to look directly at him. However, the detective needs to keep in mind that the popular polarizing sunglasses designed to reduce glare can also deaden reflections.

Peripheral Vision

You often hear someone claim to see something "out of the corner of my eye." Obviously, our eyes don't have corners, but we all have the capacity to see something without looking directly at it. Good detectives learn to rely on their peripheral vision to gather and process information. It takes a bit of practice, but a person can actually learn to expand the use of her peripheral vision.

Placement

By "placement" I refer to the practice of estimating the subject's direction in relation to yours and the speed at which he is walking. If the subject is across the street walking north at a leisurely pace, with only one doorway between him and the end of the block, the detective can estimate approximately how long it will take the subject to reach the corner. That allows the detective to look elsewhere for a period of time. There is only so far and so many places the subject can go in that time.

The trick—one of the tricks—in tailing by foot is not to grow complacent, not to take too much for granted. Simply because the subject has taken the same route from his office to the parking garage four days in a row does not mean he will do the same on the fifth day.

Tailing by Motor Vehicle

I dearly love to watch television and movie detectives tailing folks by car. They drive the most inappropriate vehicles, they use the most absurd tactics, they never get caught by traffic signals and they always find good parking places. My favorite was the Hawaiian private detective who tailed folks in a bright red Ferrari. It looked like a UFO tooling around the island of Oahu. And this detective would usually follow almost directly behind his subject so that the subject's rearview mirror must have been filled with the sight of this brightly colored exotic car. Yet the PI never got burned. Bright red Ferraris must be as common as Toyotas in Honolulu.

Although many detectives use electronic vehicle-tracking devices (covered in a later chapter), this chapter will concentrate on visual tailing.

Preparation

Again, preparation is vital in tailing by car. Obviously, the detective needs to become familiar with the subject vehicle, but the detective also needs to prepare the vehicle in which he'll be conducting the tail.

Preparation for the Subject Vehicle

A good detective always learns as much as possible about the vehicle he'll be tailing. In fact, a really good detective tries to learn more than is necessary, and is never surprised to discover that it's not enough. In addition to the most obvious factors (make, model, color, year, license number), the detective should attempt to become familiar with individual aspects of the subject vehicle, including:

- dents, nicks, scrapes and other blemishes
- bumper stickers
- taillight assembly (especially important when tailing at night)

If tailing in a rural area it's also appropriate for the detective to examine the vehicle's tire tread. Not only do different brands and models of tires have distinctive treads, the older the tires are, the more distinctive the tread becomes. A set of well-used tires can leave tracks as distinctive as a fingerprint.

Preparation of the Pursuit Car

Much of what is discussed here is just common sense, but it's amazing how often detectives—even experienced detectives—neglect to make sure their vehicles are properly prepared for tailing jobs. The smart detective plans the tail as if it's going to last all day and cover hundreds of miles—even if he's *certain* he's only going to follow the subject the usual 7.4 miles from her office to her home. Most detectives have been caught short once; good detectives try to make sure it's only once.

The following should always be checked prior to beginning the tail:

- Gasoline. Always have a nearly full tank.
- Maps, both highway and local street maps.
- Spare change for tolls, phone calls, unexpected road emergencies and snacks.
- Sunglasses. These should be polarized, unlike the sunglasses used for tailing on foot. Road glare can be a killer.
- Flashlights. And, of course, a trunk full of extra batteries.

Obviously, the vehicle should be in good working order. You don't want backfires and clouds of blue smoke calling attention to your car.

A few minutes of preparation can spare the detective untold hours of regret and self-recriminations.

Concealment

This is primarily a matter of common sense. A pursuit vehicle should be as inconspicuous as possible. This means no bright red Ferrari. When choosing a pursuit vehicle, a detective might want to consider the following:

- It should be clean, but not obsessively so. People tend to pay more attention to meticulously maintained cars.

- It should be a common color. A neutral blue is good.

- It should be free of bumper stickers, decals, antenna art or anything else that might attract attention.

- No vanity license plates.

I knew a man who obtained his private investigator's license, left his job as an insurance adjustor and opened a small detective agency. One of his first concerns was to get a vanity license plate for his car. It spelled "SNOOP." How could he expect to tail anybody? How could he expect to be taken seriously as an investigator? Nobody was surprised when his business folded in less than a year.

Tactics

There is one primary disadvantage to tailing by car: the inability of the detective to respond as quickly or readily as he could on foot. Even the most nimble of cars is still a ton of steel on rubber wheels. In addition, cars are bound by tens of dozens of purposely restrictive traffic laws. You can't just go anywhere you want, when you want. You're required to stay on a road and in an assigned lane. You're restricted from turning except at certain designated places. You're compelled to go in one specific direction. You're not even allowed to stop where and when you want.

Fortunately, those same restrictions apply to the subject being tailed. Although a lot of people routinely violate traffic laws, the scale of those violations is limited. The subject is unlikely to suddenly stop the car in the middle of the street and begin backing up. It's not impossible, but it's unlikely.

As with tailing on foot, tailing by car is best done with a team of at least three operatives. Again, this ideal is more likely to take place with police detectives than with private detectives. Private investigators often find themselves forced to engage in solo tails. Since solo tails are more common in fiction, I'll focus on them.

There are two factors to consider when engaged in a solo tail: interval and the number of shield cars. We've discussed the concept of interval already. The same vague rule applies to tailing by cars: The detective needs to be close enough but not too close, far enough but not too far.

Shield cars are vehicles the detective allows between himself and the subject vehicle. The number of shield cars depends on the detective's self-confidence and a variety of external conditions, including:

- traffic density, speed and flow
- lighting conditions
- weather

Too many shield cars makes it difficult to maintain visual contact with the subject, increasing the odds of losing her. Too few shield cars increases the likelihood of getting burned. On an interstate highway—where exits are limited and fewer surprises can happen—the detective can allow more shield cars. City traffic, on the other hand, is much more treacherous; fewer shield cars are appropriate. In poor lighting and bad weather conditions, tighten the interval.

Some writers seem to think the most difficult people to tail are those who race madly down the highway. Not so. They may be a danger to other drivers, but speeders are usually fairly easy to follow. Speeders are paying attention to the road, looking for openings in the traffic. When they look in their rearview mirrors, they're usually watching for traffic cops.

Loafers, on the other hand, are exceedingly difficult to tail. They drive so slowly that it's difficult to remain behind them without attracting attention. They disrupt traffic patterns, and they spend a great deal of time glancing fearfully in their rearview mirrors. Slow drivers are also far more sensitive to cars behind them. They're expecting to get either rear-ended or honked at, so they spend more time studying the traffic behind them.

Getting Burned

Regardless of how well prepared the detective is, regardless of how skillful and methodical the detective is, something will inevitably go wrong. It's yet another universal truth of detective work: Every detective eventually gets burned—or at least singed around the edges.

It's important to remember that all detective work is, at its heart, intrusive. It consists of poking around in the personal affairs of other people. Most folks, if they discover they're being followed, tend to resent it, especially if they've been doing something they shouldn't be doing. This is much more of a problem when tailing on foot than when tailing by car. The subject is less likely to be able to physically confront the detective when both are in cars.

So how should a detective behave when he gets burned or is about to get burned? If burned, or almost burned, when tailing in a car, the detective can simply drive away. And never use that car again to tail that subject.

If burned, or almost burned, when tailing on foot, all the rules go by the board. The only thing the detective can do is to rely on his wits. Every situation is different, and every detective will respond to the situation differently.

Usually when I found myself face-to-face with the subject I was tailing—whether I'd been burned or not—I generally did something physically rude and repulsive. I scratched my crotch or picked my nose or let some slobber dribble down my chin. That sort of offensive behavior usually makes people look away, or at least it keeps them from looking you in the face. It costs a little dignity, but it usually kept me from being confronted— and sometimes allowed me to continue the tail on another day (although more cautiously).

Conclusion

Following people is like good jazz, a heady mix of improvisation grounded in a deep understanding of fundamental principles. When it all comes together it can be an exhilarating experience; when it doesn't, it's terribly frustrating and exasperating.

As a writer you should be aware of the perverse thrill that comes from successful tailing, but it's also important that you understand tailing is a difficult process that must be grounded in dull, routine preparation. In a way, it's this contrast that makes it difficult to find detectives who are adept at solo tailing. Those detectives who are good at routine tasks may lack the boldness and audacity required to work a tail; those who have the requisite brashness may not have the patience to do the necessary preparation.

INFORMATION SOURCES

There are some facets of detective work that rarely appear in detective and mystery fiction. Perhaps the most important of these ignored facets is the amount of time detectives spend either gathering information or maintaining the networks necessary to gather information. I suspect the reason this aspect of investigative work is ignored by writers is because it's, well, sometime's it's pretty dull. Unfortunately, it's also pretty important.

We live in an information age. Information is a commodity, just like coal, coffee or ball bearings. You can buy and sell information. You can even buy and sell *access* to it. Although all detectives, police and private, deal in information, only private detectives treat information as their stock in trade. Police detectives use their information-gathering skills to serve the community at large; private detectives use their skills to serve their clients and make a buck. But both need to build and nourish information networks, both need to find their way through the bureaucratic maze of information available to the public, and both understand information as an object of value.

There are two basic sources of information available to detectives: people and archives. A good detective needs to be able to work with both.

Human Sources

We've already discussed techniques of interviewing and interrogation. Those techniques are merely the final step in the information-collection process. Think of interviewing and interrogation as different ways of cooking. Before you can cook, you have to know where to get the ingredients. You can't make a filé and andouille gumbo unless you can track down the filé and andouille sausage. One of the sources for the fixings of detective work is people.

It's more difficult to get information from people than from documents. People have to be coaxed, flattered, threatened, charmed. People are complicated creatures. But they respond well to genuine interest. The best detectives have a deep and abiding interest in and concern for people. They may have ulterior motives in some of their working relationships, but they genuinely like people. And people recognize that and respond to it.

Good detectives cultivate a variety of contacts—people in information-rich environments. Clerks, bartenders, secretaries, social workers, probation and parole officers, nurses, receptionists. The world is full of people who have access to unique information, information that is difficult or impossible to obtain anywhere else.

Cultivating Contacts

How do investigators acquire and maintain networks of contacts? It's a long process, one that can't be rushed. Cultivating a contact is rather like growing bonsai, those tiny, twisted Japanese trees. Contacts don't need constant, lavish attention, but they do need careful, periodic, thoughtful attention. It's important for the detective to take the long view. A contact may not produce any worthwhile information for a long time, and may not produce it often. What the detective is really cultivating is the *potential*.

To develop a contact the detective needs to consider:

- the purpose of the contact
- the contact's daily routine and interactions
- a contact maintenance program

These are general guidelines, of course. (I know I keep repeating

The Hidden Power

It's not widely recognized, but clerks and secretaries run the entire world. They are the glue that binds organizations—private and public—together. They control access to the people who manage the organizations. They produce the documents necessary for organizations to operate. They schedule appointments. They know where everything is located. If every secretary and clerk in the world refused to go to work one day, the world would rapidly grind to a halt. Nothing would get done.

Good detectives recognize this fact and treat clerks and secretaries with the respect they deserve.

the phrase "general guidelines," but detective work isn't like engineering; general guidelines are all we have.)

Purpose of the Contact

The first thing the detective needs to consider is *why* she needs to develop a specific contact. The obvious answer would be that the person has access to information the detective needs. That's why detectives develop relationships with secretaries and phone company employees and petty criminals.

But the truth is detectives often develop contacts who produce no information at all. Some contacts simply produce *access* to other folks who have information. Some produce introductions. One of my best contacts was an old retired woman who volunteered her services at the information desk of a county courthouse. Every time I went to that courthouse I stopped to visit with her. She had friends in every department of the court. Whenever I needed to go to a particular department to get information, I'd stop at the information desk, chat for a bit and ask who I should talk to in that department. She'd give me a name and would sometimes even call that person and say she was sending me. It made my life a lot easier. Besides, she was a cheerful old woman who'd lived an interesting life.

Private detectives tend to have a wider, more varied network of contacts than police detectives do. That's because a PI has a more diverse caseload. Police detectives are restricted to criminal work; private investigators often work several types of cases simultaneously—a criminal case, an asset location case, an insurance fraud case. Each type of information requires different sources. On top of that, PIs have to cultivate sources in areas where police detectives get information as a matter of course (criminal records clerks, for example).

Police detectives, on the other hand, tend to have a more extensive network of contacts in the criminal world (snitches). This, of course, is a reflection of the purpose of their work.

Private investigators also generally put more effort into cultivating and maintaining sources. As noted in the chapter on interrogation and interviewing, police detectives tend to rely on the authority of their position to compel folks to give them information. It's not uncommon for police detectives who enter into private investigative work on retirement to discover that many of their sources dry up; the basis of their relationship ended when the detective turned in her badge.

Contact's Daily Routine and Interactions

When developing a contact, the detective needs to understand the nature of the contact's work life. Take, for example, a low-level clerk in a city hall office. The work is often dull and unrewarding. Clerks are often treated like serfs by members of the public and by their own superiors. All day long clerks face people who are impatient and inconsiderate. Members of the public view the clerks as the physical manifestation of a malevolent bureaucracy. Their own superiors tend to see them primarily as adjuncts to the computers and typewriters—mere extensions of the machines they work. Clerks often feel alienated from the people they work for, from the people who give them orders and from the product of their work. It's little wonder they are sometimes less than enthusiastic in their interactions with others.

Knowing that, consider the best way to approach a clerk in a city hall office. Try to consider the daily routines and interactions of, say, an emergency room nurse. Or a police dispatcher. Or a waitress in a bar frequented by lawyers, or one in a bar frequented by firefighters. Really think about who and what they face every working day. Each of these potential contacts faces radically different social situations.

A good detective makes the necessary effort to understand the reality of the contact's work life. This is necessary for the detective to both empathize with the contact and develop a pattern for maintaining the contact.

Contact-Maintenance Program

Once the detective determines the need for a contact in a certain situation, she needs to cultivate a relationship with that contact. It's a flagrant error for the detective to seek out the contact only when information is needed. The contact will feel used—and rightfully so. Good detectives develop *relationships*. It's critical for the detective to show herself routinely, to be friendly, courteous and genuinely interested.

I used to make rounds. Periodically I'd spend an afternoon and evening visiting bars, letting the bartenders and wait staff see my smiling face, engaging them in casual conversation, asking them nothing important, leaving them a healthy tip. Or I'd visit city hall, or a courthouse or a hospital and do the same thing (without the overt tip, of course, although I might bring along a few boxes of chocolates or fresh-baked cookies).

Short-Term Contacts

For every long-term source of information a detective cultivates there are three or four short-term contacts. These are people who have information the detective wants, but who aren't in positions the detective will routinely find useful. For example, a detective based in Ohio may find himself needing information from a clerk in a social services office in Wisconsin.

When there is no need to cultivate the source as a long-term contact, the detective has more options. What matters is getting the information as efficiently as possible. These are Capone situations. Al Capone is credited with saying, "You can get farther with a kind word and a gun than with a kind word alone." I'm speaking of a metaphorical gun, of course (although I suspect Capone wasn't). A Capone situation is merely one in which the detective is free to use *any* technique to get the needed information. This includes intimidation, threats, bullying or bribery.

Capone situations may allow the detective a broader range of options, but just because you *can* do a thing doesn't mean you *should* do it. A good detective uses rude behavior as a last resort

A Bribery Primer

Bribery of public officials is a crime. Committing a crime is a bad thing. Nonetheless, detectives (mostly private detectives) occasionally find themselves in situations in which the offer of a little financial assistance is needed to obtain the information desired. There is an unspoken etiquette about those situations.

- Discretion is advisable. Don't make an overt offer. Simply put the money where only the target can see it.

- Avoid any suggestion that the money is a bribe. Offer it to defray copying costs, for example. Or don't mention it at all; simply let the target know you need the information. The target will know what the money is for.

- Don't scrimp. No singles. No fives. No tens. Never offer anything less than a twenty. This is a *bribe*, even if neither of you acknowledges it.

- Don't be smug. If the target accepts the offer, thank him sincerely. *Never* let the target think you look down on him for accepting a bribe.

- Accept a refusal gracefully. Apologize and leave.

even in Capone situations. Remember, even Capone stressed the importance of the kind word.

Archival Sources

As noted earlier, it's easier to get information from a document than from a person. A document is like physical evidence; it's just there. It can be held in the detective's hot little hands, it can be read, it can be photocopied, it can be faxed, it can be scanned onto a computer diskette. Archival information is available to anybody who knows where to find it.

I'm not going to spend a great deal of time on the traditional archival sources. It would take an entire book to accurately convey the breadth and depth of the amount of information available to the general public. Indeed, there are several decent guides to help people maneuver their way through the intricacies of bureaucratic and private archival sources (see the bibliography). Instead, I'll simply give a general overview of the types of information available through traditional sources, then turn our attention to a less traditional source of archival information—the trash can.

Traditional Sources of Archival Information

Certain types of information, such as arrest records, are theoretically available only to police officers (I say "theoretically" because most private investigators who need that sort of confidential information have usually developed contacts willing to provide it). Still, the vast majority of information of use to detectives is available to the public—if they know where to look.

Below I've listed places where certain types of information can be obtained. All the detective needs to do is go to those places and politely ask for the information. Again, most clerks will be helpful *if* they are treated decently. Far too many detectives, both police and private, expect clerks to drop whatever they're doing and offer assistance.

If the clerk can't help, she (since most clerk positions pay relatively poorly and these employees are expected to take abuse, they are staffed almost exclusively by women) can usually suggest another option.

Financial Information

- Clerk of Court, Civil Files. It's a common practice in a divorce for the parties involved to be required to provide accounts of their financial statuses—income, debts, expenses and so forth. The Clerk of Court will also have a record of bankruptcy and possibly small claims suits.
- City Clerk. Maintains files on deeds, mortgages and liens against property.
- Tax Assessor. Records location, purchase price and current value of real property.

Legal Matters (Criminal and Civil)

- Clerk of Court, Criminal Files. Criminal convictions are a matter of public record, as are appeals.

- Department of Corrections/Bureau of Prisons. Sentences, inmate behavior infractions are available.

- Clerk of Court, Civil Files. Documents lawsuits (both plaintiff and defendants are named), personal injury matters, awards of damages and judgments (both for and against), certain contracts and names of representing attorneys.

Family Information

- City Clerk/County Recorder/Department of Vital Statistics. Files birth certificates (which include dates, times, places, names of parents, mothers' maiden names, parents' occupations, attending physicians), death certificates (which include causes of deaths, next of kin, burial locations), marriage licenses (which include names of witnesses, names of parents, maiden names of mothers, signatures of both parties) and marriage applications (not every marriage license applied for is used).

- Public Library. Newspapers on microfiche include information on births, deaths and marriages, and generally include more detailed information on families than provided in public records. City directories list the number of dependents and sometimes their names.

Business Information

- Better Business Bureau/Chamber of Commerce. Maintains files of complaints against specified businesses.

- Clerk of Court, Civil Files. Records civil suits and criminal complaints against businesses.

- Alcoholic Beverage Control Board. Collects information on tavern owners (including names, addresses, DBAs—doing business as, names under which businesses operate—and fingerprints).

- Public Library. Keeps registers of corporations that list subsidiaries (Dun and Bradstreet, Standard and Poor's, Moody's). Newspapers on microfiche often note staff promotions and other pertinent information.

- Secretary of State, Corporate Division. Maintains files of DBAs. Sometimes oversees professional licensing (physicians, nurses, private detectives, haircutters, lawyers, bondsmen, etc.).

- Securities and Exchange Commission. Holds records of public corporations, investment services and stockbrokers.

Property

- Department of Motor Vehicles. Operator licenses (including restrictions; also give weights, heights, eye colors of operators), vehicle registrations (include descriptions of registered vehicles, including boats), vehicle identification numbers (VINs), accidents and revocations of licenses.
- Tax Assessor. Records location, purchase price, current value and description of real property.
- City Clerk/Clerk of Court, Civil Files. Plat books give boundaries of property, restrictions on property use and improvements to property.

These are, of course, only a few of the traditional sources of archival information. Should you, as a writer, need to know where to find more obscure information, I've included a couple of appropriate texts in the bibliography.

Dumpster Diving

Some of the best information isn't given away, isn't purchased, isn't delivered; it's tossed in the trash. The garbage cans and dumpsters of the nation are an overlooked and valuable source of information.

According to waste management professionals, there are two types of refuse: trash and garbage. Most people aren't aware of the distinction—nor do they need to be. In general garbage consists of organic remains, such as leftover food, cigarette butts, bones, rinds. Everything else—empty bottles, burned-out lightbulbs, cereal boxes, that old manuscript—is trash. Both contain useful information.

Garbage

Garbage is most commonly found in the trash cans of dwelling places rather than businesses. The information found in garbage may be interesting, but it is of limited use to most detectives.

By and large, only private detectives engaged in child neglect cases find garbage of much benefit. The organic remains can give the detective some insight into the children's diet.

Trash

Trash is the more revealing aspect of refuse. Trash comes in two general categories: personal trash and business trash. Personal trash consists of the trash found in the home trash can; business trash is, obviously, trash that comes from businesses.

Personal Trash

Unless the detective is searching for a particular item (a telephone bill, for example, or credit card receipts), *everything* should be examined.

The following is a partial list of things that might be found in personal trash:

- Empty prescription medicine bottles. These are always labeled with the patient's name, and are usually labeled with the name and dosage of the drug. The drug can be looked up in the *Physicians' Desk Reference (PDR)*, which can be found in the reference section of most public libraries. Prescription medications can provide insight into an individual's medical and/or emotional condition.

- Credit card receipts. These list the cardholder's name, credit card data and often the items recently purchased. An interesting sidenote: A new criminal market has sprung up, sparked by dumpster divers who search for all those preapproved credit card applications that get tossed as junk mail. The applications are filled out, the credit cards are sent to post office boxes, and the thieves have the chance to max out brand-new credit cards.

- Personal letters. Gentlemen may not read other people's mail, but detectives do. Then again, nobody every accused a good detective of being a gentleman.

- Empty alcohol containers. Obviously, it can be important to know how much a person drinks—and how much money is being spent on drink.

- Contraceptive materials, such as condom wrappers, birth control pill packages and empty tubes of spermicide. These give some indication of the subject's sexual habits.

- Telephone bills. These list all the long-distance numbers called, including the dates and durations of the calls.

- Magazines, newsletters and other materials that provide some indication of the reader's political, religious and social interests.

Even hard-boiled detectives often find it morally distasteful to nose around in other people's trash, but it remains a source of valuable information.

Business Trash

Nearly half of all the nation's trash is paper. Almost one million tons (that's two billion pounds) of office wastepaper find their way to the nation's landfills every year. Some of that wastepaper contains information of value to the detective.

Legally, a business has no right of privacy. The courts have concluded that the concept of privacy attaches only to individuals, not corporate entities. Businesses, however, do have certain rights that are analogous to the right of privacy. For example, corporate espionage might be prosecuted as an improper acquisition of a trade secret. A PI who finds a document containing a trade secret of an engineering firm may be within the law to remove the document from the trash, but he might be committing a crime if he sold that information to a competing firm.

Many businesses (and some individuals) attempt to protect themselves by shredding sensitive documents. This is not always as effective as people like to think. Cheap shredders simply don't slice the documents into small enough strips. Further, they tend to clump the strips together so that it's easy to know which strips go together. A determined and patient investigator can often reassemble these "shredded" documents. In fact, by shredding the document the business is in some ways making the detective's job easier; it points out which documents are the most important.

Legal Considerations

As it currently stands, federal law states that individuals have no reasonable expectation of privacy in regard to the contents of personal trash cans, even when the trash and/or garbage is placed in opaque bags (*California v. Greenwood*, 486 U.S. 35 1988). In effect, individuals relinquish their property interests in their own trash when they place the trash cans out for collection.

However, some individual states offer their citizens somewhat more protection against this sort of intrusion. California, Hawaii, New Jersey, Washington and Vermont all have laws limiting access to trash. Other states will likely follow suit. It would be wise for writers to research the laws of the states where their stories are located. This can be done at a local law library with the help of a reference librarian or, for those writers with access to the World Wide Web, by accessing one of the legal reference URLs listed in the bibliography.

While the law generally says trash set out for collection is fair game, detectives cannot trespass on private property to take it. Trespassing is a crime.

Conclusion

OK, I admit gathering information is not the most exciting aspect of detective work. It doesn't offer the dramatic opportunities of tailing or undercover work. Maybe it's the groundwork that allows detectives to do the more interesting things, but it's not always easily translated onto the page.

And yet, it can add something to the depth of the character or the breadth of the narration. It can offer writers the opportunity to instill a sense of verisimilitude, an aura of authenticity, into their work. All too often we see fictional detectives spend hours running around trying to track down information real detectives can get in half an hour of talking to a contact or looking in a plat book. It can also allow the writer to develop the character a bit more.

One of my favorite scenes in the movie *Chinatown* (one of the best detective movies ever made, in my opinion) takes place in a dusty county clerk's office. Watching how Jake Gittes, the protagonist, interacts with the clerk tells us a lot about the sort of person Gittes is.

Gathering information *can* be made interesting.

E I G H T

UNDERCOVER WORK

Undercover operations are certainly the most dramatic of the various investigative roles available to detectives. They are also the most dangerous—dangerous to the undercover investigator (both physically and emotionally) and dangerous to the unsuspecting public.

Undercover operations are those in which the investigator purports to be somebody or something other than what she actually is. They are used by both private and police detectives, sometimes even operating in conjunction. The range of undercover operations is remarkably diverse—from police operations designed to catch drug dealers to private investigations designed to uncover and deter property theft in a nuclear plant.

Private Undercover Operations

The vast majority of undercover operations carried out by private investigators have one main purpose: to reduce corporate financial losses. Corporations lose over two billion dollars annually due to internal employee theft and sabotage. Another source of financial loss is underproduction and absenteeism as a result of drug use during working hours. In addition, corporations engaged in unpopular business practices find their profits are threatened by protestors and critics.

Corporations large and small often find it is more cost effective to hire private investigators to infiltrate their own workplaces or the organizations of their critics than to change the internal structures of their plants or alter the nature of their business practices.

Internal Investigations

Corporations hire private investigators to infiltrate the workplace and uncover employee crime or policy violations. These undercover operations generally follow one of two patterns: reactive or proactive.

Reactive Operations

Reactive operations take place when the corporation becomes aware of, or suspicious of, an internal problem and feels it necessary to take drastic steps to resolve it. Private investigators are hired and inserted into the workplace as either new or transferred employees. Once in place, the investigators attempt to blend in with other employees and eventually ferret out the problem.

The three most common reasons for hiring undercover investigators are:

- internal theft and pilferage
- employee drug use
- employee sabotage

We all know what internal theft is. Drug use is equally clear. Employee sabotage, however, is less well known to the public. This form of deviance takes place when alienated workers deliberately damage either the product they are producing or the machinery that manufactures the product.

An example of a reactive undercover operation took place at a large Midwestern soup production plant. The managers suspected some of their employees were selling and using drugs during one of the shifts. They hired a small investigative agency to discover (1) *if* drugs were being sold; (2) if so, *who* was selling them; and (3) *who* was using them.

A Shoe in the Works

It's interesting to note that the term "sabotage" is derived from the very type of activity many corporations hire private investigators to prevent. A *sabot* was a type of wooden shoe worn by French laborers during the early days of the Industrial Revolution. Workers in that era often worked fourteen hours a day under horrific conditions. People were treated as adjuncts to the machinery. One way for workers to stop the machinery and provide themselves with a well-needed break was to toss a wooden shoe into the gears. Sabotage.

Several operatives were sent undercover into the plant as new employees. After a period of time, the operatives reported to the managers that drugs were, in fact, being sold in the plant on a regular basis. They also provided the managers with a list of names of sellers and users. The offenders were given the opportunity to resign, not so much to protect their reputations but to protect the reputation of the company. It wouldn't do for the public to think that one of America's favorite brands of soup was being made by drug users.

Proactive Operations

In some instances corporations want to stop detrimental activity before it starts. These are proactive operations. Some investigative firms specialize in proactive operations. The purpose of proactive operations is to deter those employees who might be tempted to engage in pilferage or product sabotage.

Again, an undercover operative is inserted into the company workplace as a new employee. Shortly after beginning the job, the operative begins to pilfer or sabotage company products. This is done openly enough that other employees become aware of the activity, but not so openly that it is apparent the operative wants to get caught.

After a period of time the operative is, of course, "caught." He is then publicly humiliated and fired. The other employees, having witnessed the process, are less likely to engage in similar behavior.

Although some of these internal investigations result in criminal prosecution, the vast majority are resolved through unofficial means. The offending employees may be sued for restitution but are usually simply terminated. The intent of the investigation, after all, is not to punish the offenders but to reduce corporate losses. Criminal prosecution only advertises the fact that there are problems within the corporation; most corporations would rather settle the matter as quietly as possible. Firing the offenders not only gets rid of undesirable employees, but is believed to act as a deterrent to other employees who might be involved in the offending activity.

External Investigations

Corporations involved in certain unpopular business practices, such as polluting streams and rivers, deforestation, the production of nuclear energy or the manufacture of certain chemicals, often hire private investigators to infiltrate their critics. The function of these undercover operatives is threefold:

- Discover the plans of the critical organizations.
- Disrupt or sabotage those plans.
- Gather gossip and scandal on the members.

The primary targets of these external investigations seem to be environmentalist organizations. Lumber companies have commissioned external investigations against those who protest clearcutting of old forests. Oil companies have hired investigators to infiltrate and gather dirt on organizations attempting to stop drilling in, or the laying of pipelines through, environmentally sensitive wilderness areas. Nuclear energy companies have investigated antinuclear protest organizations.

The purpose of these investigations is to neutralize critics who may affect either legislation or public sentiment on company practices. I have to admit these operations sometimes make me ashamed to have been a private investigator.

Police Undercover Operations

Unlike the undercover operations of private investigators, police undercover operations are designed strictly to catch and punish criminals. Police officers pose either as criminals or as potential victims of crimes. These operations generally fall into three broad categories:

- sting operations
- decoy operations
- drug cases

There are, of course, other variations of undercover work (such as the infiltration of criminal organizations), but the vast majority of police undercover operations fall into these categories.

Sting Operations

Sting operations are those in which police officers pose as criminals in order to catch other criminals. Some sting operations are elaborate and require months of undercover work; others are fairly simple and require only a few hours of preparation.

Here are some examples of classic police sting operations. A joint operation of Washington, DC, and FBI agents set up a bogus fencing enterprise. They rented a warehouse, had business cards printed (calling themselves PFF Inc., which stood for Police-FBI Fencing) and began to make the rounds of area bars and clubs. They let folks believe they had ties with organized crime in New Jersey and were in the market for just about anything they could buy and sell. In six months they'd bought stolen property worth over $2.5 million and had arrested over one hundred folks. They repeated the operation about a year later, this time calling themselves GYA Enterprises. What did GYA stand for? Got You Again.

In Portland, Oregon, undercover police officers bought a bunch of cheap, used televisions. The officers then went around to area bars saying they had stolen televisions they wanted to sell. Several people bought them and were subsequently arrested for receiving stolen property. (When these cases were brought to trial, the charges were reduced from felonies to the misdemeanor crime of intent to buy stolen property; the televisions weren't actually stolen, after all. The judge also ordered the police to return the "stolen" televisions to the folks who'd bought them. The fines the offenders were ordered to pay didn't cover the costs of the televisions.)

As this book is being written, federal agents have just completed a two-and-a-half-year sting operation. The operation started as an inquiry into organized crime in Cleveland, Ohio. The agents were primarily interested in money laundering, drugs, gambling and firearms violations. However, as the investigation progressed, the agents encountered a corrections officer who worked in the Cuyahoga County Sheriff's Department. This officer not only allegedly sold drugs to the undercover agents, he also allegedly offered to arrange for security for other illegal operations. The agents accepted the offer. As of this moment, the federal agents have arrested seven of the original targets of the sting and forty-four officers from five different law enforcement agencies.

Just a Little Sting

Not all sting operations involve desperate crimes and hard-eyed criminals. For example, police departments are increasingly running sting operations that target convenience stores that sell cigarettes to minors. Departments in Hawaii, Virginia and Washington have all initiated operations in which undercover teens work in conjunction with detectives to to bust the errant clerks.

Decoy Operations

Decoy operations are those in which police officers pose as potential victims. The purpose of these operations is twofold: (1) to catch the criminal and (2) to displace the crime that might have victimized an innocent citizen so that a police officer becomes the potential victim. For example, an undercover might pose as a drunk, a handicapped person or a taxi driver in order to be an attractive target for an offender.

An example would be the Manhattan dentist who was suspected of fondling his women patients while they were under anesthesia. A female officer made an appointment with the dentist. She brought along a video camera and transmitter concealed in her handbag. As the operative drifted off under the anesthetic, the dentist began to fondle her. Other officers, watching the video transmission from nearby, busted in and arrested the dentist.

Undercover police units in Atlantic City routinely pose as intoxicated tourists who are in town for the gambling. They stumble through bad neighborhoods—under the watchful eye of other undercover officers—hoping to attract robbers.

Death, Where Is Thy Sting?

A popular sting operation involves placing a false obituary in a local newspaper. Many professional burglers habitually read the obits; they not only identify the deceased and the next of kin, they inform the burglars when those folks will definitely be out of the house. With a little research, the burglars can determine if anybody in the family lives in a neighborhood attractive to burglars. When the burglars arrive to rip off the address from the fake obituary, the police are waiting to arrest them.

Drug Cases

Drug cases have become one of the most common types of undercover operations. Although some drug cases are technically sting or decoy operations, they are qualitatively different. Drug deals bring together a volatile mixture of large amounts of money, paranoia and high-powered weapons that make them wildly unpredictable.

Perhaps the most frequent type of drug undercover operation is the "buy and bust." In these operations, an undercover detective is disguised as a drug buyer and equipped with a concealed audio transmitter. The detective makes the purchase using cash that has had its serial numbers recorded. Two undercover officers referred to as ghosts pose as passersby. Their assignment is to watch over the buyer and to track the seller after the buy has been made. Also hidden nearby are another half-dozen backup officers wearing jackets labeled "Police." Their job is to converge on the suspects and arrest them after the sale has been completed. This operation is used often (approximately five thousand buy and busts take place annually in New York City alone).

Drug operations have caused a radical change in the nature of undercover work. Far more police officers are finding themselves involved in undercover operations that are far more dangerous than ever before, often for far less amounts of money. Buy-and-bust operations routinely target low-level drug dealers, and busts are made for sales amounting to only five or ten dollars. In a process known as "shaking the trees," these low-level dealers are arrested in the hope that they will inform on higher level dealers, who are in turn arrested in the hope they will inform on dealers at still higher levels.

Less common, though more dramatic, are deep-cover drug operations. This is where an agent maintains a cover in the drug trade for a long period of time—months, perhaps even a year. Obviously all the problems of undercover work are magnified in such a long-term operation. The demands and dangers work on deep-cover operatives with a sort of tidal force, slowly eroding their ability to maintain the cover or, worse, their grasp on their real identity.

Demands and Dangers of Undercover Work

Undercover work is often the most dangerous type of detective work, for both private and police detectives. The dangers faced by detectives are both physical and emotional. Undercover operations also pose a physical risk to the safety of civilians.

Physical Danger

The most obvious danger faced by detectives in undercover operations is the physical danger. Even those cases that don't involve drugs, guns or huge amounts of money can still spark violence. After all, the nature of undercover operations is such that somebody is being betrayed. The detective is undercover to fool *somebody*; when that somebody discovers the betrayal, feelings are apt to run high and turn violent. Employees who have lost their jobs as a result of information obtained by an undercover private detective have been known to assault the detective who turned them in. Undercover police detectives face considerably greater physical dangers.

Danger to the Undercover Operative

Although private investigators are occasionally injured during undercover operations, police undercover operatives face the most danger, especially those officers involved in drug cases. This danger comes from three sources:

- criminals
- other officers
- otherwise law-abiding citizens

Danger From Criminals

As police become more effective in closing open-air drug markets, the drug dealers are forced to move inside. This escalates the risk to the undercover officer for several reasons:

- The closed space means that when things go wrong, they go wrong faster and with more deadly results. It's more difficult to run away, and there are fewer places to run.

- The undercover officer is not only out of sight of the "ghosts" and backup officers, there is often at least one locked door separating them. It takes longer for help to arrive.

- The relative privacy increases the odds that the dealer will frisk the undercover officer. This means fewer undercover officers are willing to wear Kevlar vests for risk of blowing their cover.

- The increased privacy means more officers are being forced to sample the drugs they're buying. In New York City this now takes place on the average of six times a month.

According to newspaper sources, a New York undercover officer is wounded during a staged purchase at least twice a month. Shortly before this was written, an NYPD officer acting as a ghost was fatally wounded during a ten dollar buy-and-bust operation. The officer was shot in the shoulder; a Kevlar vest would likely have saved his life.

Undercover officers are also at risk from criminals who suspect the officers are either rival gang members or simply other criminals who intend to rip them off.

Danger From Other Officers

Undercover officers, obviously, don't look like cops. They aren't supposed to. If they're at all competent they look like criminals. Since undercover operations often take place in high-crime neighborhoods, it's not uncommon for uniformed officers to mistake undercover officers for criminals.

As mentioned in chapter two, the classic example of this sort of mistake took place in 1975 when undercover Drug Enforcement Administration operatives arranged to sell a shipment of heroin to a gang that turned out to be undercover customs agents. Everybody showed up at the exchange armed to the teeth. It was only because one of the DEA agents and one of the customs agents recognized each other that an armed encounter didn't take place.

Far more common are cases like that of Desmond Robinson, an undercover NYC Transit Police officer working the subways. Robinson and other officers were chasing two youths reported to have been armed. An off-duty NYPD officer saw Robinson sprinting down the subway platform with a gun in his hand and mistook him for a criminal. The off-duty officer shot Robinson four times.

A similar incident took place two years earlier, when an undercover Transit Police officer attempted to arrest a fare-jumper. Three uniformed officers saw the incident and opened fire, shooting twenty-one rounds at the undercover officer.

Danger From Citizens

Undercover operatives are also at risk from ordinary citizens. These are often well-meaning citizens who understandably misinterpret what they see. Incidents in Boston and New York

---

How to Tell the Cops From the Criminals

How are uniformed officers supposed to tell an undercover officer from a criminal? Big-city police departments designate a color of the day (or week). Undercover officers are supposed to make sure they wear a prominent article of clothing in that color. Uniformed officers who see an incident involving somebody prominently wearing the color of the day are supposed to give the person the opportunity to identify himself before opening fire. Of course, in the heat of the moment such niceties are sometimes overlooked. Officer Robinson, who was shot four times while chasing a youth armed with a shotgun, was wearing the appropriate color.

City illustrate the problem. Two Boston College students interfered with what they thought was a mugging. It was, in fact, an undercover officer attempting to arrest a woman. The woman ran away when the students accosted the officer. The students were arrested and charged with assault and abetting an escape.

In a similar incident in New York, a man interfered with what appeared to be a racial attack—several white men assaulting a black man on the ground. The white men, of course, were undercover narcotics officers. The man who interfered was also beaten by the police and jailed for over thirty hours.

Emotional Danger

Although the physical dangers of undercover work are the most obvious, the emotional dangers are equally formidable. This is especially true for investigators who are in deep cover.

Deep undercover operations, whether conducted by police or private investigators, pose unique problems and require a special type of operative. Beyond the obvious complications of masquerading as somebody else—foremost of which is keeping the cover story straight—there are potentially debilitating emotional demands. Undercover operatives are often required to make friends with the subjects of the investigation and then to betray that friendship.

Deep-cover operatives also have less contact with their handlers (the officers who oversee the undercover operation). Where most undercover detectives lead normal lives when not on duty, deep-cover operatives are *always* on duty. They do not go home to their families. They do not report to the squad room. They do not maintain any of their normal relationships or engage in their normal activities. This, of course, only exacerbates their feelings of isolation and alienation.

Once again, the dangers are greater for police investigators. Not only are they faced with the standard emotional difficulties of deep undercover cases, they are also often subjected to tremendous temptations, especially in drug cases. There are two constants that can always be found in drug cases: sex and huge amounts of money. It's a combination that is sometimes more than an undercover officer can resist.

The newspapers are filled with stories of undercover officers gone bad. Consider the case of Tampa police officer Javier Guzman. In 1991 he was named Officer of the Year by the Tampa PD. A short time later, after approximately eleven months working undercover on drug and money laundering schemes, Guzman found himself facing an eleven-year prison sentence. Guzman apparently realized he was getting in too deep; he told a department psychologist that he was experiencing depression, marital problems, sleeping disorders and loss of appetite. He even requested a transfer off the case. Unfortunately, the case had reached a critical stage, and Guzman stayed on. Not long afterward Guzman found himself under arrest by DEA agents, charged with laundering over a million dollars for the very drug dealers he had been assigned to investigate.

The need to remain undercover and in character can also do terrible damage to relationships. It's often difficult for wives, siblings and parents to understand the pressures faced by undercover operatives. When the cover requires a radical change in appearance, the undercover investigator often begins to avoid the people and places he would ordinarily frequent—the difficulty in explaining the change is simply too awkward. This, of course, tends to further isolate the investigator. Although some departments require undercover agents to maintain weekly, or even daily, contact with police officials and psychologists, it is rarely the sort of contact that the agent really needs.

Conclusion

Undercover operations are heady stuff for the writer. The possibilities are dazzling. Adventure, deceit, high and low drama, danger, pathos, dark comedy. However, writers often fail to consider the stark isolation of the work, the deep loneliness that accompanies the increasing isolation, the sympathy that undercover operatives may come to feel for the targets of their investigation, and the self-loathing that comes from the inevitable betrayal. Because somebody or something is always betrayed in undercover work. Usually it's the target of the investigation, sometimes it's the agency or department, and sometimes it's the investigator's integrity.

THE WIRED
INVESTIGATOR

We've all heard the story of the private detective who hid a radio transmitter in an olive in a martini glass. This is no urban legend—at least not entirely. The olive was, in fact, the handiwork of the late Hal Lipset. Lipset was one of the most influential private investigators in history; his creative uses of technology changed the nature of investigative work. The olive bug was not part of Lipset's standard equipment; it was created solely as an exhibit for Lipset's testimony before a 1968 senate subcommittee examining privacy laws. But it doesn't matter that the olive was fake, or that the transmitter was severely limited in range, or that the entire device almost certainly would not have worked at all if real gin and vermouth were used in the martini glass. What matters is that Lipset was defining the cutting edge of investigative technology.

Investigators have always lurked around the frontiers of technology. The purpose of technology, of course, is to make our lives and work easier—and that's as true for investigators as it is for architects, housekeepers, factory workers or accountants. But as we begin to look at the technology of investigation, it's important to remember that every technological advance heralded as

The Conversation

Hal Lipset is said to have been the model for Harry Caul, the protagonist in Francis Ford Coppola's movie *The Conversation*. Lipset did, in fact, serve as a technical adviser on the set and even played a small cameo role in the film. Although the technology in this film is now outdated, it remains one of the finest examples of the realities of private investigative surveillance work to be found in the movies. It also provides a disturbing, if somewhat exaggerated, look at the ethical and moral dilemmas inherent in PI work. Go to your local video store and rent it. Do it now.

the next great investigative tool has also turned around and bitten investigators on the butt.

Let's take a quick look at the historical record. One of the earliest and most significant technological aids to detectives was the telephone. Suddenly, amazing new lines of communication opened up. Before the advent of the telephone, a police detective in New York City who wanted to ask a question of a detective in Philadelphia would have to leave his office, go to the telegraph office and send the telegram to a similar office in Philadelphia, where it would eventually be delivered to a detective in the Philadelphia police. If the New York detective was lucky, the delivery boy would wait for an answer rather than force the Philly detective to leave *his* office, walk to the telegraph office . . . and the green grass grows all around all around. With a telephone, such questions became easier to ask and therefore more likely to *be* asked.

However, the telephone also served to increase the workload of all police officers, including detectives. It became both easier to report a crime and easier to do with anonymity, and more victims and witnesses did so. It also made it easier to file false reports of crimes (which, nonetheless, had to be investigated). Even as the telephone increased the amount of information available to the police, it also increased the amount of time spent following false leads, answering questions from detectives from other towns and responding to queries about the progress of investigations. If that wasn't enough, the invention of the telephone also created entirely new criminal behaviors, including telephone fraud, obscene phone calls and theft of services (the use of telephone lines without paying for them).

The same is true with every advance in investigative technology. Cameras, computers, radios—each makes the investigator more effective and makes investigative work easier. However, we must not forget that technology will, at some point, always let us down. Computers will crash, batteries will fail, static will disrupt a signal, ambient noise will interfere—something, somehow, *will* go wrong.

The forms of technology that are of most use to investigators are those that enhance the scope of their traditional skills: watching and listening. The most widely used investigative technologies are those that extend the reach of the detectives' eyes and ears. Vision is enhanced through the use of devices such as telephoto lenses, miniature surveillance cameras, pinhole lenses, night vision equipment and infrared photography. Hearing is enhanced through wiretaps, bugs, sound amplification dishes and radio transmitters/receivers.

Vision Enhancement Devices

The term "private eye" (which, by the way, I have never heard used by anybody in the business) is said to have originated from the logo of the Pinkerton Detective Agency: The Eye That Never Sleeps. Certainly, the eye reference is appropriate since so much of the work of investigators involves observation. Nor is it surprising that so much technology has been developed to extend the range of observation.

The investigator's sense of vision has been enhanced by technology in a variety of ways. Technology allows us to see across great distances, to see in extremely low light—or no light at all—even to view and record in absentia. In the case of vehicle tracking systems, the technology permits us to be aware of a vehicle's location without actually having to see it.

Binoculars, Monoculars and Spotting Scopes

These are the most common vision enhancement devices used by detectives. They're useful and relatively inexpensive—an irresistible combination.

The Law of Unintended Consequences

Every meaningful technological advance also creates entirely new and unanticipated problems. The advent of computers is a perfect example. Computers allow investigators to store, sort and analyze data in entirely new ways—and to do so with amazing speed. Computers, however, also exacerbate errors—and do so with amazing speed. Every year we hear of dozens of incidents in which entirely innocent people are mistaken for dangerous felons because they share similar names or the same dates of birth (policing agencies sort arrest records by the offender's DOB; there may be several people in the United States named Mortimer Matthews, but how many of these Mortimers were born on 04/18/74?)

The law of unintended consequences is not an artifact of modern society. It's been around since the earliest days of technology. For example, when Gutenberg invented the printing press in 1455, it allowed an unprecedented dissemination of information. In addition to printing Bibles, however, early printing presses were also used for the mass production of pornography (most folks couldn't read, but anybody could understand a picture). Early presses also churned out clerical indulgences (a document forgiving the holder of a sin, a sort of spiritual get-out-of-jail-free card), which were often "given" to wealthy sinners in exchange for contributions to the church.

The invention of the railroad made the mass transit of people, livestock and heavy goods possible. It opened up the American West (and helped destroy the culture of the native peoples who lived there). It also created an entirely new form of robbery. Since trains necessarily traveled set routes (they are, after all, dependent on laid track) and since they maintained strict time schedules, any enterprising robber with a watch could know where a train laden with bullion would be at any given moment in time. In effect, railroads acted as robbery delivery systems. The robbers simply had to wait beside the tracks for the train to arrive.

Binoculars are classified by a simple numerical code, for example 7 × 35 or 10 × 50. The first number refers to the magnification power of the binocular. With a 7 × 35 binocular, the object being viewed appears to be seven times closer than you would see it with the unaided eye. The second number refers to the diameter in millimeters of the objective (front) lens. The larger the second number, the more light the binocular gathers and the brighter the image will be.

For general purposes, 7 × 35 binoculars are perfectly fine, although I personally prefer 8 × 40s. I have known detectives who carried a pair of 10 × 50s, but they tend to be very large and, to my mind, far too heavy. The combination of weight and high magnification makes it difficult to keep the object in the center of the viewing area, and the size makes them difficult to use inconspicuously. In recent years pocket-size 10 × 25 binoculars have become popular. These are wonderful in good light conditions, but as the light begins to fade they are less useful.

Monoculars and spotting scopes are essentially low-power telescopes. Monoculars are single-barreled binoculars; they operate on the same principle, though are usually considerably smaller and often slightly less powerful. Monoculars are almost always intended to be handheld. Spotting scopes, on the other hand, have a magnification that ranges from 8x up to 40x. As the magnification increases, so does the need for a tripod (see the sidebar on tripods on page 154). Tripods, of course, are both conspicuous and cumbersome. As in so much of investigative work, a balance needs to be found between technology and circumstance.

Night Vision Devices

Night vision devices (NVDs) allow investigators to see in low-light situations—even no-light situations. NVDs may be used as independent units, which enhance the investigator's ability to see in the dark, or in conjunction with a still or video camera, which allows the investigator to record what is seen.

There are two basic types of NVDs used by investigators: image intensifiers (usually referred to by marketers as I^2 devices) and forward-looking infrared (FLIR) devices.

Image Intensifier Devices

These are by far the most common NVDs used by police and private detectives. The technology was developed by the military and first saw extensive use during the war in Vietnam. They come in four forms: sights, bioculars, monoculars (or scopes) and goggles. Sights are attached to weapons and are used by police snipers to target offenders in low-light situations. Biocular and monocular simply refer to whether the NVD has one or two eyepieces. A biocular NVD may look like binoculars, but it isn't; it lacks the magnifying power of binoculars. A biocular NVD simply allows the investigator to look at the image with both eyes, which reduces eyestrain. Goggles can be either binocular or monocular; they are worn on the head like, well, like goggles. They have the advantage of leaving the investigator's hands free—convenient for taking notes or eating a sandwich.

I^2 night vision devices work by amplifying existing ambient light. Ambient light is the faint outdoor light cast by remote light sources. These include house lighting, distant streetlights, fire, the moon and stars. Every urban and suburban area contains a tremendous amount of ambient light. Rural areas have less artificial ambient light, but usually enough natural ambient light. By amplifying that light tens of thousands of times, I^2 devices allow investigators to literally see in the dark.

The incoming light undergoes a complicated process that eventually shows up on an imaging screen, which looks like a miniature television screen. When you look through an I^2 night vision device, you're actually looking at the imaging screen, not the object itself. The screen shows a monochromatic image. The image is often shades of green, although some of the better equipment gives black-and-white images. At present only the military has access to color I^2 devices, but they will eventually find their way into policing and civilian markets.

With the collapse of the Soviet Union, I^2 night vision devices have become relatively inexpensive. There are a great number of military surplus I^2 devices from Russia, the Czech Republic and other Eastern European nations. In addition, the factories that provided such devices for the Soviet army now manufacture them for Western public markets. It's now possible to buy a good I^2 NVD for just a few hundred dollars; the best devices available to civilians, however, cost around six thousand dollars.

Midlevel NVDs are not only sufficient for most investigative purposes, but are usually preferable. The most expensive I^2 devices are actually *too* sensitive for use in city and suburban environments, which is where the vast majority of investigations take place. Remember, this technology operates by amplifying ambient light. A unit that will provide the necessary light amplification to allow a detective to see on a cloudy, moonless night in the desert will be overwhelmed by the amount of ambient light in a typical suburb.

The biggest problem with I^2 devices occurs in situations in which the light level changes (cars driving by can cause problems) or in which point light sources appear (for example, a streetlight that is too close to the object under surveillance). This can cause blooming or washout effects. Blooming is when the light source reduces an area on the screen to an amorphous blob of light. Washout takes place when the light is too bright to allow clear resolution on the imaging screen. Another common problem with I^2 devices is the fact that they are limited in regard to the level of visual contrast available; objects of similar color will blend together and will be difficult to distinguish even when the light is greatly amplified. A person wearing dark clothing (which does not reflect light well) against a dark background will be difficult to see at night even using a modern I^2 device.

Forward-Looking Infrared Devices

This technology was also originally developed for military purposes. FLIR devices were used in a variety of attack vehicles (planes, helicopters, tanks, etc.) to target the enemy through thermal energy. For a long time the technology was too bulky and heavy for handheld use; FLIR technology in policing was limited to systems mounted in helicopters and on patrol cars. Recent innovations, however, have made it possible for relatively lightweight FLIR devices.

Everything emits infrared energy at a level proportional to its temperature. What does that mean? It means the more heat an object emits, the more infrared energy it emits. FLIR technology works because heat in the infrared spectrum behaves similarily to visible light. Like visible light, it can be gathered and optically focused. Unlike visible light, however, infrared energy is invisible to the unaided eye. FLIR technology can detect minute variations in temperature, which are then translated into video signals. Different temperature variations (temperature differentials as small as .18 degrees centigrade can be detected) are assigned different shades of gray, which are then displayed on a small imaging screen.

The fact that FLIR technology is based on heat rather than light has several implications. First, it means this form of night vision is completely unaffected by the amount of light at a scene. I^2 equipment, remember, can only amplify existing ambient light; it is useless in a totally dark situation (for example, at night in an unlit warehouse). FLIR devices, however, would still be able to detect a suspect in total darkness. Second, unlike I^2 devices, FLIR allows the detective to see people in dark areas regardless of how they are clothed and regardless of the position of light sources and shadows. Third, FLIR devices can also provide valuable intelligence above and beyond the ability to see people and things in the dark. Thermal information can be used to determine if a vehicle has been recently used (the engine will show hotter), to see objects thrown away by a suspect (for example, even an unfired handgun will retain the body heat from the suspect), even to see suspects *through* a hedge. From the air, FLIR devices are are used to identify and locate drug cultivation hothouses.

Obviously, FLIR devices are significantly more expensive than I^2 devices and less readily available. The best of these devices cannot be owned by civilians, not because of the cost but because it is prohibited by law.

Investigative Uses of Cameras

Seeing, we're often told, is believing. The power of a photograph or video image is immediate, intense and visceral. Consider the power of the video taken of Rodney King being beaten by officers of the LAPD. Consider the image of the lone protester in Tiananmen Square facing down a tank. Consider the photograph of the bloody, dying child in the arms of the firefighter outside the bombed federal building in Oklahoma City. These images bite at us; we are incapable of ignoring them.

The photographs and video images taken by investigators may not have a wide influence, in part because they are rarely seen by more than a few people—perhaps just a client, perhaps a jury. Still, the effects of investigative photographs on individual lives are often profound. They can result in imprisonment, in divorce, in shattered lives or in lives almost miraculously restored.

There are three basic types of cameras used by investigators:

Facial Thermography

Thermal imaging based on technology similar to that of FLIR has spawned new security devices to control access to sensitive areas. Facial thermography measures the characteristic heat patterns emitted by each face. Some systems can measure sixty-five thousand temperature points with an accuracy of identification that surpasses fingerprints. This technology is expected to eventually find its way into a variety of corporate and public venues. For example, instead of punching a PIN (personal identification number) onto a security keypad to enter a door or gain access to a bank account at an ATM (automated teller machine), access would be controlled by facial thermography.

One drawback, however, is that alcohol consumption radically alters the thermograms.

- Still cameras. These are just regular cameras. Although investigators may use more sophisticated camera bodies and lenses than the average tourist, all still cameras work on the same principle.

- Video recorders. Again, the video cameras used by investigators may have more bells and whistles than the one you bought at Electric Warehouse, but they're basically the same under the hood.

- Closed-circuit television (CCTV). These cameras provide a live feed to an observation post. Although they are more commonly used for security purposes (you see them discreetly located in shopping malls, banks, factories, etc.), investigators use them covertly to observe real-time activity. For example, a PI may plant a CCTV camera in a false clock to determine if an employee is committing theft.

Each of these types of camera is also routinely used in conjunction with other devices described in this chapter. For example, an investigator may attach a camera body to a night vision device, allowing him to take photographs under extremely low light conditions.

There are two significant differences between the equipment most photographers use and that used by investigators: lenses and film. Investigators use a wider variety of lenses, ranging from extremely long lenses (up to 1,800mm) to pinhole lenses (as small as 3.5mm). In addition, investigators may use different types of film, or have ordinary film processed differently.

Long Lenses

Perhaps the most common photographic tool used by investigators is the telephoto lens. The standard lens (the one that comes with most 35mm cameras) is a 55mm lens; it has approximately the same focal length as the human eye. The smallest telephoto lens is usually considered to be 135mm—too small for most covert investigative purposes. Telephoto lenses used by investigators range from 200mm up to around 1,800mm. An 1,800mm lens will allow the investigator to take photographs from about a mile away from the subject.

The obvious advantage of these lenses is that they eliminate the need for the investigator to get close to the subject. The disadvantage is that most long lenses will require a tripod. Under good conditions an experienced photographer with a steady hand can usually shoot with a 200mm lens without a tripod; any lens over 200mm should be used with a tripod. There may only be one chance to get the photograph you want. It would be shameful if that one photograph was too blurry to be useful. A good investigator doesn't take any unnecessary risks.

All good-quality extremely long lenses have a tripod mount built into the lens body. With shorter lenses, the camera body is attached to the tripod and the lens is attached to the camera body; with extremely long lenses, the lens itself is attached to the tripod and the camera body is attached to the lens.

Pinhole Lenses

At the other photographic extreme are pinhole lenses. These lenses are exceptionally small, ranging from around 11mm down to about 3.5mm. They are designed to be concealed in unlikely places, such as false ceiling sprinklers, beepers, clocks and lamps. These are most commonly used with video cameras. The video transmitters used in conjunction with pinhole cameras may be as small as a coin. Despite their small size, pinhole lenses can be extremely versatile. Some can pan and tilt, zoom in or out, and be remotely focused.

One odd investigative use of pinhole lens technology has been adapted from medical use. A prefocused, self-illuminating fiber optic lens/probe designed for assisting surgeons in examining the interior nooks and crannies of the human body has been used by investigators to examine the contents of unopened envelopes.

Fast Film

Film speed is expressed as an ISO (International Standards Organization) number or an exposure index (EI). Essentially it refers to the film's sensitivity to light; the higher the film speed, the more sensitive to light. A fast film requires less light for proper exposure than a slow film. That has two implications: First, fast film can make photographs possible under low-light conditions (assuming the investigator is not using a night vision device), and second, fast film means the investigator can use a faster shutter speed. That's important when using long lenses. The longer the shutter is open, the greater the chance for lens wobble or vibration—which will result in a blurry image.

The problem with fast film is that it generally produces a grainier photograph. However, odd as it sounds, juries and clients tend to believe that a grainy photograph is somehow more authentic. It "feels" more real.

Most standard-speed films (100 to 400 ISO) can be "pushed." That is, the film can be exposed as if it were faster (for example, when using a 400 ISO film, the photographer can set the camera ISO speed to 800 or 1,600). Pushed film has to be processed differently at the lab. Almost every professional lab, if informed the film has been pushed, can adjust the processing to ensure the proper exposure.

One tenet all detectives believe is this: Film is cheap. They take a lot of photographs, often varying the exposure. It's better to waste a roll of film than to miss getting the photograph.

Infrared Film

As noted earlier, light waves in the infrared spectrum aren't visible to the human eye. We can't really see heat. However, infrared (IR) film can. The advantage to this is obvious: We can take photographs of things we can't see with the unaided eye.

Just as FLIR technology can let us see in total darkness, IR film lets us make photographs in total darkness.

IR film is available in both color reversal (slide) and black-and-white versions. Because the film is sensitive to light the human eye can't see, the film, when printed, presents an odd-looking image. People look ghostly, but are recognizable.

IR film can be used in regular still cameras. However, there are some extra precautions to be taken. Because IR film is so sensitive to such a wide spectrum of light, it must be loaded in the camera in total darkness. Care must also be given when changing lenses. With ordinary film the photographer can change lenses anywhere. With IR film the photographer should do so in at least subdued light, otherwise the film may become fogged.

Another problem with IR film is that many modern cameras have an integrated automatic film advance. Many of these devices use an IR system to control the film movement. This will result in fogging the film, or fogging a portion of it (for example, the Canon EOS 5 uses such a system and will fog the lower third of the film). It's not pleasant to go to all the effort to take IR photographs only to discover you've been betrayed by your camera.

Finally, IR film requires a slight change in focusing. On the body of a lens there is usually a red mark, adjacent to the normal focusing mark, that denotes where the point of focus should be when using IR film. Auto-focus lenses may not show the IR focus mark; some modern optics don't require a focus shift.

Vehicle Tracking Devices

Tracking devices aren't actually vision enhancement devices; they don't actually extend or enhance the investigator's ability to *see* anything. Instead, they allow the investigator to know the location of a subject's vehicle when it's out of sight. More accurately, they allow the investigator to know the location of the tracking device; we've all seen movies in which a tracking device is discovered by the subject and attached to another passing vehicle.

These devices (which are also called bird dogs, homers or bumper beepers) make solo tailing of a vehicle remarkably easier.

A Few Words About Tripods

Any investigator who frequently uses long-lens photography in surveillance must have several types of tripods. It's difficult for the average person to avoid lens wobble when using any lens with a focal length of over 200mm, unless the lens or camera is attached to some sort of stable platform. Lens wobble results in blurry photographs. Blurry photographs suck—for both police and private detectives.

In addition to a sturdy fluid head tripod, investigators often use the following:

- A window mount. This clamps onto a side window of a vehicle. The clamps are wide and flat and covered with rubber or felt to prevent damage to the window. On top of the clamp is a standard, swiveling tripod mount to which a camera, lens or spotting scope can be attached.

- A suction cup mount. This curious mount has a large suction cup on one end and a gimballed tripod mount on the other. The advantage of a suction cup is that it will attach to any flat surface. The gimballed mount makes it possible to keep the camera/lens/spotting scope level despite the surface to which it is attached. At the base of the mount is a button or lever that releases the vacuum, allowing the suction cup to be detached. The suction will hold for several hours.

- A monopod. This is simply a one-legged tripod (which, I realize, makes no literal sense). A collapsible monopod is convenient for those situations in which it is physically difficult to set up a tripod (in the bushes, for example) or when the investigator is in too big a hurry to set up a standard tripod.

They don't, however, allow the investigator to see what behavior is taking place inside the vehicle.

There are two basic designs for vehicle tracking devices: radio frequency (RF) systems (although the name is misleading since both systems use radio frequencies) and global positioning satellite (GPS) systems.

Radio Frequency Tracking Systems

These systems consist of a transmitter and a receiver. The transmitter is usually attached to the subject's vehicle (almost always underneath the vehicle) by a magnet. The transmitter emits an RF signal from which the receiver can calculate certain spatial relationships between the locations of both components.

Now, just what does that mean? It means the investigator can determine where the target vehicle is in general relation to his own vehicle. It can also tell the investigator if the target is moving away or getting closer. Some systems are capable of scanning a 180-degree arc in front of the tracking vehicle; other systems can scan a full 360 degrees. Since most tracking is done from behind the target vehicle, the 180-degree systems are good enough for most detectives. Besides, the 360-degree systems are, as might be expected, more expensive.

Radio frequency systems are really rather simple. The 180-degree systems have two small antennae located near the front of the vehicle (the 360-degree systems have four antennae—two in front, two in back). The signal from the transmitter arrives at each antenna at slightly different times (measured in fractions of seconds). The difference in the times indicates the direction from which the signal is being sent—and therefore, it's to be hoped, the direction of the target vehicle (see diagram next page). The investigator determines the direction by looking at a simple zero-center meter. The approximate distance between the target vehicle and the tracking vehicle is indicated either by a tone (which changes pitch as the distance varies) or by a series of lights.

This is not a highly precise technology. The system will not inform the detective that the target vehicle is, say, three blocks in front and two blocks to the right. All it will do is inform the detective that the target vehicle is up ahead a short distance and slightly to the right. But that's almost always enough information.

RF systems are often advertised as having a range of up to ten miles. Quite frankly, I don't trust them at that distance—or anywhere close to that distance. I'm uncomfortable with the thought that the target is that far away. In truth, I'm a wee bit uncomfortable with the idea that the target is out of my direct line of sight, but I trust the technology to the extent that I'm willing to take some minimal risks. Even so, I think it would be

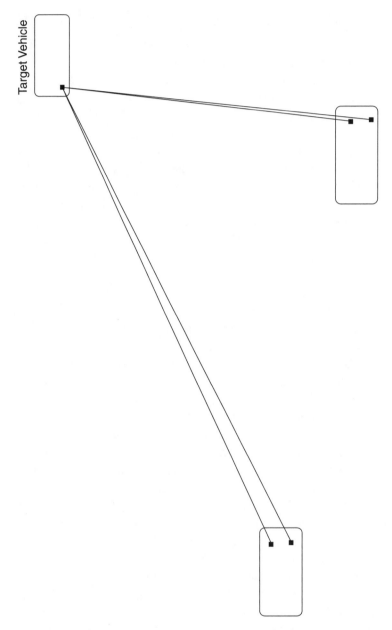

The signal sent from the transmitter attached to the target vehicle is received by the antennae attached to the detective's vehicle. By measuring the slight difference in the time each antennae receives the signal, an RF tracking system can determine the direction of the signal and its approximate distance.

unwise to allow the target vehicle to get more than a mile or two away, especially in urban areas.

The problem with RF systems is that in large urban areas the signal bounces off all sorts of surfaces (tall buildings, bridges, etc.). This has the effect of blurring the received information; in effect, the receiver is hearing lots of echos. Better RF systems include an indicator of the purity of the signal. The purer the signal, the more accurate the information.

But even a dirty signal still provides a general distance and direction. When a signal gets dirty, the best plan is for the investigator to head in the direction of the signal. That will usually bring the investigator closer to the target vehicle, reducing the number of surfaces the signal is reflecting off and clearing it up.

In those dreadful situations when the signal is lost altogether, the investigator has two options. First, hurry to high ground, which improves the chance of reacquiring the signal. Second, hurry in the direction of the last decent signal and begin to drive in a grid pattern. If you're lucky, the signal simply became too degraded from bouncing off various buildings; if so, it can often be reacquired. If you're unlucky, the batteries on the transmitter have died (batteries are generally reliable for over twenty-four hours); if so, you're done for the day.

Global Positioning Satellite Systems

In the 1980s the U.S. Department of Defense placed twenty-four global positioning satellites in orbit 20,200 km above the earth. These satellites continuously broadcast signals that contain the time and identifier codes (each satellite has its own code). A GPS receiver acquires signals from several satellites (at any given time, at least six satellites are in position to be acquired by the user) and uses those signals to determine the receiver's position (including height above sea level). The GPS system works on the same mathematical principle as the RF system: The minuscule time differential between when the signals are received (measured in nanoseconds) provides the location of the receiver—and does so with remarkable accuracy. A quality GPS receiver can pinpoint its location anywhere on the planet to within a few *feet*.

Although the technology was developed for military use, it has been adapted for a variety of nonmilitary purposes. Obviously, the use we are most concerned with pertains to GPS

Attaching a Bumper Beeper

Despite this device's name, a vehicle's bumper isn't an appropriate place to attach tracking equipment. First, fewer and fewer bumpers are made of metal and most transmitters attach by means of a magnet. However, even if the bumper is metal, it rarely offers a surface flat enough to attach the transmitter. The most common places to attach it are the frame and inside the wheel well.

Before attaching the device, it's a good idea to scrape off as much of the accumulated grime, oil and dirt as possible (investigators who do a lot of this work always carry around a putty knife for scraping and those odd-smelling towelettes for cleaning their hands). Although the magnets on these devices are usually quite powerful, a careful detective also secures the unit to the vehicle with a length of tape (electrical tape is good; it's dark and won't be quite as visible if the subject, for some reason, looks under the vehicle).

In theory there is no advantage to attaching the transmitter to the rear of the car. The signal will be the same whether it comes from the front of the car or the rear. However, most detectives tend to plant the devices at the rear. Go figure.

technology as a covert means of tracking a vehicle. A GPS tracking system is composed of a transmitter, a receiver/decoder and a laptop computer loaded with a mapping program.

The transmitter is planted on the target vehicle in the same way as an ordinary RF system transmitter. It transmits a brief (two milliseconds), digitally encrypted signal (so that only the owner can decode it) every few seconds. The satellite obtains the signal from the transmitter, and the receiver/decoder obtains the data for that particular transmitter from the satellite. The data is then plotted in real time on the mapping program, showing the investigator the location of the target vehicle and the distance from the target vehicle in feet (seventy-five to sixty-five thousand), as well as its speed and the direction in which it's moving. The computer program can even be manipulated so that it can alert the investigator if a stationary vehicle begins moving again.

Good GPS tracking systems can simultaneously monitor up to ten separate targets.

Secondary investigative uses of GPS technology are to assist the investigator in finding an unfamiliar location and to prevent him from getting lost. A handheld GPS system contains both the transmitter and the receiver. When used in conjunction with a computer mapping program, the system will show the investigator's precise location. This may sound like a small thing, but consider how often investigators find themselves in strange cities, and consider how poorly street names are marked in some cities, and consider how difficult it is to find a specific intersection on a map when you're unfamiliar with the landmarks of the city. Now consider doing all that late at night—in a bad neighborhood.

Although GPS technology has become increasingly more common and lower in price, it remains fairly expensive. Still, it offers tremendous benefits to investigators of all sorts.

Laser Range Finder

It's often important for detectives to make precise measurements of long distances. The distance from the site of an assault to the nearest streetlamp, for example, or the distance between the suspected location of a sniper to the body of the victim. A steel measuring tape or a measuring wheel (a device consisting of a small wheel on a shaft, which is rolled from one location to another, the turning of the wheel ticking off the distance) is acceptable for many situations, but not always practical and not always accurate over long distances. In addition, these devices are often inconvenient. In investigating a negligent homicide case involving an auto accident, I needed to measure the length of some skid marks on a busy highway. I spent nearly ninety minutes attempting to measure the marks with a measuring wheel. Traffic kept chasing me off the road. I was eventually forced to give up and return late at night, when the highway was less busy. With a laser range finder and an assistant to stand at the other end of the skid marks, I could have done the job in seconds—at a great savings to my client.

A laser range finder operates on a simple principle. The user points the device at an object and presses a button. The device emits a harmless laser beam, which bounces off the object and returns to the range finder. The distance between the object and the range finder is determined by measuring the elapsed time between the emission of the beam and its return.

A laser range finder measures distance more quickly and with greater accuracy than other measuring devices. In addition, it provides the bearing of the target from the sighting location, both in compass points and in 360-degree notation (for example: NW, 325.8 degrees).

Hearing Enhancement Devices

Seeing what is going on is certainly important. Hearing (and, of course, recording) what is going on is perhaps even more important. Technology that enhances the investigator's ability to listen has become one of the most important areas of modern investigation.

One of the things a writer needs to understand is the distinction between wiretaps and bugs. A wiretap is just that—a device that intercepts a transmission carried over a wire or related form of telecommunication. This includes not only voice communication but also fax and computer communication. A bug, on the other hand, is any technology that transmits sound from one area to a listening post. A bug doesn't depend on telecommunications; it can be planted anywhere—in a home or office, on a park bench, on a person's clothing, in the salt cellar at the local diner. Or in an olive.

Wiretaps

Wiretaps can be yoked to a variety of wires—a telephone line (which also carries transmissions via computer Internet access or fax); a PBX (private branch exchange) cable, the telephone console that controls all the phone lines in a large company; a computer local area network; a video system; even an alarm system. There are essentially four types of wiretaps:

- Hard. A hard wiretap occurs when a section of the wire the signal travels on is physically accessed. The detective attaches a second set of wires, which connects a listening device (a handset, earphones, etc.) to the signal wire. For long-term wiretaps, the second set of wires will lead to a listening post. Otherwise the investigator may simply stand there and listen in on the signal (which may be a conversa-

Technical Surveillance Counter Measures

Although most of this section is devoted to bugs and wiretaps, it should be noted that private security personnel devote more time to *finding* these devices than to planting them. The field of Technical Surveillance Counter Measures (TSCM) is rapidly growing. Sad to say, this field also produces some of the most blatant scam artists in the business. Since the majority of clients requesting TSCM haven't a clue how the process works, they are vulnerable to any unscrupulous private detective or security firm with a suitcase full of gadgets with blinking lights. Fortunately, the majority of people requesting TSCM are *not* being tapped or bugged, so these scam artists do no harm (aside from taking money they haven't really earned).

A TSCM sweep usually involves three aspects: a radio frequency (RF) sweep to locate any listening device using a radio transmitter; a wire sweep to check communication wires (telephones, faxes, modems, etc.) for taps; and a physical sweep to search for concealed, hard-wired microphones. A physical sweep is very time consuming (and dirty); every nook and cranny, every piece of furniture, every appliance and office machine, every air duct, every office fixture (smoke detectors, sprinklers, ceiling light, clock, etc.), every electrical outlet, every*thing* must be searched.

tion or an electronic signal such as a fax or computer signal). This is a fairly crude technique, but serves for a fast and dirty means to get information. Both PIs and police investigators have used hard taps.

- Soft. A soft wiretap involves modifying the software used to run the telephone system to allow access to the signal. Police detectives (or other official public investigators) may do this at the telephone company. It can also be done at a PBX, which is the location where private detectives are more likely to install a soft tap. This is also referred to by some folks as a translation tap.

- Record. This is a common wiretapping method. In effect, a record tap is nothing more than a hard tap in which the signal is sent to a tape recorder rather than to an active listener. The biggest drawback of a record tap, of course, is the need to constantly change tapes. A voice-activated recorder alleviates this somewhat (rather than recording all the time, a voice-activated recorder only records when a sound is heard).

- Transmit. A transmit tap is essentially a radio frequency transmitter—a bug (which is covered next)—connected to the signal wire.

Bugs

This is classic detective technology—listening in on folks who aren't aware they're being listened to. As might be expected, the information obtained through listening to such unguarded conversations can be extremely revealing.

There are five categories of bugs:

- Acoustic. Actually, there is no such thing as an acoustic bug. This refers to the practice of using relatively low-tech devices to amplify sound waves through a barrier. This includes something as simple as a stethoscope or placing a water glass against a wall. These things actually work, although at a limited level. And it sounds better in your report to say you utilized an acoustic listening technique instead of admitting you pressed your ear against the wall.

- Ultrasonic. These bugs convert sound into an audio signal that exceeds the range of human hearing. The signal is transmitted to a remote listening site and converted back to normal audio range.

- Radio frequency. This is the classic bug. A small radio transmitter is surreptitiously planted in an area or a device. All sounds that occur within the range of the transmitter are sent to a nearby receiver where the transmission can be recorded. Sophisticated RF bugs can be turned on and off remotely. This not only saves on the life of the batteries, it allows the investigator to turn the bug off after normal business hours. This is the time when most TSCM sweeps are conducted; therefore the deactivated RF bug has a better chance of being missed in the sweep. When transmitting, RF bugs are fairly easy to detect.

- Optical (or laser). These devices bounce a laser beam off a window in the area under surveillance. The premise is that all sound, including conversation, produces waves. These waves make the window vibrate, which is detected by the laser beam. The vibrations are converted into an electrical signal, which is transmitted to a receiver, where it is filtered and reconverted into an audio signal. These are rather expensive devices and are of limited use. Not only do voices make windows vibrate, so does the wind and a jackhammer and unrelated building noise.

- Hybrid. A hybrid bug is one that combines any of the preceding technologies.

Sound Amplification Dishes

These are relatively inexpensive handheld sound amplification devices. They are sometimes referred to as bionic ears. In essence the device consists of a highly sensitive directional microphone centered in a lightweight, concave dish. The dish, which is usually removable, serves to expand the listening surface. The greater the listening surface, the more sound waves are captured. You get a similar effect simply by cupping your hands behind your ears. The operator listens through headphones that generally contain an automatic shutoff function for sudden loud noises.

The operator simply points the microphone and dish at the object she wishes to listen to. Sound amplification dishes are sensitive enough to capture a quiet conversation at seventy-five yards or an argument at half a mile. Most of these devices also include an audio jack that allows the operator to connect a tape recorder.

The problem with these devices, especially at the low end, is that they not only amplify the sounds the detective wants to hear, they amplify *all* line-of-sight sounds. For example, let's say the investigator wishes to listen to and record a conversation between two people on a busy beach. It is unlikely the investigator will be able to maintain a clear path between herself and the subject. In that situation the dish will pick up every conversation (and other noise) in the direct line of sight—the people in front of and behind the target, radios, perhaps even the sound of waves (if the ocean is behind the target). However, if the beach has a nearby hotel, the detective could maintain a clear line of sight from a balcony on an upper floor. (See illustration next page.)

The quality of the sound obtained through amplification dishes is not always acceptable. Sometimes the conversations recorded through these devices must be taken to an acoustics expert to filter out extraneous noise.

These devices can be found in some hunting or outdoor catalogs. Hunters use amplification dishes to help locate game; birders use them to locate birds and to record bird songs. They can usually be bought for about $150.

Two-Way Radios

When compared to the other technology we've discussed, two-way radios are ancient technology. Nonetheless, they are critical tools for investigators involved in stationary and mobile surveillance. It's important under those circumstance for a team of investigators to be able to exchange information.

As with other technologies, new developments have allowed two-way radios to become small and less expensive. The most important qualities of a two-way radio system are weight, range and clarity. Obviously, the ideal system is one of negligible weight that allows for static-free communication at a great distance.

An important accessory is a voice-activated circuit (VOX), in which the microphone automatically keys open when the user speaks into it. When combined with a lightweight earpiece and microphone headset, this allows for totally hands-free communication—definitely convenient when conducting a mobile surveillance in traffic. Modern headsets consist of a tiny ear loop and a wire-thin microphone that are virtually invisible from a short distance.

Conclusion

As a writer you should be aware that technological progress always comes at a price. Progress often exchanges old aggravations for new ones. For police and private detectives, technology promises to make them more effective and to make their working lives easier at the same time. And, for the most part, technology actually fulfills that promise.

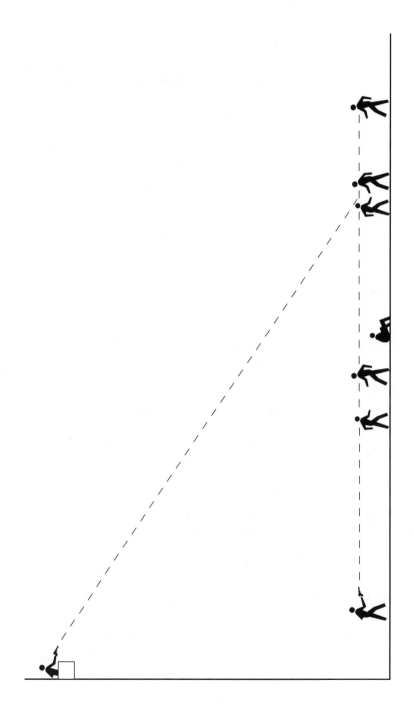

Cutting-edge technology has become integral to a great deal of detective work. No detective would willingly give up a computer, or a night vision device, or telephoto lenses. They can have my vehicle tracking system when they pry it from my cold, dead fingers.

But (there's always a "but") you need to remember that the purpose of technology is to *assist* the investigator. The vast majority of investigative work done by police and private detectives alike is still done the old-fashioned way: by spending time on the streets, by asking nosy questions, by poking around in places they shouldn't, by developing relationships, by avoiding notice and by looking at the world in ways most folks don't.

For many investigators (and, sadly, many writers as well) the reliance on technology—and always the *very latest* technology—has resulted in the neglect and erosion of traditional skills. Some detectives make the mistake of accepting new technologies simply because they are new and discarding old methods of operation simply because they are old (just as some writers spend more time searching for the perfect dictionary program than they do in the simple but necessary task of putting words in a row).

You needn't outfit your protagonist, whether a police investigator or a private detective, with the latest technology. For the vast majority of investigative chores, old technologies work just fine. An eight-year-old Soviet Army surplus night vision device may not give great resolution or work in total darkness, but it's good enough. A beat-up old 500mm mirror lens may be a bit heavy and may not provide images that are perfectly crisp at the edges, but it's good enough. The 8×40 binoculars with a scratched lens may not be pretty, but they're good enough. Good enough is good enough.

I am a big fan of technology. I purchased my first computer (a Kaypro 2) in 1983. There are times, however, when I wonder if perhaps humankind reached its technological peak with the invention of the corkscrew. Mystery and detective novels are about people and the things they do, not technology.

T E N

PULLING IT ALL TOGETHER

There you have it. Just the facts, ma'am. Well, maybe a little more than just the facts. We've talked about what it takes to be a good detective, we've looked at the differences and similarities between police detectives and private investigators, and we've compared their approaches to crime scenes. We've contrasted interrogation and interviewing, we've looked at different modes of surveillance and types of tailing, and we've discussed a variety of information sources. We've taken a peek at undercover work and examined some of the technology available to investigators.

Had I given you just the facts, this would have been an exceedingly short and remarkably dull book. In the first chapter I mentioned that "just the facts" isn't enough. Investigation is much more than simply amassing facts; it's a process, a constantly evolving inquiry.

And yet, "Just the facts, ma'am" isn't *entirely* inappropriate. A good investigator needs to know *how* to get the facts, how to determine *which* facts are important, what to *do* with the facts and what *not* to do with the facts. A good mystery writer needs to know this as well.

Here, then, are some facts about facts. More accurately, here are some opinions about facts.

Not All Facts Are Created Equal

Facts are facts. It's hard to argue with that. But some facts weigh more than others. An elephant and a mouse are both miracles of creation, but one is much more impressive than the other. One draws the eye; the other often escapes notice. The existence of an elephant is much harder to overlook. This doesn't mean elephants are more important or significant than mice. The relative importance of these two creatures depends entirely on the problem under examination. If the problem is the spread of disease, mice are far more significant; if the problem is cleaning up after them, well . . .

One of the things that distinguishes good detectives from bad ones is the ability to sift through facts and determine which are the important ones. The more obvious facts aren't necessarily the ones most deserving of attention.

Consider the following case: A young man has been having some financial difficulties and has fallen behind on car payments. One evening he calls the police and reports his car has been stolen. A few hours later that night, in the parking lot of a convenience store not far from the young man's apartment, a car is discovered enveloped in flames. It is, of course, the young man's vehicle.

The police and fire departments respond to the convenience store. The heat of the fire is so intense the dashboard melts. After the fire is extinguished and the vehicle examined, it's obvious an accelerant was used to start the fire. This was a clear case of arson. Also found in the burnt-out car are a couple candy bar wrappers.

The police showed the convenience store clerk a photograph of the young man. The clerk recognized him, stating the man had been in the store the night the car was torched. In fact, the clerk said the young man often stopped by the store. He usually bought a lottery ticket, a soft drink and a couple candy bars. The clerk, however, couldn't recall the brand of the candy bars.

The young man filed an insurance claim. A couple days later he was arrested and charged with fraud and filing a false report (he wasn't charged with the crime of arson; it's not against the law to burn your own car, but it *is* against the law to try to defraud an insurance company). The young man, of course, claimed he was innocent.

Here are the facts: (1) The young man was having financial trouble; (2) he reported his car was stolen; (3) from the damage to the dashboard and the presence of accelerants, it's clear his car was deliberately torched; (4) he was known to have been in the convenience store the night of the fire; (5) he was known to have bought candy bars; (6) candy bar wrappers were found in the burned hulk of the car; and (7) the young man filed an insurance claim on the car. Which facts are the most important?

At first I thought the most important fact was the damage done to the dashboard. It takes a lot of heat to melt a dashboard. Certainly enough heat to incinerate any candy bar wrappers. When I interviewed the clerk at the convenience store, I discovered that both the firefighters and the police officers had come into the store during and after the fire, buying snacks, drinks and candy bars. It's likely the candy bar wrappers were dropped in the car by a careless firefighter. In truth, the most important fact in this case wasn't even considered by the police. The most important fact was that the car happened to get torched in the parking lot of a convenience store—a place where the police and firefighters had access to snacks.

The evaluation of facts during an investigation is an ongoing process. As more facts are obtained, the existing facts must be reevaluated. As new facts become known, the importance of old facts may change. Facts that seemed important at the beginning of the case may seem irrelevant by the end. It can be terribly frustrating for an investigator, but it works well in a detective story.

Facts in Isolation Are Pointless

Here is an indisputable fact: The brains of women are smaller than the brains of men. Of course, not every male brain is larger than every female brain, but on average the brains of men weigh about a hundred grams more than those of women. It's a fact. You can look it up.

Now, what does that fact mean? Surely, all that extra brain matter must mean something. A century ago the larger male brain was considered conclusive proof that men are more intelligent than women. Not just smarter, but more rational and more analytical. Superior, in other words. (Would you be surprised to learn that the scientists who reached this conclusion were men?)

In fact, the only conclusion we can gather from the sex difference in brain size is that an isolated fact has little value. Yes, it's true that male brains are larger than female brains. So are male arms. So are male legs and feet and hands. Men, in general, are simply larger than women.

In order to be meaningful, a fact needs to be interpreted in relation to other facts. It's possible during an investigation for a detective to develop a form of investigative tunnel vision. There are times when a detective can focus on a single fact to the degree that he becomes blind to all other facts. This is almost always detrimental to the investigation.

I've heard of a police detective who was called to the scene of an apparent suicide. The victim, a woman still in her pajamas, was hanging by a length of clothesline cord tied to a beam in the kitchen. A chair had been kicked over. The woman's slippers were on the floor beneath her. It appeared she'd removed her slippers, stood on the chair, tied one end of the clothesline cord to the beam, tied the other into a noose, slipped the noose around her neck, then kicked the chair out from underneath her. According to others, the woman had a history of depression brought on by severe chronic back pain, and she had attempted suicide in the past.

All the facts pointed toward suicide. All but one: The woman's slippers were on the wrong sides. The left slipper was on the right, the right slipper on the left. How could that have happened? Was she wearing the slippers on the wrong feet? Were the slippers put there *after* the woman died?

The detective remained puzzled until he consulted another investigator at the scene. The second detective looked at the slippers and recalled how his wife removed her slippers. She sat on a chair, removed the left slipper with her right hand, dropped it, then removed the right slipper with her left hand. When she finished, the slippers were always on the wrong sides.

The slippers, seen in isolation, could have led the detective to the wrong conclusion. However, when seen in relation to other facts—especially the chronic back pain, which would have forced the victim to sit to remove her footwear—the position of the slippers made sense.

I mentioned earlier that to focus on a single fact is almost always detrimental to the investigation. There are, of course, some cases in which it is beneficial. But even in those situations what makes that fact meaningful is its relationship to other facts in the case.

Facts Are Cold

Bertrand Russell once remarked that the degree of one's emotions varies inversely with one's knowledge of the facts: The less you know the hotter you get. To allow yourself to become too emotionally involved is a cardinal sin in investigative work. Passion interferes with reason (and so it should; it's one of the most attractive aspects of passion). It's fine for an investigator to have an agenda (a political stance, a religious perspective, a philosophical ideology), but the agenda must always be secondary to the case.

Facts are cold. They have no agenda, no cause to espouse, no motive. They can, however, sometimes be twisted by an investigator who allows her own personal convictions, needs or desires to interfere with the course of the investigation.

I once had a client, a woman in her late twenties, who was charged with murder and arson. She lived in a rather seedy old apartment building with her boyfriend. Their relationship could only be described as stormy. On the night of the fire she had learned her boyfriend was having an affair with another woman. After an argument, the boyfriend left the apartment. The young woman gathered his clothes, put them in the hallway, doused them with lighter fluid and set them on fire. The fire department responded to the building, found the burning clothes and put out the fire. Fortunately, no real damage was done (except, of course, to the boyfriend's clothes). Since nobody had seen the woman put the clothes in the hall or start the fire, she was not arrested.

In the wee hours of the following morning a second fire erupted in the building. This one, however, was far more severe. During the fire an old man jumped from a fourth-floor window.

He died at the scene. Several other folks were seriously injured, including a toddler who died a few days later at the hospital. The apartment was, for all intents and purposes, destroyed. Because of the earlier incident, the young woman was arrested and charged with murder and arson. An investigator in the fire marshal's office spent a morning rummaging through the debris. He declared the point of origin to be near the front door of the young woman's apartment and stated the fire had been a spite arson.

Any criminal defendant accused of harming a child or an old person draws a lot of negative attention. This young woman was vilified in the press, and there was a tremendous amount of pressure put on the prosecutor, the police and the fire marshal to convict her.

A week or so after the fire, the defense team, with our own arson expert, walked through the apartment building. We examined and photographed every apartment on every floor. Our arson expert stated the fire had been the result of faulty wiring in a maintenance closet. His opinion was that a short had occurred in the wiring and had probably smoldered for some time before erupting into flames. The fire, he claimed, had likely started at least two hours before the first alarm.

The attorneys reported our findings to the prosecutor, hoping to get the charges dismissed. They weren't. In fact, on the first day of jury selection the prosecutor gave us a series of photographs taken inside various apartments in the building. In each photograph we could see a clock, the hands of which had stopped at the approximate time the fire marshal claimed the client started the fire.

It was a catastrophic blow to the defense. But then we looked at our own photographs—the ones I had taken a few days after the fire. Since we had photographed every apartment in the building, we were able to compare our photos with the new ones we were given by the prosecutor. In our photographs the hands of the clocks were stopped at a totally different time—the approximate time our expert had suggested the faulty wiring had shorted.

At some point after we'd done our examination, somebody had entered the apartment building and adjusted all the clocks to support the prosecution's case. We later discovered it was done by an investigator from the fire marshal's office. There was a great deal of pressure—by the public and his superiors—to get a conviction in this case. On top of that, this fire marshal investigator would soon be having his annual review, and putting away a major case would look good. But most of all this man was entirely *certain* the defendant had started the fire. In his mind he'd done nothing terribly wrong; he was simply making a minor change in the evidence to ensure she was properly punished for the crime. He had allowed his passion for what he considered justice and his own personal agenda to get in the way of the case. The charges against our client were, of course, dismissed.

Good detectives accept the facts as they are. They work with the facts they have at hand and never allow their own agendas to distort their visions. It's important to distinguish between treating the facts with imagination and imagining the facts.

Facts Are Facts, and Only Facts

Every investigation involves amassing a huge number of facts. A great number of those facts can simply be gathered and promptly ignored; they'll have absolutely no bearing on the result of the investigation. Still, the wise detective collects them as a matter of course. For example, consider a detective called to a murder scene in a home in a suburban middle-class neighborhood. Parked in the attached garage is a car. There is absolutely nothing to suggest the car has anything to do with the crime, yet as a matter of routine somebody is likely to look at the vehicle registration. It will almost certainly be registered to somebody who lives in the house. Even if it isn't, it's highly improbable the car is significant. But you never know. So the fact is collected and stored, and available if by some fluke it turns out to be important.

One of the most interesting murder cases I worked involved two Cuban immigrants. The murder had the most common murder ingredients: a hot summer night, two men who know each other, alcohol (both had been drinking beer all day), some sexual jealousy (both were interested in the same woman), an argument (they'd been playing cards) and ready access to a weapon (a knife). Put them all together, mix well and you often end up with a bleeding body. It didn't look like a very interesting case.

Then I discovered that both men were Marielitos. In 1980 there was a tremendous influx of Cubans who fled the island and attempted to sail the ninety miles from the harbor of Mariel,

Cuba, to the Florida Keys. These folks were called Marielitos. They made the voyage in anything that could float—motorboat, sailboat, raft. Unable to stop the emigration, Fidel Castro decided to rid himself of those he found undesirable. He opened his prisons and mental hospitals and sent the inmates along to the United States with the other immigrants. A significant portion of the 125,000 Cuban immigrants who arrived during the five months of the boat lift were convicted criminals or mentally unbalanced.

How does one determine Castro's undesirables from those who simply wanted to escape Cuba? The undesirables often had similar tattoos—a five-pointed star on the web of the hand between the thumb and forefinger. Both the victim and the accused murderer had star tattoos.

The investigation began to take on a new and interesting angle. Not only were they both Marielitos and both ex-convicts, it turned out they were both practitioners of Santeria. Santeria is a religion that is a curious fusion of Catholicism and the religion brought to Cuba between the sixteenth and nineteenth centuries by slaves from the West African Yoruba tribe. Santeria stresses respect for one's ancestors and the use of ritual music, usually drumming, to communicate with the spirit world. Priests called Santeros toss cowrie shells or use numerological methods to divine the future. They make frequent offerings to the gods, including, at times, the sacrifice of live animals. Followers of Santeria believe the gods intervene in the day-to-day lives of believers. The believers are occasionally possessed by an Orisha, a spirit that represents both a force of nature and a set of human behavioral characteristics.

Needless to say I spent weeks acquiring a huge fund of knowledge on the religion, on Marielitos and on Cuban prison culture. I reported all of it to the attorney assigned to represent the accused murderer. We pored over the details of the crime, looking at them from a religious angle (could the murder somehow be related to the practice of Santeria?), from a feud angle (maybe the two knew each in a Cuban prison or mental institution and carried a grudge to their new home in the United States) and from a cultural angle (perhaps there was something in Cuban culture that made the fight inevitable). Surely, we thought, there was bound to be something in all that information that would explain why the murder had taken place.

In the end, it turned out to be just another pointless murder. No old prison grudge. No curious religious overtones. No Cuban cultural explanations. Just a couple of drunk guys who got in a fight on a hot summer night, and one of them wound up dead. I had gathered all those facts—those lovely facts—for nothing.

But you never know. You collect the facts, you try to determine which ones are important, you examine the facts in relation to other facts, you keep your own attitudes and beliefs out of the investigation, and you remind yourself that much of your investigation is simply gathering irrelevant information.

During a brief period as an academic I learned a valuable lesson. There are two ways of teaching: You can fill the bucket, or you can start a fire. You can give people the information they need, the *facts* on which they can build their own ideas—you can fill the bucket. Or you can inspire folks to *think*, to take those facts and run wild with them—you can start a fire. Sometimes you can do both. Fill the bucket with gasoline, then hope it combusts.

That's the idea behind this book. To fill the bucket *and* start a fire. I have, I hope, filled the bucket. You now have a few more facts about how police and private detectives go about their business. My hope is that you will also be inspired to think about those facts, to consider as many permutations of the facts as you can.

For example, you now know a bit more about tailing by car. Try to imagine a variety of possible tailing situations (and as creative as you are, you'd be agape at the sorts of situations that actually take place in real life).

What would your detective do if he's conducting a tail and the subject's car gets a flat tire? Does your detective stop to help? That's a great way to blow a tail. Does he break off entirely and try again the following day? Does he simply drive calmly by and begin to search for a place to park and wait, hoping to pick up the tail later? What if the subject is an old woman (that's right— an old woman; it happens more often than you'd think)? Does that make a difference in your detective's decision? Should it? What if the car got a flat on a country road, where nobody is likely to pass for a while? Or in a bad neighborhood late at night? Or in the middle of the local "miracle mile" of car dealers and fast-food outlets? What if the flat tire happened downtown during rush hour? What if, what if, what if?

There are no right answers to those questions. The answers are entirely dependent on the circumstance, and one of the eternal truths of detective work is that no two circumstances are exactly alike.

We often hear that old cliché "Truth is stranger than fiction." Well, of course it is. Truth doesn't have to make sense. Truth isn't bound by a narrative tradition. As a writer, you're expected to make your work internally logical. Truth isn't under any pressure to tie all the loose ends together; readers of mystery and detective fiction abhor loose ends. Truth can be corny; you can't. Truth can revolve around the most unlikely coincidences; readers hate coincidence.

Whenever people scoff at the notion that truth is stranger than fiction, I like to tell them the story of Wilmer McLean. In July of 1861 McLean owned a small farm near the village of Manassas Junction, Virginia, on the banks of a small stream called Bull Run. The first real battle of the American Civil War took place all around McLean's farmhouse. During the battle a shell actually smashed through one of his windows. After the battle McLean decided to take his family farther south, away from the war, where they could live in some semblance of peace and safety. And he did—for nearly four years.

Then, on April 9, 1865, in a small Virginia village called Appomattox Court House, it came time for Robert E. Lee to formally surrender to Ulysses Grant. An aide to General Lee was sent to find an appropriate building for the ceremony. He selected a sturdy-looking brick farmhouse. It belonged to Wilmer McLean. The bloody war that began on his doorstep ended in his parlor.

What writer would have the nerve to include a coincidence of that magnitude in a novel? What editor could read such a coincidence without groaning and reaching for the red pen? It's so incredibly improbable, and yet it's true.

It's possible to create realistic characters and put them in realistic situations and still tell a good story. Hammett did it. Mosley still does it. So do Lawrence Block and Liza Cody and dozens of others. And so can you.

E L E V E N

CASE STUDIES

In order to give you some idea how real cases begin and evolve, I'm going to present a couple of the cases I've worked on, a civil case and a criminal case. Obviously, the names of the folks involved and some of the facts have been altered to protect, well, whoever needs protecting. I must also say that the cases have been radically condensed. Although I include some of the false leads and dead ends, it is impossible to include every detail of each case. The actual case files are thick with information that turned out to be of no use. The civil case file is nearly one hundred pages long; it took six weeks to conduct the investigation. The criminal file is close to four hundred pages; the defense investigation took five months to complete. Still, the essence of each case remains.

The case studies will necessarily reflect my own personal experience as a private investigator. In presenting the criminal case, however, I'll attempt to demonstrate the process by which the police detectives worked the case. I will not attempt to make these cases into mysteries; I will simply report what took place. These examples are for education, not entertainment.

Civil Case
Getting the Case

In movies and novels, most cases seem to begin with a prospective client coming to the detective's office. Most of my cases began, like this one, with a telephone call. It was from an acquaintance—a friend of a friend, a man who had been lawyering for only a year or so. As a new lawyer, this man generally got the cases nobody else in the law firm wanted. This particular case involved doing a favor for one of the firm's senior partners. More accurately, it involved the aunt of one of the partner's oldest clients.

Several weeks earlier the old woman, a widow, had accidentally stepped in front of an ambulance on a run. She'd been struck by the ambulance and injured. As an older woman on a fixed income, she found herself facing disastrously expensive medical bills (this was one of those bureaucratic nightmares in which the woman's health care provider refused to cover many of the treatment expenses because the trauma center to which she was taken was not on the list of authorized centers). Despite the advice of every lawyer in speaking distance, the old woman wasn't looking to sue the ambulance company for damages; she said the accident was largely her fault. However, she also felt the ambulance company had some level of responsibility for the accident and wanted that company to help with the medical expenses.

My instructions were simple: Look into the accident. In other words, there was no real direction to the investigation; I was simply asked to nose around and see what I could find out about what happened. This is a tad unusual. Most cases have a fairly clear objective. Had the widow been suing the ambulance company for millions of dollars, for example, I'd probably have been asked to investigate the driver of the ambulance, the crew of the ambulance and the safety record of the company. But since she had openly admitted that she was primarily at fault, the lawyer simply wanted me to see if there was any sort of hook we could use to pry some cash out of the ambulance company.

Eyewitness Report

The lawyer had already obtained copies of the police reports (which were sent to me by messenger) but hadn't yet received any material from the ambulance company. This was hardly surprising; the company would stall as long as possible.

I began by reading the police reports. They were straightforward. At approximately 6:40 P.M. an ambulance (identified by number) from a private company (rather than from a fire department) had been running with emergency lights and sirens. Witnesses had observed the woman step directly into the path of the ambulance. Most of the witnesses stated the woman had appeared distracted. The ambulance attempted to stop. The woman seemed to be too surprised and frightened to avoid the ambulance. Although the ambulance was able to slow down and swerve, the left front fender still struck the woman and knocked her to the street.

The police reports included the names, addresses and telephone numbers of five eyewitnesses. The reports also included the names of the three men in the ambulance crew, but only listed their work address. The reports also included the dates of birth for each of the witnesses and crew members. Getting a DOB is a habit with the police; criminal records are generally categorized by DOB rather than by name. It was interesting to note that only one member of the ambulance crew was older than twenty-five.

The statement from the ambulance driver was brief (not a surprise; some ambulance crews are trained to give only the information necessary, in order to limit liability). He stated he'd seen an old woman step into the road, he'd slammed on his brakes, he'd tried to swerve to miss her—all to no avail. The ambulance crew reported that they provided care to the old woman until a second ambulance arrived to transport her to the nearest trauma center.

The police reports also included a statement from the old woman. In the statement she acknowledged the accident was mostly her fault, that she'd been inattentive and hadn't paid close enough attention to the ambulance's siren. She'd not only stepped in front of the rushing ambulance, she'd failed to try to get out of its way. It wasn't a statement that would help her case.

Although the police statements were clear, it was necessary to reinterview everybody involved. Even when the police are competent (which they generally are in such routine matters), they often omit details that are important to civil lawyers. The police don't always ask the questions civil lawyers want answered. The police, after all, aren't interested in civil liability; their job is to catch criminals. That often leads to the police being less than thorough in getting the statement of a witness.

In both civil and criminal matters, private investigators routinely reinterview the witnesses, generally asking the same questions of the same people and getting the same answers. But it pays off. It's surprising how often you get a different answer, or a more complete answer, or perhaps an answer that's open to a different interpretation.

The Investigation Begins

I went to see the old woman at her home. She was a fairly sturdy and tough specimen—not one of those delicate, birdlike, grandmotherly types. In fact, despite the fact that her leg had been broken and she was forced to use a walker, she was still pretty active and surprisingly perky. While that was admirable of her, it was bad for her case. A pale, trembling, debilitated old woman would have been more likely to engender sympathy— from the ambulance company or from a jury.

I asked the old woman to tell me what had happened, beginning an hour or so before the accident. She told me she had attended an aerobics class for seniors at the YWCA and then had been running errands. As she walked down the sidewalk toward an intersection, she saw the "Don't Walk" sign turn to "Walk." She was looking in her handbag for a cigarette (she smoked unfiltered Camels—a *tough* old bird) as she stepped off the sidewalk to cross the street. She admitted she'd heard the siren of an ambulance, but for some reason thought it was off on another street. As she pulled the cigarette pack out of her purse, she looked up and saw the ambulance. She thought she might have been able to jump out of the way, but instead she froze. Then the ambulance hit her.

The old woman's recollection of the events immediately after the accident were, understandably, confused and scrambled. She recalled another ambulance arrived to transport her to the hospital, and she remembered giving a statement to the police while in the emergency room. She was uncertain about what medications had been given to her in the emergency room. I had her sign a form granting me access to her medical records. It might make some difference if she'd given her statement to the police while she was under the influence of painkilling drugs.

Over the next week or so I managed to track down all five eyewitnesses. They all basically repeated the statements they gave to the police, with minor variations. All of them had heard the sirens before seeing the ambulance. All had seen the flashing lights. And all had seen the old woman, seemingly oblivious of the lights and siren, walk into the street and get hit by the ambulance. A couple of the witnesses felt the ambulance driver didn't try hard enough to avoid the woman. Others felt the driver had made a truly heroic effort to miss her. One witness thought the old woman had made a motion—shifting her weight—as if she was going to move out of the way but didn't. That witness felt the old woman's motion might have confused or misled the driver, convincing him that she was getting out of the way.

I went to the ambulance company to talk to the ambulance crew, but didn't even get past the front office. I was turned away at the door on the advice of the company lawyer. Lawyers always advise their clients not to talk to anybody, whether they have anything to hide or not. The lawyers are usually right.

Something Is *Not* Quite Right

I hadn't found anything significant that would help the old woman. But I had the feeling I was missing something. Sometimes in novels you'll read something about a detective's instinct. I don't buy into that myself. But I do believe that if you do the work long enough you begin to develop a feel for it, and sometimes you get a sort of subliminal message that something is not quite right, that something is slightly out of whack. It isn't instinct; instinct is what makes geese fly south for the winter. It's like getting your pictures back from the one-hour photo mart and the color of the prints is off just a tad; it takes you a while to realize you don't own a sweater quite that particular shade of blue.

It took a couple of days for me to realize what was troubling me. I'd neglected to ask where the ambulance was going. Was it going *to* the scene of an emergency or returning *from* a scene? If it was returning from a scene with the sirens and lights operating, there should have been a patient in the back. If it was returning from a scene without a patient but was still running with the lights and sirens operating, then the old woman had a potentially lucrative case.

I looked once again at the police reports. Most of the witnesses mentioned a second ambulance arriving to treat and transport the old woman, but nobody reported a third ambulance for the original patient. Nor did any of the police reports mention a patient in the ambulance. It seemed likely then that the ambulance had been going *to* a scene.

But how to be certain? One way was to check the 911 logs. Every call to 911 is logged—the time of the call, the name of the caller (if given), the nature of the problem and the address to which the police/ambulance/fire engine responds.

If the ambulance was on its way to a scene, then the call to 911 probably had been made shortly before the accident. Since the ambulance had been unable to complete the run, another ambulance would have to have been called. Therefore there should be at least two calls for the same address: one before the accident and one after the accident.

I had the lawyer get a copy of the logs for the day of the accident. There was no record of duplicate calls around the time of the accident. It looked, therefore, as if the ambulance was *not* on its way to an emergency scene. That seemed to suggest the ambulance was either returning from a scene or wasn't involved in an emergency at all. And that was good news for the old woman.

So I was immediately suspicious of my own findings. The problem was I *liked* them. It pleased me to think that somehow the ambulance crew had been involved in something it shouldn't have been involved in. It appealed to me, partly because it would benefit the old woman and partly because it would make the case more fun for me. However, a detective should always be doubly suspicious of a theory he finds attractive. It leads to wishful thinking.

Getting Closer

Obviously, more work needed to be done. I went back to see the woman and asked her if there had been a second patient in the ambulance that brought her to the emergency room. She said no, she'd been in the ambulance alone. Nor could she recall another patient being brought to the emergency room at about the same time she arrived. That was far from conclusive, of course, but still helpful.

I tried to interview the police officers who had responded to the scene, but without success. Police officers are notoriously unwilling to get involved in civil cases. I can't blame them. They are paid for the time they spend in court testifying in criminal cases, but they respond to civil matters on their own time. And in this litigation-crazed culture there is always somebody looking for a reason to sue a cop, so anything a police officer says in a civil matter is usually scrutinized with the intensity of an anthropologist poring over hieroglyphics.

There was no point in returning to the ambulance company and asking exactly what the ambulance was doing when the accident happened; employees there had been adamant about not cooperating with me. But I went there and asked anyway. You never know. As expected, they had nothing to say to me and sent me on my way with a demand that I never darken their doorway again.

I went back to the 911 logs. If the ambulance wasn't going to an emergency scene, it was probably returning from one. The fact that there was no patient in the back might mean they had treated and released the patient at the scene. Or perhaps another ambulance had beaten them to the scene.

It was also possible the ambulance hadn't been involved in an emergency at all. Perhaps the crew had simply been out getting lunch or was bringing the ambulance back from having the tires balanced and rotated. It's not unheard of for an ambulance (or a police cruiser, for that matter) to try to beat traffic by using its sirens and lights.

It seemed worthwhile to try to establish where the ambulance had been immediately before it hit the old woman. And it seemed easiest to work on the assumption that it was returning from an emergency call.

If the ambulance was returning from a run, it was likely the call had been placed to 911 within ninety minutes before the accident. Just to be certain, I focused on the calls that had been made within three hours prior to the accident.

After narrowing the time range, I tried to hone in on the location. Fortunately, the ambulance had been in the southern part of town traveling east when it struck the old woman, so I concentrated my search in the southwest quarter of the city. There were only five ambulance calls from that quarter of town in the three-hour time period.

I visited each of those addresses. Of the five emergency calls made in that particular part of town during the right period of time, only one had not resulted in the patient being transported to the hospital. A rather obese man had experienced chest pains and shortness of breath after eating supper—a large bowl of linguini and sausages with peppers, a third of a loaf of garlic bread and two or three beers. His wife had believed he was having a heart attack and called 911.

The ambulance crew responded and diagnosed the man as simply suffering from severe indigestion and heartburn. He was treated at the scene, and the ambulance crew left.

It didn't prove anything. There was no guarantee that this was the ambulance crew I was after. Still, it seemed likely. And it suggested there had been no need to run with the emergency lights and siren, that the driver had no reason to be speeding as fast as he was. But again, it didn't prove anything.

The Key Witness

What I really needed was to talk to the ambulance crew. The lawyer would, of course, go through the process of deposing them, but that could take months. Civil cases move at a glacial pace. Delays and continuances are routine. But the client had bills to pay *now*. Even if she decided to file suit, took it to trial, won and received a judgment in her favor, the judgment might be appealed. The old woman might not see a penny for years.

However, I'd been able to get tolerably good descriptions of the three-man crew from the woman and her chubby husband. The police reports gave me names of three ambulance crew members. All I needed to do was match up the names with the descriptions.

Where to start? With the names and a telephone directory. There were, of course, problems. Of the three crew members, two were under twenty-five years of age. Young people are less likely to be listed in telephone books. They move more frequently, they often share houses (and telephones), they may be students and live in dorms, or they may be living with their parents.

The oldest of the crew members was named Peter Harriman. Harriman had also been the driver of the ambulance. There were only about twenty Harrimans in the telephone book. The youngest of the crew was named Alan Smith. Not at all helpful. There were far too many Smiths. And while there were only a few variations on Alan Smith (A. Smith, Allan Smith, Allen Smith), there was no guarantee my Smith was one of them.

The last crew member, however, was named Martin Haywood. There were only a half-dozen Haywoods—none of them Martins. Still, I decided to start with him.

I decided to call each of the six Haywoods and ask for Martin. On the second call I spoke to a woman who said she was Martin's aunt. I told her I'd lost Martin's number and was just trying random Haywoods. She kindly gave me the correct phone number.

I didn't call him, of course. It's far too easy to refuse to talk to a person over the telephone. It's not so easy to say no to a smiling, cheerful, polite person standing right there in front of you. With only half a dozen Haywoods, it was easy to check his phone number with the addresses listed.

Martin Haywood lived in a neighborhood of working-class homes and apartment houses. The address listed in the phone book turned out to be a pleasant two-story house with a nice porch and a neat little fenced-in yard. It was near one end of the block. I assumed the house belonged to his parents. At the end of the block, the street intersected with a fairly busy thoroughfare. There was a convenience store with a couple of gas pumps and a Burger King at the intersection. It would be fairly easy to park in the lot of the burger joint and see the front gate and front door of the Haywood house.

It was early evening during the middle of the week when I found the Haywood house. I drove around the neighborhood for a while, getting familiar with the area. The next afternoon, around 3:30, I went to the Burger King and took a parking spot facing the Haywood house. I went into the Burger King and spoke to the manager. I showed him my detective's license and told him I was doing a surveillance of a house down the street—that his restaurant was in no way involved in my investigation. I just wanted him to know I would be parked out there and sitting quietly in my car. I didn't want him getting nervous and calling the police (fast-food chains handle a lot of cash and are popular spots for armed robbers). The manager found the whole thing terribly exciting and offered me a free meal.

Why didn't I just go knock on the door and ask to speak with Martin? Because I suspected he lived with his parents. Parents want to protect their children. They might discourage Martin from talking to me. I wanted to talk to Martin alone, informally.

So I sat in my car, repeating in my mind the descriptions of the two youngest members of the ambulance crew. Around 5:30 P.M. a little Toyota pulled up to the curb in front of the Haywood house and a young man stepped out. He was wearing what appeared to be an emergency medical technician (EMT) outfit and matched one of the descriptions. Before I could get out of my car, the young man had bounced up the porch steps and entered the house.

Trusting to luck, I ran into the Burger King, used the toilet and ordered a large order of fries (no catsup) and a large water with lots of ice. I was gone less than five minutes. The Toyota was still there.

I settled in, hoping young Martin might wander out later that night. The only other action at the Haywood house took place about fifteen minutes later when an older man in a late-model Dodge pulled into the driveway. Martin's dad, I decided. Dad kept his car in the drive; Martin parked at the curb. Made sense to me.

When Martin hadn't shown his face by 9:00 P.M. I gave up and left.

I was back at the Burger King at 6:00 A.M. At 7:15 the young man came out of the house, hopped in his Toyota and started down the street. I had my car started and was ready to pull out when he pulled into the Burger King lot and parked near one of the doors.

I shut off my car and opened the door. We both got out of our cars in unison, like Busby Berkeley dancers.

I called out, "Martin Haywood?"

The young man stopped and turned toward me.

I showed him my detective's license and told him my name.

Martin's plan was to get a sausage biscuit to go and eat it in his car on the way to work. But I never gave him the chance. I told him we needed to talk about the old woman he'd hit with the ambulance (I knew, of course, that Martin hadn't been driving the ambulance, but there's no drama in saying we needed to talk about the ambulance he'd been a passenger in).

Martin Haywood was a nice, decent young man. I bought him his sausage biscuit and led him to a booth. I pulled out a small voice-activated tape recorder (for his sake, I told him, to ensure I didn't misquote him) and put it on the table between us. When I started to talk about the old woman, he caved in immediately. The whole incident had been weighing heavily on him. He was torn between doing what he thought was right and what he thought was smart. The smart move, of course, was to listen to the company lawyers and not discuss the incident with anybody. The right thing, however, was to admit that Peter Harriman, the driver of the ambulance, had been irritated and in a hurry after leaving the indigestion case. He'd been irritated that the run was over nothing more critical than heartburn and indigestion and in a hurry to get home—he was going to a friend's house, where a lot of folks were gathering to watch a heavyweight championship boxing match on a big-screen television. Harriman had turned on the lights and sirens simply to get through the late-afternoon traffic.

But the incident, Martin said, wasn't Harriman's fault. The old woman had stepped right in front of them. There was absolutely nothing Harriman could have done to avoid her.

Resolution

Since the incident, all three members of the ambulance crew had been assigned to routine maintenance work at the ambulance yard. Martin disliked the new work. He wanted to go on emergency runs. That was what he'd trained for. He was considering leaving New England and going to stay with an uncle in Arizona.

I gave the tape to the old woman's lawyer. He used it to pry an agreement to pay for the old woman's medical care (she still refused to bring suit).

I don't know what happened to young Martin—whether he was fired from the ambulance service or moved to Arizona. I doubt the ambulance service allowed him to return to the work he wanted to do.

Criminal Case

Since my involvement in the case did not begin until approximately a month after the crime, I am relying on police reports for information on the early stages of the police investigation.

You'll note that during the initial phases of the police investigation a great deal of information is accumulated. If it seems disorganized and confused, that's because it is. That's how the police get it. In fact, you're getting a tidied version of what took place; most of the rumors, suggestions and gossip have been omitted.

Finding the Body

Frank DePrizio had simply stopped at the garage to check on the price of some tires. It was shortly after 11:00 A.M. on a Saturday morning in the middle of summer. As he talked to the clerk—just a kid, really—an old man entered the garage. The old man, whose name was Lemuel Hawkins, was clearly upset and confused. He wanted to use the telephone, he said, to call for an ambulance; he lived across the street, and his friend was hurt and lying on the floor. The young clerk seemed uncertain what to do, so DePrizio borrowed the telephone and called 911, requesting an ambulance. He then accompanied Hawkins across the street to 15 South Main Street—a shabby, two-story clapboard house—to see if he could offer help.

Riverton was a small, rather impoverished lumber town in rural New England, and the neighborhood around South Main Street was the poorest section of Riverton. If a railroad had run through the small town, this neighborhood would have been on the wrong side of the tracks. Aside from the garage, a squat cinderblock structure surrounded by vehicles in various states of repair, there were a few sad-looking houses and cheap apartment buildings.

Hawkins led DePrizio to the house. Although there was a front entrance, they entered through a side door, which opened directly into the kitchen. That's where DePrizio found the body. The dead man was a rather large man, and he'd died in a rather undignified position—his butt on a chair, his torso slumped forward, his head only inches from the floor. The dead man was prevented from completely tumbling out of the chair only because his shoulder had struck the refrigerator, leaving him wedged between the chair and the refrigerator. A large amount of blood covered the floor under the body and had pooled beneath the kitchen table. DePrizio could see the feathered fletching of two arrows protruding from the body's chest.

A short time later an EMT arrived in her personal car, followed almost immediately by an ambulance with two attendants. All three medical personnel entered the house and observed the body. They noted the body had bled from the mouth and nose as well as from the two arrow wounds. From habit they checked for a carotid pulse. Of course, there was none. The body, they noted, was stiff and rigid, and livor mortis had set in—the blood had pooled internally in the dead man's head and arms, which were lower than his torso. They notified the police.

As a very small town, Riverton had a very small (fewer than ten full-time police officers) and poorly trained police force. The first officer on the scene, Officer Felder, arrived at the scene at 1141 hours. He examined the body and noted the two arrows protruding from the victim's chest (including the one that passed completely through the victim's right arm before burying itself in his chest). He called the incident in as a suicide. He also requested the state police be notified of an unusual death. At that point Felder did one thing right: He herded the witnesses out of the house and secured the scene (note that so far six people have entered the small crime scene—Hawkins, the good Samaritan, the three ambulance personnel and the officer).

The first state police officer, Officer O'Toole, arrived shortly thereafter. He briefly looked at the body and recognized it for what it was—a murder. O'Toole then checked the first floor of the house to determine if anybody else was present. The front door to the house, he noted, had a chair in front of it. It clearly hadn't been used for some time. The door to the second floor was closed. O'Toole decided to wait until further assistance arrived before exploring the second floor.

Outside, O'Toole reminded Felder to guard the scene and not let anybody enter. Felder mentioned to O'Toole that Hawkins lived in the house and had discovered the body. Hawkins told O'Toole the body was that of Will Cartman.

When the next officer, State Trooper Dave Brion, arrived, he and O'Toole explored the second floor of the old house. Nobody was there.

The Police Investigation Begins

Once the death was labeled a murder, local and state police officers began to gather at the scene. Within ninety minutes of the initial request for an ambulance, a dozen police officers (five state police and seven local police officers) were on the scene. A member of the County Attorney's Office and the county medical examiner were there as well. Most of the officers entered the tiny kitchen on arrival to look at the body and nose around. This stopped on the arrival of State Trooper Wethers, who truly secured the premises until the arrival of the forensics team.

Given that five of the first six people to see the body were civilians, it's not surprising that word of Cartman's death spread rapidly. It was, after all, a small town, and murders were infrequent. And a murder with a bow and arrow—well, it was unheard of. The number of civilians gathering near the victim's house grew as quickly as the number of police personnel.

Several civilians, mostly people from the neighborhood, mentioned informally to the police that they had occasionally seen a man carrying a compound bow[1] in the area. They described him as a tall, skinny man with a beard and long hair pulled back in a ponytail. Others reported seeing two men practicing shooting bows and arrows in a field across the street. In fact, one of the men lived almost directly across the street, in one of four apartments in a converted liquor store. His name was Martin Becker.

A Suspect Develops

The local officers knew the name. Becker had come to their attention before. One of the officers on the scene, Riverton Police Officer Green, recalled an incident that took place around a month earlier. While on routine patrol at 0300 hours, he encountered Becker walking down the road carrying two bows and some arrows. Green had given Becker a ride home. The arrows, Officer Green informed State Trooper Brion, were green and yellow. At Brion's request, Green looked through the kitchen door. Although it was difficult to see the arrows in Cartman's chest, Green stated they appeared to be the same as the ones he'd seen Becker carrying.

They had a dead man with arrows in him; they had a neighbor known to mess about with bows and arrows, a man known to the police as a bad actor. In other words, they had a suspect. With that, the machinery of law enforcement began to focus.

State Trooper Mike Russell was designated the principal investigator; he would coordinate the investigation from that

---

[1] A compound bow is a hunting bow. It uses a pulley arrangement that allows the hunter to deliver the arrow faster and with more power than an ordinary bow.

point on. He delegated some of the police officers on the scene to control the growing crowd of onlookers. Others began to interview members of the crowd. Still others began to canvass the neighbors.

Russell ordered the Riverton Police Department to find out who owned the house at 15 South Main Street (it was owned by Bert Stanton, who had lived there with Cartman and Hawkins until a couple of months earlier when he was hospitalized after a seizure). Russell also wanted to know who owned the apartments where Becker lived. They'd need that information for a search warrant.

While all this took place, two young boys, John Deiter (age thirteen) and Gary Lyon (age sixteen), sat on the porch a few houses down from the murder scene, watching the excitement.

Among the crowd of onlookers was Charles Deiter, the father of one of the boys on the porch. Deiter told Officer Felder, the officer who'd reported the incident as a suicide, that he'd seen somebody in front of the house at 15 South Main Street at around 2130 hours the night before. Deiter couldn't identify the person. It appeared to Deiter that the person was trying to look in a front window. After a moment, the person entered the house by the side door. Deiter said he knew Becker and agreed it was possible the person might have been him.

The onlookers supplied the investigators with a great deal of gossip about Becker and his relationship with Will Cartman, including suggestions that Becker's mother had once been Cartman's lover, and that Becker and Cartman had been involved in a serious fight, either because of Cartman's behavior toward Becker's girlfriend or because of a threat Cartman had made to Becker's brother Theo.

At 1315 hours Dr. Wilson, the medical examiner, arrived. He pronounced Cartman dead and began to photograph the body and the area around the body.

Officer Healy of Riverton PD spoke to Steve Adderly, a friend of Cartman. They had spent much of the day before in Cartman's house playing cards and drinking whiskey. At approximately 1400 Martin Becker dropped by the house; he joined the card game but not the drinking. According to Adderly, this wasn't unusual. Becker and Cartman got along, although they'd had trouble in the past. They'd once had a fistfight in Adderly's house.

The fight was about money: Cartman suspected Becker had taken some money from Cartman's wallet while he was unconscious after an accident. Adderly also said Cartman suspected Becker of burgling the house once. Still, it wasn't uncommon for them to visit each other and play cards. Adderly stated Cartman and Becker hadn't argued on this occasion. Becker left at approximately 1530. As he was leaving, Adderly stated Becker said, "I'll see you later." Cartman responded by saying, "I'll be here." Becker, Adderly said, had been wearing a long-sleeve white shirt. Not long after Becker left, they ran out of alcohol. Cartman called a taxi and had another bottle delivered to the house. At approximately 1830 Adderly's wife arrived and they continued to drink and play cards until around 1930, at which time the couple left. Only Cartman and Hawkins were in the house when they left.

Riverton Police Department Officer Denice Phelps was also involved in the investigation. She spoke with Carol Washburn, who lived in the same apartment building as Becker. Washburn stated she had often seen Becker with a hunting bow. She had been at home the night of the murder, playing cards with friends. At around 2230 she had seen somebody walk by her door a couple of times, but it was dark outside and she couldn't identify the person.

Trooper Russell spoke to Lemuel Hawkins, the man who shared the house with Will Cartman and had discovered the body. Hawkins stated Becker had been at the house the preceding day, but he was uncertain of the time. He and Cartman had been drinking a bit, he said. He usually went to bed early (his bedroom was on the second floor of the house), and he generally slept late in the morning. He wasn't sure what time he'd gone to bed the preceding night, nor could he say who was in the house when he'd gone to bed. He'd heard nothing unusual during the night and had awakened around 1100 when his dog woke him. Hawkins said he always slept with the door to his room closed. The dog slept in the room with him. When Hawkins arose in the morning and went downstairs to let the dog out, he saw Cartman's body.

More Information, More Questions

One of the onlookers, a man named Albert DeRozier, spoke to Officer Danton, the only plainclothes officer on the Riverton PD. DeRozier said he'd once heard Bob LaFrank, who had once lived in the house with Cartman and Hawkins, threaten to "blow off Cartman's head."

At approximately 1345, investigators located Cartman's next of kin, his sister, Maureen Goodkind. Because of the amount of blood and the unpleasant lividity of the victim's head, she was not asked to visually identify the body. Goodkind informed the police she hadn't seen or talked to her brother in approximately ten days. Goodkind stated Cartman had been receiving threatening phone calls for six months or so. The threats were all made by a male caller. She had also heard that Cartman had taken a shot at somebody about four months earlier; she thought it might have been at one of the Becker brothers, but she didn't know which one.

In the early afternoon, Becker, his brother Theo Becker and their mother, Jane, arrived at the scene and joined the onlookers. Trooper Wethers reported hearing a man later identified to him as Martin Becker asking Trooper Brion about the murder. "How did he die? Was it a gun? Knife? Or what?"

Shortly thereafter, Wilbur Shearing from the state crime lab arrived at the scene. With the help of Trooper Russell, Shearing processed the scene. He noticed and photographed a kick mark on the kitchen door; apparently the door had been kicked open at some point. On the exterior doorknob, Shearing discovered a bit of blood with some fiber stuck in it. He removed the doorknob and sealed it in an evidence bag. All the appropriate aspects of the downstairs of the house were dusted for fingerprints. In addition, Shearing seized some of the contents of the kitchen: a deck of cards, a pack of Pall Mall cigarettes, two packs of Camels, a cribbage board, two small glasses, one large glass, four empty bottles of Mr. Boston's whiskey, one empty Gordon's vodka bottle and one empty bottle of Michelob beer. All were transported to the lab to check for latent prints.

As the crime scene was being processed, attendants from the Scott Funeral Home arrived to remove the body and transport it to the funeral home for the autopsy. The body was removed at 1605 hours.

Most of the onlookers left the scene shortly after the body was removed. Those officers doing crowd control duty were reassigned to help canvass the neighborhood.

A Second Suspect?

Not long after the body was removed, Officer Phelps spoke with Charles Halburton, a neighbor of the deceased. Halburton reported seeing a man walk by his house with a bow and arrows on at least six occasions over the past few months. He described the man as tall with long dark hair tied into a ponytail and a full beard. An onlooker suggested the description sounded more like Weldon Becker than Martin Becker; Weldon was one of Martin Becker's brothers.

Both Martin and Weldon Becker were approximately 5'10", 160 pounds with dark hair. Weldon wore his hair long, usually in a ponytail, and had a full beard. Martin had short hair, trimmed above the ears, and a mustache.

Based on this information, Russell sent Riverton Police Officer Green to interview the neighbors of Weldon Becker. Weldon lived approximately one-half mile north of the murder scene.

At 1645 Troopers Russell, Shearing and Wethers went to the funeral home to witness the autopsy. Also present were Riverton's Chief of Police Karl Hendricks. Hendricks identified the body as that of Will Cartman. He knew Cartman as a long-term resident of Riverton; Hendricks had, in fact, arrested Cartman on a number of occasions. In a wallet found in Cartman's trousers was an expired driver's license in the name of Will Cartman. The photo was consistent with the features of the body.

Late that afternoon Officer Phelps found Norm Eggles, another neighbor of the victim, who had observed a man with a bow walk down South Main Street on at least three occasions. The man was described as being approximately 5'10", with dark hair and a beard.

Based on information developed by talking to some of the onlookers, Trooper Brion and his partner, Trooper Consodine, went to Stan's Gun Shop, where Becker was believed to have bought his bow. They discovered that Becker had, in fact, purchased the bow there. But they had not sold him any arrows.

By 1900 hours the autopsy had been completed, and Trooper Russell and the others returned to the scene. Officer Green reported to Russell that he'd finished talking to Weldon's neighbors. All of them stated they'd seen Weldon with a bow and arrows, often in the company of another man, perhaps one of his brothers. One neighbor stated she believes she saw Weldon out in his yard, alone, at some time between 2130 and 2300 hours on the preceding night. Weldon didn't appear to be doing anything in particular.

Russell went with Officer Danton and Trooper O'Toole to talk to Weldon. Weldon refused to let the officers into his house, although he agreed to talk to them in the police cruiser. Weldon said he knew Cartman well; they were both incarcerated in the state prison at the same time. Weldon stated Cartman had enemies from prison, where he had been burned out of his cell on two occasions. He also told the officers Cartman had mentioned he'd been getting threatening phone calls. Weldon said he got along pretty good with Cartman, as did everybody in the Becker family. Weldon told the officers he'd spent the previous night at home, but had no witnesses other than his wife to prove it. When asked if he owned a bow and arrows, Weldon had his wife fetch the bow and arrows to the cruiser. The arrows, they noted, had brown fiberglass shafts with black and red feathers. Two were missing from a set of twelve. Weldon also told the police he owned a muzzle-loading rifle. However, Weldon stated, "That's only good once. The bow you can keep shooting."

During this period, Officer Green located the owner of the house in which Weldon Becker lived and obtained permission to search the premises (according to the law, the owner of a property can give consent to search even if the tenant opposes the search). No search was conducted, however.

The Prime Suspect Tells His Story

At approximately 2130 hours, Martin Becker went to the Riverton Police Department and asked to speak to Trooper Brion. Brion and Consodine were out conducting interviews, but responded to a radio request. They returned to RPD and met with Becker. Brion read Becker his rights, which he agreed to waive (and signed a form stating so). Becker told them he knew rumors had been circulating around town that he'd killed Cartman and wanted to set the record straight. He stated that he'd gone across the street to see Cartman and play cards at approximately 1300 to 1330. He stayed until around 1430. Steve Adderly was also visiting with Cartman. Both Cartman and Adderly had been drinking whiskey, Becker told them, but he'd only had coffee. When he left at 1430, Adderly was still there. As he left Becker told Cartman he'd see him later; it was an expression, not an appointment. Later that afternoon Becker got a ride from a friend, Eddie Barton, into Rochester, a nearby town. Becker was planning to buy a truck, and they went to the Ford dealership. After talking to a salesperson, they went to the home of Harris and Deanna Priest. Priest's wife was the sister of Becker's live-in girlfriend, Sylvia Lawrence. There they played cards and began drinking beer. He stayed at the Priest home in Rochester until around 2130, returning home to Riverton at approximately 2145. Becker stated he stayed in the apartment and watched television, first a boxing match and then an adult movie. His girlfriend, Sylvia, wasn't home when he arrived but returned shortly thereafter. She was angry because Becker had been drinking. She decided to take their child and spend the night at her mother's house. Sylvia called her mother, who worked the second shift at a nearby shoe factory. Her mother said that as soon as she got off work, which, according to Sylvia, was 2300, she would come fetch Sylvia. She then went into the bedroom to wait for her mother. Becker left the apartment shortly before 2300 in order to avoid meeting Sylvia's mother. He decided to walk into town and have another beer. As he walked by 15 South Main Street he saw no light in the kitchen, although he thought there might have been a light on upstairs. The bar Becker went to (Catton's Place) was already closed, so he went to a convenience store to buy a six-pack. Once there, however, he considered his girlfriend and changed his mind. He walked around a bit at random, then returned home. As he was returning home on foot, Becker met Riverton Police Officers Kelly and Krawczyk, who offered him a ride, which he refused (the two officers confirmed they had met Becker at approximately 0100 to 0130 that morning). Becker stated that ever since he was a boy he had known Cartman and often played cards with him. Becker admitted to having owned a bow but had sold it recently to man named John LNU (last name unknown, generally pronounced "Lanue") at a bar called Mike's Tavern in the nearby town of Rochester. Becker also admitted he'd bought a dozen arrows around the time he'd bought the bow. The arrows had field tips (practice tips), not hunting tips (also called broadheads; these lethal tips have three to six razor-sharp blades designed to inflict massive tissue damage, causing the prey to quickly bleed to death). He'd sold the arrows with the bow, although he'd only had six left; he'd lost the other six practicing. The arrow shafts, he said, were green aluminum with green and white fletching. Becker stated all his brothers also owned bows. When asked if Cartman and Becker's mother ever had anything going, Becker angrily responded that she'd never had sex with Cartman. When asked if he had anything to do with Cartman's death, Becker replied he hadn't. He stated he'd learned about the death from a friend at approximately 1130, after which he called his brothers and told them. He gave the officers consent to search his apartment and agreed to take a polygraph test, but only after talking to a lawyer. Becker refused to write his statement. As the interview was ending, Becker said he wanted to talk to a lawyer because he'd lied about how he learned about Cartman death's. He refused to comment any further.

The Police Investigation Continues

While Becker was talking to the police at the Riverton Police Department, Trooper O'Toole and four uniformed officers arrived at the apartment Becker shared with Sylvia Lawrence. She agreed to allow them to conduct a search of the premises. During the search they seized five arrow field tips, a small pillow with blood on it and a pair of work boots. Officer Danton observed four Michelob beer caps in an ashtray. Lawrence stated the pillow belonged to her baby and that the blood was from a scratch. She admitted that Becker owned a bow and arrows and stated he kept them in a closet. She thought the arrows were silver with green feathers; she didn't know what sort of tips were on the arrows but knew they weren't bladed. The bow was not there when the police looked for it. Lawrence stated she'd last seen the bow three or four days earlier when she went to the closet to fetch a blanket for her baby to lie on outside. On the preceding night she'd been out with a girlfriend. When she came home she noted that Becker had been drinking, which made her angry; he'd promised to stop. She called her mother at work and asked to spend the night with her. Her mother said that as soon as she could get away from work she'd pick Lawrence up. She then went into the bedroom and lay down. Her mother, she said, arrived shortly thereafter. She estimated the time to be around 2130 to 2145. Becker was gone by the time her mother arrived.

It was late at night by the time two state troopers located and spoke to Jane Becker, the mother of Martin Becker. She said she'd known Will Cartman most of her life. Two years earlier Cartman had lived with her for about four months after he'd been released from prison. She had asked him to leave because of his drinking. Mrs. Becker said Martin and Cartman had had words about a year earlier after Cartman had been in a fight with another of her sons, Theo. During that fight Cartman had put a gun to Theo's head and threatened to kill him. Despite all that she and Cartman remained friends. She had spoken to Cartman by telephone at approximately 2030 on the night of the murder. Cartman said he'd seen Martin Becker earlier that day and that he was just sitting at home drinking and playing cards with Steve. Mrs. Becker assumed he meant Steve Adderly. That morning Becker and Theo had come by her house at approximately 1000 to drop off some money. They stayed for about half an hour and visited. They seemed perfectly normal to her. Martin called her at around 1330 and informed her Cartman had been killed. She had met Becker and Theo and they had all gone to the scene.

Mrs. Becker was the last witness interviewed that night. The case was now twelve hours old.

The Investigation, Day Two

The next day was Sunday, but none of the police investigators rested. Trooper Russell sifted through the accumulated information obtained the day before. As the primary investigator, it was his job to direct the investigation.

Russell assigned Trooper Brion and Officer Danton to discover where Martin Becker had purchased the broadhead tips for the arrows. In addition to their other investigative duties, these officers spent the next few days canvassing all the sporting goods shops and hunting supply stores in a three- or four-county area. In all, over fifty stores were queried. None had any record of Becker buying broadheads.

Brion also interviewed Harris and Deanna Priest, the couple with whom Becker had spent the afternoon and evening of the night of the murder. The Priests confirmed that Becker had, in fact, been with them until sometime after 2100. He had been drinking a great deal of beer—Michelob, his favorite brand. The Priests told Brion they'd never seen Becker with a bow of any sort. They were aware that Becker and Cartman knew each other and played cards together, but they were unaware of any dispute between them.

An investigator also spoke to Bob LaFrank, who was said to have threatened Cartman. LaFrank acknowledged that he used to live in the house on South Main Street with Cartman, but stated he moved out because Cartman used to beat him up. He described Cartman as a bully who also used to beat up Lemuel Hawkins. LaFrank also stated that during the time he'd lived in the house, Cartman had received three or four threatening telephone calls. LaFrank told the investigator that Cartman and Becker had once argued over comments Cartman had made to Sylvia Lawrence, although he was uncertain of the nature of the comments. LaFrank also stated Cartman suspected Becker had stolen a sum of money from him on one occasion. LaFrank was also aware of an incident in which Cartman had put a revolver to the head of Theo Becker and threatened to kill him.

Closing In On the Prime Suspect

The main focus of the investigation remained Martin Becker. Although he was only in his mid-twenties, Becker had a long history of arrests and convictions for minor crimes and one major felony conviction. At the age of eighteen Becker had been convicted of kidnapping and sentenced to three to six years in prison. He served a little over two years.

Russell wanted to confirm Becker was the person seen carrying a bow in the area of the murder scene. He sent Officer Danton to reinterview Carol Washburn, the woman who lived near Becker and who had seen somebody walk by her door. It proved to be a significant decision.

Over the course of the night, Washburn had remembered something. On the night of the murder she had been playing cards with Ellen Bujold and Jack DeWitt. At approximately 2230 that night her thirteen-year-old brother, John Deiter, had come to her apartment (John was about fifteen years younger than his sister). She thought John may have been in the company of Gary Lyon, although she was uncertain. John told her he'd just seen Martin Becker outside the apartment carrying a bow and arrows and heading across the street (in the direction of Cartman's house). She stated John told her he'd said "Hi" to Becker and Becker had said "Hi" back. Washburn said her brother also mentioned that

Becker was carrying a bottle of beer, which he dropped or threw away. The bottle had broken. Washburn stated she hadn't mentioned this in her first statement because she'd forgotten about it.

Officers Healy and Jemmins went to get a statement from John Deiter. The Deiter family lived almost directly next to Will Cartman. After getting permission to talk to John from his parents, the investigators asked John what he had seen on the night of the murder. John said he and his friend Gary Lyon had spent most of the evening goofing off. They had decided to go across the street and visit John's sister. As they approached the apartment building they saw a man carrying a bow and an open bottle of beer. John stated the man was wearing a brown T-shirt, jeans and sneakers. He recognized the man as Martin Becker, who lived in the same apartment building as John's sister. John stated he said "Hi" to Becker, who had replied, "Hi, I'm going to Will Cartman's house to have a beer." John was certain it was Becker because he was coming from the direction of the last apartment in the building. John had seen Becker at that apartment once before and had talked to him about lifting weights. He also stated he recognized Becker's voice and the brown T-shirt he was wearing. Before entering his sister's apartment, John said he turned and looked again at Becker. Becker was heading directly for Cartman's house. As he turned to go into Washburn's apartment, John heard a door open. He thought it was probably the door to Cartman's house. He told his sister and her friends about Becker, but none of them had seemed very interested. John also said he saw the same man the next day. John was sitting on his porch with Gary Lyon when Martin Becker arrived driving a blue car. He'd seen Becker talk to one of the police officers.

Upon hearing this, Trooper Wethers recalled seeing a man later identified to him as Martin Becker asking Trooper Brion about the murder.

While John Deiter was being interviewed, Officer Danton located and spoke to Ellen Bujold, one of the people playing cards at the apartment of Carol Washburn. Bujold stated she remembered the incident and had just discussed it by telephone with Washburn. According to Bujold, John had come to the apartment at approximately 2230 hours. He'd told the card players that he'd seen a drunk man with a bow and arrows outside the building. The drunk man had told John he was going to kill somebody. He was also carrying a bottle of beer, which he threw at John and his friend.

After interviewing John Deiter, Officers Healy and Jemmins talked to John's friend Gary Lyon. Lyon was sixteen, three years older than John. Lyon stated he and John had watched television until approximately 2100 on the night of the murder, then had goofed around until around 2230 to 2300. At that time they decided to go see John's sister, though he couldn't recall why. As they came to her apartment building they saw a man carrying a compound bow come around the corner of the apartments. The bow was dark—green or black. The man, according to Lyon, had long hair down to his shoulders and a pullover shirt. He stated John knew the man and spoke to him. The man crossed the street as Lyon and John entered Washburn's apartment. Lyon thought he also heard a bottle drop and break. The next morning, as he was sitting with John on John's porch watching the excitement, he saw a man arrive in an orange car. John pointed him out, saying that was the man they'd seen carrying the bow the night before. The man was wearing a blue windbreaker, jeans and cowboy boots.

In the meantime Officer Danton interviewed Jack DeWitt, another of the card players. DeWitt lived near the apartment building shared by Washburn and Martin Becker. He had often seen Becker and another person practicing with bows and arrows. The arrows, he stated, were either green or brown. On the night of the murder he had been playing cards with his girlfriend, Ellen Bujold, and Carol Washburn. At approximately 2230 John Deiter had entered the apartment and said something about somebody being drunk and throwing a beer bottle. John also told them he'd said hello to the person carrying the bow and that the person had responded by saying something like, "I feel like killing somebody."

At around this time, Officer Danton recalled seeing a broken beer bottle near the scene of the crime. Concerned that somebody might step on it or a car might drive over it, he'd picked up the bottle and tossed it into some bushes. He and Russell returned to 15 South Main Street and found the broken bottle in the bushes. It was a Michelob bottle. They put it in an evidence bag and sent it to the crime lab to be checked for fingerprints.

Other investigators were also busy. They began to take formal statements from many of the people they'd spoken to informally the day before. They tracked down the cabdriver who had delivered the bottle of whiskey to Cartman (he had nothing new to add).

The Arrest

At 1415 hours, Detective Russell and Deputy Attorney General Harris Offutt presented their case to Municipal Court Judge Nute and petitioned him for an arrest warrant for Martin Becker. Their theory of the crime was that an angry and intoxicated Becker, for some unknown reason, took it into his head to kill Will Cartman. He took his bow, went to Cartman's door, saw Cartman through the window, kicked the door open and, as Cartman raised his arm in self-defense, shot him with one arrow and then another. After the murder, they theorized Becker somehow disposed of his bow and arrows and went into town for more beer. Becker, they told the judge, had no alibi between approximately 2100, when his angry girlfriend went into the bedroom, until shortly after 0100, when he was observed walking in town by two Riverton Police officers. Despite some inconsistencies in the evidence, the petition was granted.

At 1600, four officers from the Riverton police and one state trooper arrested Becker at his apartment. When told he was being arrested, Becker asked, "What for?" The state trooper merely showed him the arrest warrant, which stated Becker was being charged with purposely causing the death of Will Cartman by shooting the said Will Cartman with a bow and arrow. Becker's only response was to say, "I kind of figured this was coming."

Martin Becker was taken to Riverton Police Department, where Russell read him his rights. Becker stated he knew his rights and wouldn't say anything until he had a chance to speak to an attorney. No questions were asked of him.

At 1730, Becker was quickly arraigned on a charge of murder in the first degree. His bail was set at fifty thousand dollars, and he was transported to the county jail to await trial.

The case was thirty hours old.

On Monday the investigation continued. In addition to continuing to look for evidence to link Becker to the arrows, investigators were sent out to dig up background information on both Becker and Cartman.

Officer Consodine talked to the mail carriers who delivered mail to the Becker apartment. None could recall Becker receiving packages big enough to contain arrows. However, Consodine did locate a UPS employee who recalled delivering a package from an archery company to Weldon Becker.

Russell spoke to Will Cartman's parole officer. Cartman had been convicted of an alcohol-induced assault and sentenced to five to ten years. He had been paroled two years earlier and was scheduled to be on parole for another five years. The probation officer informed Russell that he also supervised Weldon Becker. He stated it was Weldon who had called him on the day after the murder was discovered to tell him Cartman had been killed. According to the probation officer, Weldon said the reason he was calling was because there were a lot of rumors flying around and he didn't want to get in any trouble.

Also on Monday afternoon, the preliminary autopsy report was completed. In short, the medical examiner found that Will Cartman bled to death after suffering massive tissue damage. The relevant portions of the autopsy are discussed in the sidebar on the next page.

After the arrest of Martin Becker, the pace of the police investigation became less pressured. The number of investigators assigned to the case was gradually reduced. Nonetheless, there were a great many areas of investigation the police needed to explore. The most important aspects were to dismember Becker's alibi (that he'd watched television, then went out for a beer), to find the murder weapon, to match Becker's footwear to the kick mark on the kitchen door and to discover where Becker obtained the broadhead arrow tips.

Russell, the principal investigator, also wanted to establish some sort of motive for Becker to kill Cartman. The state, of course, is under no obligation to determine *why* a person commits a crime; it only needs to prove that the person did commit it. But juries like to hear a motive, to understand the reasoning behind the crime.

The Police Investigation Slows Down

The investigative work that followed over the next three weeks was mostly slow, grinding routine work. The eighty-six-year-old man who owned the house, Bert Stanton, was interviewed at the hospital. He said he'd lived there with Cartman

Background

This fifty-five-year-old man was reported to have been alive and well on the evening of June 25 by friends who had visited him and played cards with him. He was last seen alive when they left at approximately 1730 hours.

The deceased was found sitting in the kitchen of the house, slumped over in a chair, with two hunting-type arrows in his chest and extensive bleeding, at about 1100 on the morning of June 26 by Lemuel Hawkins, a cotenant.

Death Scene

The scene of death was the kitchen of a small two-story home on South Main Street in Riverton. The kitchen appeared to be relatively orderly except for the pool of blood on the floor around the victim. The deceased was seated half on and half off a chair, slumped over, with his head down and right shoulder against a refrigerator in the corner. There was a telephone on the table along with a deck of cards, a cribbage board and other items.

The rest of the house was relatively orderly (for a bachelor's apartment) and did not appear to have been the scene of a disruption or fight. There was an entrance to the front of the house, but it was blocked by furniture. The only apparent entrance to the house was the door to the kitchen, which showed evidence of having been kicked open. The windows and screens were closed and showed no evidence of breakage or perforation.

Examination and Removal

The body was reported to have been discovered at about 1000 hours on June 26, 1982. This examiner was notified at 1230 hours and arrived at the scene at 1310 hours. Deceased was pronounced dead at the scene at 1315 hours. The body was left undisturbed for the documentation of the scene and not removed until 1600 hours. The body was taken to the Scott Funeral Home in Riverton for autopsy. The autopsy was begun at approximately 1615 hours and completed by 1900 hours.

Identification

The deceased was known in the community and was personally identified by Chief of Police Karl Hendricks. A photo ID driver's license #xxxxxxxx was found in his wallet and corresponded with his appearance. Lastly, fingerprints were taken by the state police after the autopsy.

External Examination

Shirt: Orange lightweight sweatshirt, with blood staining over the front. No undershirt.

Pants: Dark green (olive drab) work type with a black web belt. Right front pocket contains a button, nail clipper. Right rear pocket contains wallet and comb. Left rear pocket contains handkerchief and buck knife. Left front pocket is empty. There was no money in the wallet.

Socks: Gray-tan lightweight dress socks.

Shoes: Loafers.

Jewelry: None present on the body; no watch, rings or neckwear noted.

General Features

The body is that of a middle-aged Caucasian male measuring 5'8" in length and estimated to weigh 200 to 220 pounds. He is moderately obese. His nutritional status is good. He is well preserved and has not been embalmed. There was intense livor of the head and neck due to the head-down position of the body. Livor mortis was fixed (did not blanche on pressure or disappear with removal of body).

Rigor mortis was established when the body was first encountered at 1300 hours and was still present at the end of the autopsy at 1900 hours.

Temperature: The core temperature (liver) was 88.5 degrees Fahrenheit at 1700 hours. Note: Temperature during the night was approximately 60 degrees and during the day had been in the seventies.

Specific Features

Hair: Mostly bald with a narrow rim of gray-white hair, one-half inch in length.

Facial hair: Clean shaven.

Eyes: The irises are brown. The pupils measure 5mm in diameter and are round, regular and equal in size. The conjunctiva are markedly congested (attributed to the head-down position and lividity).

Ears: Normal. No evidence of injury. No bleeding.

Nose: No evidence of injury. Some bleeding from the respiratory tract.

Mouth: No evidence of injury of the lips or mucous membranes.

Teeth: Present upper and lower. No evidence of injury.

Neck: No external evidence of injury.

Shoulders and Upper Extremities:

    Right arm—See next paragraph.

    Left arm—No evidence of injury. No tracks of scars noted.

    Hands—Fingernails are dirty. None are broken.

Chest: See next paragraph.

Abdomen: No external evidence of injury.

Findings

1. Adult Caucasian male, identified as Will Cartman, age fifty-five, of Riverton.

2. Arrow wound of right arm and chest. Entrance: right fifth rib, anteriorly. Track: right heart, right lung, diaphragm, right lobe of liver to hepatic vena and inferior vena cava. Direction through body: front to back, right to midline and more or less horizontal (slight downward angle). Projectile: arrow with light-green aluminum shaft and 4-blade hunting tip recovered.

3. Arrow wound of left chest. Entrance: left fifth interspace anteriorly. Track: left diaphragm, left lobe of liver, stomach, pancreas to inferior vena cava. Direction through body: Front to back, left of midline to slightly left, and in a downward direction. Projectile: arrow with light-green aluminum shaft and four-blade hunting tip recovered.

Summary

The immediate cause of death is attributed to extensive bleeding from two chest wounds due to hunting arrows. The right arrow pierced the right arm, which appears to have been raised in a defensive gesture, before it entered the right chest. The plane is more or less horizontal to slightly downward direction (assuming the body to be in an upright position). The left arrow enters at the same level but has a more downward direction.

Both arrows inflicted potentially lethal injuries, and although death is attributed to both wounds, either wound could have resulted in death from internal and external bleeding. The sequence and timing of the wounds cannot be determined; however, both appear to have occurred either simultaneously or within a few seconds, resulting in hemorrhage from both wounds. The nature of the injuries was such that the victim would not have been rendered immediately unconscious and may have been able to move a considerable distance before collapsing from the loss of blood.

The time of death cannot be determined with accuracy, but from the degree of central cooling, the extent and degree of rigor mortis, and the increase in potassium of the vitreous fluid (eye fluid), death probably occurred twelve to eighteen hours before autopsy. This would place the time of death around midnight (plus or minus one to two hours) to the early morning hours.

The deceased appears to have been in good health and had no other underlying disease except for a minimal degree of coronary artery disease and changes in the liver consistent with alcohol effect. The manner of death is considered to be homicide.

Sweatshirt, trousers, briefs, shoes, socks, wallet, arrows (two), liquid blood, stomach content and inked fingerprints all sent to the state crime lab for analysis and storage.

and Hawkins until a couple of months before the murder. He told police investigators that Cartman moved into the house after being kicked out of his previous residence for fighting with the owners. Cartman wasn't a particular friend, but was an old drinking buddy. In all the time he lived there Cartman paid no rent; his contribution was to help take care of the house. Stanton reported that Norm LaFrank had also lived in the house, and for much longer than Cartman. LaFrank moved out after a fight with Cartman. The fight was sparked by two unrelated events: first, the fact that LaFrank had been sleeping with Cartman's sister and second, the fact that LaFrank had accused Cartman of raping a woman in the nearby town of Rochester. When asked about Becker, Stanton stated there was a long history of antagonism between Becker and Cartman. He described the fight that had taken place at Steve Adderly's house and mentioned an incident in which Cartman put a knife to Becker's throat. He believed the antagonism was rooted in the fact that Cartman had lived for a time with Becker's mother after being released from prison. Becker had also warned Cartman not to talk to Sylvia, Becker's girlfriend, after Cartman had made some offensive comments to her. Despite that antagonism, Stanton said Becker often came to the house to play cards with Cartman. To his knowledge, Becker was the only person in the house ever to drink Michelob beer.

Investigators also searched the area in which Becker and Weldon practiced with their bows, a field with a backstop made of bales of hay and old tires. They found no arrows, but did find a number of aluminum foil pie plates with holes in them. Apparently they had been used as targets. All of the holes were circular, indicating the use of field tips rather than broadhead tips. This was no surprise; field tips are designed for practice, and broadheads are designed for hunting. To practice with broadheads would only dull the edges of the blades.

Detectives also talked to the bar manager at Mike's Tavern, the bar where Becker claimed to have sold his bow to a man named John LNU. The bar manager knew Becker and said he'd had problems with him in the past. The problems were mainly just incidents of rowdy, obnoxious behavior. According to the manager, Becker was usually accompanied to the bar by another person, a man with long hair in a ponytail and a full beard. The manager stated he'd never seen Becker with a bow and had no idea of any transaction between Becker and a client named John.

Over the next few days, detectives also spoke to five of the other employees of Mike's. They had nothing new to add.

A week after Becker's arrest, the crime lab completed the fingerprint analysis of the evidence seized at Cartman's house. The fingerprints on the items were compared to the fingerprint cards of Cartman, Becker, Adderly and Hawkins. The only matches were with Cartman's prints. Several sets of unidentified prints were found, as were several prints that weren't clear enough for comparison.

The lab had also attempted to match the boots seized from Becker's apartment to the kick marks on Cartman's kitchen door. There was no match.

The Defense Team

During the three-week period after Becker's arrest, his attorney realized he had neither the expertise nor the time to conduct a proper homicide defense. Nor, if truth be told, did he have the desire. A homicide defense is a staggering task because so much is at stake—the client's life. It's difficult, maybe impossible, for a single lawyer to prepare all the necessary legal motions and to prepare for a complicated, lengthy trial while trying to maintain a routine law practice. To make matters worse, Becker was a manual laborer; even if he was not in jail awaiting trial, he simply would not have been able to afford the hourly rate charged by his attorney.

The case was therefore transferred to a law firm with a team specializing in indigent homicide defense. The defense team now consisted of two lawyers and two investigators (I was one of the two investigators; Kevin Sanders was the other). In contrast, the prosecution team consisted of a squad of lawyers, dozens of investigators from at least four jurisdictions, and a state-of-the-art crime lab. While this may seem unbalanced in favor of the prosecution (and, in fact, it *is* unbalanced), it must be remembered that the prosecution team also bears the greater burden: They have to prove beyond a reasonable doubt that the defendant committed the crime. The defense team only has to establish reasonable doubt of the defendant's guilt—a formidable task, but lacking the burden of proof. The balance is most definitely in favor of the prosecution, but not quite as much as it may appear.

The Defense Investigation Begins

Where does one start a defense investigation? The obvious place to begin was with the client, the accused murderer. The four of us went to talk to Becker in jail. We asked Becker to tell us what happened (we carefully avoided asking him if he'd killed Cartman; if he had killed him and wanted to tell us, that was up to him, but we had to defend him anyway). Becker volunteered that he didn't kill Cartman and didn't know anything about it. He repeated his alibi, though in a bit more detail than the story he'd given to the police. We asked about his comment to the police that he'd lied about how he'd learned about the murder. He told us that hadn't happened, that the police had just made that up.

After our interview, the four of us exchanged our impressions. We all agreed Becker was being somewhat less than honest with us.

We then drove to the small town where the crime took place and looked at the scene. Obviously, the house containing the murder scene was locked and sealed, but we hadn't expected to get to see it. Mainly we just wanted to fix the general area in our heads, to become familiar with the situation. We took a few site photographs and quickly sketched the area. Afterward, we drove around the town to locate the other significant locations—the bar Becker said he walked to, the convenience store where he considered buying beer, the house of his brother Weldon and the field where the two practiced with their bows.

It was only then that we decided on the course of the investigation. I say *we* decided; that's inaccurate. The lawyers decided. They were, after all, the ones who were going to take the case into the courtroom. More importantly, they were the ones who cut the checks that paid us.

We investigators disagreed with the lawyers on the course of the investigation. We felt the obvious place to start was with the ponytailed man who had been seen toting a bow in the weeks preceding the murder. After all, of the witnesses (the two young boys) who claimed to have seen a man carrying a bow from Becker's apartment building toward the murder scene, one had stated the man had a ponytail. Our client had short hair. From the police reports we even knew the name of one person who had long hair in a ponytail, a full beard *and* a bow: Weldon Becker, the defendant's brother.

The lawyers, however, wanted to take a more routine approach: Reinterview all the people who had spoken to the police, and confirm as much as possible of the statement Becker gave to the police.

The Dull Routine and a Few Nasty Rumors

My assignment was to trace Becker's movements beginning from the moment he went to work on Friday, the day of the murder, until the time he joined the crowd of onlookers outside the murder scene on Saturday afternoon. Sanders was assigned to begin reinterviewing all the witnesses (except, of course, those who were part of Becker's alibi; they fell under my assignment).

I discovered what time Becker had gone to work that morning (0645), who drove him to work (his brother Theo—they both worked as lumberers for the same company), what he did that day at work (cut down trees on a tract of land north of Riverton), what time he left work (1240) and what time he arrived home (1305). I talked to Becker's foreman, who said he hadn't noticed any unusual behavior on the part of Becker on the day of the murder. I also had him describe Becker's appearance on that day (in case he'd cut his hair since the murder): mustache and short hair. I spoke to Eddie Barton, who gave Becker a lift from his apartment to the Ford dealership in nearby Rochester. Barton said he hadn't noticed any unusual behavior by Becker, although he had seemed excited about the prospect of buying a pickup. I made an unannounced visit to the dealership and talked to the woman who had discussed the truck with Becker. She had nothing to compare his behavior to (since she'd never met Becker before), but she didn't observe any unusual behavior or moodiness on his part. I spoke with Harris and Deanna Priest, the couple with whom Becker had spent part of the evening prior to Cartman's murder. They reported Becker had been cheerful, happy and enthusiastic about buying the pickup. He had bought a case of Michelob, and they had spent the next few hours drinking beer and playing video games at the Priest house.

I spent several days doing all that, and I learned absolutely nothing new, except for a few wild rumors about Cartman. Harris Priest, who also knew Cartman, had mentioned he didn't like Cartman being around his children. He stated he'd heard rumors that Cartman had been in trouble for molesting young men and boys, that it was a taste he'd developed in prison. I made a note that we needed to look into Cartman's prison career.

A Waste of Good Detective Work

I also discovered a time discrepancy. Becker had told us and the police he'd left his apartment shortly before 2300 in order to avoid the arrival of his girlfriend's mother who, we were told, worked the second shift (3 to 11 P.M.) at a shoe factory. Sylvia Lawrence, however, had told the police that she'd called her mother shortly after 2100 and that she arrived shortly thereafter, at which time Becker was already gone. A two-hour discrepancy.

I interviewed Lawrence's mother, Twyla. The first thing I discovered was that the second shift at the factory did not run from 3 to 11, but from 4 to 12. Twyla's shift did not end until midnight. She said she'd left work when her shift ended and went directly to pick up her daughter, arriving there at approximately 0020 hours. Becker wasn't there when she arrived, but Twyla stated that wasn't unusual; he usually left on those occasions when she would come pick up Sylvia after an argument. Becker and Sylvia often fought over his drinking, Twyla said, and it was not uncommon for Sylvia to spend the night with her. I had her sign a form authorizing me to get a copy of her time card.

I then went to the personnel department of the shoe factory to get the copy of the time card. Despite the signed authorization, the secretary refused to give me a copy, as did her supervisor. I had to talk my way to the head of the personnel department in order to actually get the copy of Twyla's time card. The time clock used by the factory was graduated in six-minute increments based on a twenty-four-hour clock. For example, a notation of 15.1 would indicate a single six-minute increment after 1500; that is, 3:06 P.M. A notation of 15.5 would indicate five six-minute increments—3:30 P.M. On the night of the murder, Twyla's time card read 0.1, or 0006 hours (12:06 A.M.).

Lawrence had told the police she'd gone into the bedroom after her fight with Becker and lain down. When I spoke to her she admitted she'd fallen asleep while in the bedroom. When her mother arrived, Lawrence assumed she'd only been asleep for a moment. In fact, she'd slept for approximately three hours.

While this cleared up a discrepancy and made me feel like a detective, it did not help Becker. It was, in fact, a tremendous waste of time. There was still nobody to confirm what time Becker had left the apartment.

I checked both the bar where Becker said he'd gone to buy a beer (he'd reported the bar was closed when he arrived) and the convenience store where he'd considered buying a six-pack of beer. The bar, Catton's Place, was a well-known "bucket of blood" joint, a bar for serious drinkers whose primary interest was in getting drunk quick and staying that way. Catton's Place was the scene of frequent assaults and attempted murder cases. Only a few weeks before, patrons had become angry when "last call" was announced; they'd left the bar and set fire to three cars parked outside.

I spoke with the owner/manager of Catton's Place. He told me that the bar had been closing at 2300 hours since the incident with the burned cars. He was certain the bar had closed around that time on the night of the murder. That was consistent with Becker's alibi.

Becker had also said he'd considered buying more beer at the convenience store, implying that the store was open. In fact, I discovered the convenience store had also closed at 2300 on the night of the murder. Had Becker actually attempted to enter the store he'd have known that. However, the store manager stated the store's interior and exterior lights are kept on all night for security purposes; from a distance, it *appeared* to be open.

Later I asked Becker whether he'd actually gone into the convenience store. He stated he hadn't, that he'd only looked at it from across the street. He also admitted his decision not to enter the store had nothing to do with any concern about disappointing his girlfriend (although that was what he'd told the police). He said the real reason he didn't go into the convenience store was because he realized he didn't have enough money to buy a six-pack. He appeared surprised when I told him the store wasn't open. He said he'd simply assumed it was open.

The Defense Gets a Break

Sanders, in the meantime, had completed his assignment with similar results. By and large, the interviews as they appeared in the police reports were accurate. There were a few minor discrepancies, but nothing that affected the case.

He did, however, make the first truly important contribution to the defense. He discovered the source of the kick marks on the kitchen door at Cartman's house. The police appeared to suspect that the murderer had kicked the door open before shooting Cartman full of arrows. In fact, the kick marks were several months old. One of Cartman's drinking buddies, a man named Billy Nantes, had become rowdy during a heavy drinking session. He had punched holes in the plaster walls (and, in fact, photos of the crime scene showed unpainted, recently plastered spots on the kitchen walls) and kicked the door. Sanders interviewed Nantes, who admitted the incident. He also stated Cartman had called the police that night and had been arrested by Officer Green (one of the officers involved in the Cartman murder investigation). Sanders checked with the police and confirmed that about four months prior to the murder at the Cartman house, Officer Green had, in fact, arrested Nantes for disorderly conduct.

It wasn't much, but it was the first nick in the state's case.

After completing my assignment, I began to help Sanders in the chore of reinterviewing the police witnesses. We agreed three of the witnesses would be the most interesting: the two boys who saw somebody with a bow on the night of the murder and Weldon Becker. We both wanted to conduct those interviews; we compromised and agreed to do them together.

We first interviewed Gary Lyon, who elaborated on what he'd told the police. He and his friend John Deiter had gone to visit John's sister on the night of the murder. As they approached the building the sister lived in, they met a man carrying a compound bow (with arrows in a quiver attached to the bow). The man had long hair pulled into a ponytail that hung down onto his shoulders. He was wearing a dark pullover shirt—heavier than a T-shirt, but not as heavy as a sweatshirt. He didn't notice whether the man was carrying a beer bottle, but as they walked away from each other Lyon did hear a bottle drop and break. He told us that John seemed to know the man and that John greeted him and the man mumbled something back. The next morning Lyon was sitting with John on a porch when John pointed out a man getting out of an orange car. John told him that was the man they'd seen the night before. The man was wearing a lightweight blue windbreaker, faded jeans and cowboy boots.

The Police Witnesses Falter

Next we interviewed John Deiter. The first thing we discovered was that John was a wee bit slow for his thirteen years. He was a sullen and surly boy, alternating between cranky confusion and insolence. Even though it had been only a month since the murder, John seemed uncertain about what he'd seen. He stated that on the night of the murder he and Gary Lyon had gone to his sister's apartment and met a man carrying a bow and a bottle of beer. The man had the bow in his right hand and the beer in his left. He couldn't provide a description of the man, couldn't say whether the man was wearing a jacket or not, whether he wore a long-sleeve shirt or a short-sleeve shirt, whether he wore boots or sneakers, even whether or not the man wore a hat. Nor could John recall pointing out the man to his friend Gary the following morning. He did recall speaking to the man and that the man muttered something in response, though he couldn't remember what either of them said.

I contacted the school John attended and requested information regarding his intellectual status, his grades and any IQ test results. The administration correctly refused to discuss any of this without the permission of John's parents (I hadn't really expected to get the information that easily, but it never hurts to try). Since John was such an important witness, however, the attorneys were able to get a court to order a psychological and intellectual evaluation. After being given a battery of tests, John was found to have a full-scale IQ of 67. The psychologist who conducted the evaluation reported that in order for John to retain any information it had to be repeated frequently. In addition, John's memory deteriorated rapidly. The psychologist thought it unlikely John's current memory of the incident was reliable, that his memory of the incident the morning after would be suspect, but that his memory of the incident immediately after it happened would probably be fairly reliable. However, the psychologist also noted that John's ability to retain visual and auditory information was faulty, and in testing he was unable to accurately describe items even a few minutes after being shown them.

In essence this meant John was an unreliable witness.[2] The statements he made to the police the day following the murder were suspect. The most accurate information he could offer would have been the comments he made to the people that night at his sister's apartment.

Sanders and I decided we had to curb our desire to interview Weldon Becker and instead to reinterview Carol Washburn, Ellen Bujold and Jack DeWitt—John Deiter's sister and the friends who were playing cards with her on the night of the murder. We began with Washburn and immediately discovered a fact either overlooked or omitted by the police. All three adults in Washburn's apartment were drunk by the time John Deiter and Gary Lyon arrived. Washburn admitted they'd been drinking all afternoon and evening; they had finished off two cases of beer and were deep into a bottle of peppermint schnapps by the time the boys arrived. She was uncertain exactly what John had told her on that night. She knew it involved a man and a bow and a bottle of beer; she knew her baby brother had apparently seen the man who killed Will Cartman. But she wasn't sure if she could distinguish between what John had told her that night and what she'd heard from others over the next few days. Washburn admitted she hadn't even recalled the incident the first time she'd talked to the police. Somebody else, she told us, must have sparked her memory.

As witnesses, Ellen Bujold and Jack DeWitt weren't much better. Both admitted they had been drinking heavily the night of the murder. Both admitted they didn't pay much attention to John when he talked about seeing the man. They could not recall in any detail what they had told the police. When shown his police statement, DeWitt was surprised to discover he had reported to the police that John had said the man said he felt like killing somebody that night. DeWitt admitted he may have said that to the police but couldn't recall it, nor could he recall John saying it. Both DeWitt and Bujold, however, were convinced John Deiter and Gary Lyon had seen Cartman's murderer that night.

---

[2]John Deiter was later interviewed by several more police detectives, by a pair of lawyers from the Attorney General's Office and by a psychologist hired by the prosecution. By the time the matter came to trial, he was suffering from insomnia, acting out in school and reporting bouts of depression.

The Defense Investigation Narrows Focus

Finally Sanders and I could turn our attention to Weldon Becker. Although the law only requires the defense to establish reasonable doubt in order to win an acquittal, juries usually feel unsatisfied unless the defense can point the finger toward somebody else. If the defendant didn't do it, they ask themselves, who did? If possible, the defense team likes to have one or more people it can point to as potential suspects. We usually referred to those people as The Real Killers, even if the case didn't involve any killing at all. It's a concept stolen from television, where the defense always finds The Real Killer.

Sanders and I knew Weldon was almost made to order for the part of The Real Killer (the lawyers knew it as well, but probably felt it would be unprofessional to admit it so soon). Weldon matched the majority of the descriptions given to the police of a man carrying a bow. We also knew Weldon had been in prison with Cartman (although we didn't yet know why Weldon had been incarcerated). And we knew that a lot of townspeople were uneasy about Weldon. From what we'd heard, Weldon apparently saw himself as a mountain man, a modern-day Jeremiah Johnson in New England, a loner who lived in town only to please his wife.

The only problem with marking Weldon Becker as The Real Killer was that he was Martin Becker's brother. Pointing the finger at our client's brother would probably not endear us to the client. That, we figured, was the reason the lawyers were being so cautious. Since Sanders and I had less contact with Becker, we could afford to jump the gun a bit.

We went to Weldon's small house one evening at about 2000 hours. We didn't announce we were coming; we just showed up and knocked on the door. Weldon's wife answered the door, and after we identified ourselves as working for her brother-in-law, she invited us in. Weldon was in the living room watching television. A .50 caliber muzzle-loading rifle was propped in the corner of the room. Although we knew Weldon had at least two children (and we saw a few toys in the kitchen), there was no sound of children playing in the house. I had the feeling Weldon didn't like to be disturbed when he was watching television.

Weldon Becker looked the part of a mountain man—tall, wiry, a full bristly beard and long hair. His hair was untied and hung down onto his shoulders. He was an imposing figure, and I was glad I hadn't gone to his house alone. He didn't invite us to sit, but he did turn off the sound on the television. He let us know he very much did not want the interview tape-recorded. In fact, he told us he didn't want to talk to us at all, that he didn't know anything about anything. We attempted to ask him a few questions, to which he responded primarily with single-word responses, a nod or shake of the head or sometimes just a grunt. We learned that he had owned a bow but had recently traded it, although he didn't say what he had traded it for. When asked how he got along with Cartman, Weldon simply shrugged. After a few minutes he said, "That's it. No more questions." So we left.

In the car outside, Sanders and I agreed Weldon Becker was one of the scariest people we'd seen in recent memory. We decided he was not only perfect to be portrayed as The Real Killer, but he might, in fact, actually *be* the real killer. We determined we should look more closely at Weldon, although preferably from a distance.

Twice during this period we discovered small notices in the area newspapers (most of which were little more than weekly shoppers—small newspapers that printed notices and advertisements for local businesses) stating a bow had been found. Both times I tracked down the person who had found the bow, examined it (mostly for show; unlike guns, there is no way to determine if a particular bow fired a particular arrow) and suggested the person notify the police detectives investigating the Cartman murder. Both times the police responded. Both times they seized the bows, labeled them as evidence and dutifully sent them to the crime lab. It was a small thing but we thought it might be useful at trial, reinforcing the fact that the police had not found the murder weapon. However, it also served to irritate the police detectives, who were still searching for Martin Becker's bow and attempting to shore up the weak parts of their case.

Some Surprising Discoveries

After talking to the lawyers about Weldon Becker, Sanders and I were turned loose to investigate him. We began by looking at his criminal history. We discovered he had been incarcerated twice, once as a juvenile and once as an adult. Although his juvenile records were sealed, we were able to discover the incarceration was a result of an arson. When he was sixteen Weldon had become angry at a man named Garson Cannady, who was dating Weldon's mother. He set fire to Cannady's garage. He did eight months in a juvenile detention facility.

Weldon's adult conviction was more serious. When he was seventeen years old, Weldon had become angry at another man who was dating his mother—Walter Brody. Weldon stabbed Brody between thirty-five and forty times with an army surplus bayonet. He was tried as an adult, convicted and received a sentence of fifteen to thirty years. He served a dozen years of the sentence and was released. He still had another ten years of parole to fulfill.

The parallels between the three cases were eerie. Cannady had been dating the mother, as had Brody. Although Cartman wasn't dating Mrs. Becker at the moment, they had lived together shortly after he was released from prison—a period when Weldon was still incarcerated and unable to do anything about it. Both of the previous crimes were premeditated but relatively unplanned. In other words, the intent to cause harm was there but the crimes themselves were impulsive. The Cartman murder appeared to have been committed in the same way. The victims of all three crimes were active alcoholics (which may have only been a reflection on the types of men Mrs. Becker dated). In all three cases the crimes were committed in the victims' homes. All three crimes were committed in the dead of night.

While there were similarities, there was one important inconsistency: In the first two cases, Weldon had been drunk when he committed the crimes. There was no indication that Weldon had been drinking on the night Cartman was murdered. In fact, most of the people we spoke to told us Weldon rarely drank, partly due to the fact that he had difficulty controlling his temper when he was drunk and partly because alcohol hurt his throat. Weldon had suffered some sort of throat injury while he was in prison.

We needed to try to ascertain if Weldon had been drinking on the night of the murder. That meant speaking once again to his neighbors. It meant canvassing the nearby convenience stores, markets and bars to see if anybody could remember him buying alcohol.

In order to do that effectively, we needed a photograph of Weldon. Rather than ask his family for a photo, thereby alerting them we were focusing on Weldon, we decided to just take one. His home was not in a good area for conducting a surveillance; there were only a few houses in the hilly neighborhood and no place to park inconspicuously. So I decided to get a photograph of him at work. Like his brothers, Weldon Becker did lumber work. All I needed to do was show up at his work site and expose a half-dozen frames of film—maybe ten seconds total. The difficulty was in finding the work site; these folks often worked out in the woods, several hundred yards off the road, if you could call the unmarked, narrow dirt tracks that wandered through the woods roads.

I spent two or three hours driving around lost and confused in the woods trying to find the work site, and another couple of hours trying to find my way back to civilization, but in between I spent thirty or forty seconds shooting a twenty-four-exposure roll of Tri-X black-and-white film. With a 300mm lens, I didn't have to get anywhere near Weldon or the other workers. They never knew I was there. Wherever "there" was.

Zeroing In On Our Prime Suspect

While I took photographs and began to check the local stores and bars in Riverton, Sanders began to look into the prison histories of both Weldon Becker and Cartman. He discovered Cartman had been a member of a prison gang called the DieHards. The gang had become extinct; the members were either dead or had been released. But there had been a time when they were a force to be reckoned with inside the prison walls. Cartman had apparently made a number of enemies while in prison. On two different occasions his cell was torched—Molotov cocktails tossed into the cell, setting everything on fire. Cartman hadn't been in his cell on either occasion.

In contrast, Weldon had almost been a model prisoner. He kept to himself, he tended not to bother anybody. He did his time quietly and with a minimal amount of fuss. However, he appeared to have angered at least one person during his twelve years in prison. Somebody apparently put some caustic solution in Weldon's food. As a result, Weldon's esophagus was damaged. His diet was limited to soft foods, such as eggs, jello, mashed potatoes and rice. An internal investigation did not reach any conclusions, but among the people suspected of having put the corrosive liquid in Weldon's food was Will Cartman.

In the meantime, I found a convenience store clerk who recognized Weldon's photograph. She recalled him in part because she was somewhat familiar with most of the people who used the small store. She'd never seen Weldon before and, as noted earlier, he is a rather intimidating figure. She couldn't say with any certainty when he was in the store, but she knew it had to be either a Friday or Saturday night. Those were the only nights she worked; her other shifts were day shifts. The clerk said Weldon had bought either a six-pack or a case of beer.

We kept the lawyers apprised of these developments. They agreed that not only could we mold Weldon Becker as The Real Killer, he might actually have murdered Cartman. They'd been busy writing motions (trying to limit the evidence, trying to confine testimony to certain topics, trying to get access to Weldon's juvenile records without alerting the prosecution) and generally churning out huge quantities of extremely clever paperwork, all of it designed to tie the prosecution into tight little knots. They were also arranging a bail hearing for Becker. His mother had agreed to put up her house and a bit of property as surety for his appearance in court.

It was the lawyers who recalled that Martin Becker, after his talk with the police on the night after the murder had been discovered, had told the police he wanted a lawyer because he'd lied about how he learned of the murder. They suggested Weldon may have killed Cartman and then told Becker. Or perhaps Weldon had even told Becker before the fact. The question the lawyers had was this: Assuming Weldon had done the murder and Becker knew about it, would Becker be willing to turn in his own brother?

A Brief Sidetrack

The lawyers felt we had enough information on Weldon for the time being (we'd be asked to get more later, they assured us). They wanted us to turn our attention to another troublesome detail: Martin Becker's bow. He continued to insist he'd sold the bow to one John LNU in a bar called Mike's Tavern in nearby Rochester. The police had investigated this, but obviously they weren't eager to find positive results. Their case would suffer if they actually found John LNU; it would show Becker didn't own a bow at the time of the murder. This isn't to suggest that the police investigators were intentionally booting that aspect of their investigation, just that their hearts weren't really in it.

The only information Becker could give us that the police lacked was that John LNU drove a small, blue pickup truck. Becker thought the truck also had either a gun rack or a fishing pole rack in the back window. It wasn't much help, but every little bit of information is important in that sort of needle-in-a-haystack search.

Sanders had good connections with the Department of Motor Vehicles (DMV), so he undertook the formidable, if dull, task of getting a list of all the people named John who owned small, blue pickups in Rochester and the surrounding towns. I began to interview the staff and regular customers of Mike's Tavern, trying to see if anybody knew anybody name John who fit the vague description provided by Becker. Basically, for a week or so I spent my afternoons and evenings sitting in the bar, talking to folks. It's not as much fun as it sounds.

The Accused Speaks Out

While this was going on I got a telephone call from Becker. He had something he wanted to talk about in person. Usually that means the client is getting a bit stir-crazy and wants to hear words of encouragement from a somewhat sympathetic face—preferably one who will also bring a couple packs of cigarettes. I picked up some unfiltered Camels (a tough guy's smoke, popular in jails and prisons) and went to the jail.

Becker, however, really wanted to talk about something (of course, he still took the cigarettes). We met in one of the small attorney-client interview rooms. Becker said he was desperate to get out of jail and was willing to do whatever it took to get out on bail (he was apparently unaware that his mother had agreed to put up her house as surety for his bond). I asked him if he was willing to reveal the name of the person who actually killed Cartman. He hesitated. I wrote the name Weldon on a piece of paper and showed it to him. Becker nodded and said, "That's right."

According to Becker, Weldon had come to Becker's apartment while he was watching the boxing match on television (approximately 2245 hours). Sylvia Lawrence was asleep in the bedroom. He stated Weldon had his bow with him. He was moderately drunk and claimed he'd just killed Cartman. Becker said he didn't believe his brother at first, but finally accepted it after Weldon continued to insist. Weldon asked for a beer, and Becker gave him one. Weldon left Becker's apartment on foot shortly before 2300 (apparently just in time to meet John Deiter and Gary Lyon). Becker said he stayed in his apartment for a few minutes, then left—he wanted to think about what Weldon had said and he wanted to avoid his girlfriend's mother, whom he expected to arrive at any moment (under the mistaken impression she got off work at 2300). From that point on, Becker said, his story was just as he'd told the police and us: He'd walked to Catton's Place, which was closed, and then to the convenience store, where he realized he didn't have the money to buy a six-pack of beer.

I asked if he'd gone to Cartman's house to check on Weldon's story. Becker hesitated, then said he hadn't. I suspected (and continue to suspect) he was lying. I also asked if he had, in fact, sold his bow to John LNU. He said that with the exception of denying any knowledge of the murder, everything he'd told us had been the truth.

Most important (to me, at any rate), Becker informed me that his brother Theo had been to visit him a week or so earlier. Theo had told him that Weldon was aware we were asking questions about him and was concerned we were going to try to pin the murder on him. Becker told me Sanders and I should be cautious around Weldon, that he had a volatile temper.

I reported all this immediately to the lawyers and Sanders, of course. We had an emergency strategy session, out of which came the following plan. Sanders and I would finish our attempt to locate John LNU then turn our attention back to Weldon Becker. The lawyers told us we were not to go to Riverton alone, and that when we went to Riverton one of us should be armed. The question that remained unresolved was what the lawyers should do with Becker's admission. Should they save it for trial? Or reveal it to the prosecutors in the hope they would dismiss the charge against Becker and file one against Weldon. That decision, we decided, could wait. In the meantime, we would continue our investigation.

Cleaning Up Loose Ends

I spent a few more days in the bar, then gave it up. I'd met several people named John. I'd met a few who owned blue pickup trucks. But I met nobody who had bought a bow, not from Becker or anybody else.

Sanders had been cold-calling the names on his DMV list of Johns with small blue pickups, and having the same luck I'd had. While he did that, I began to look for a way to tie Weldon to the broadhead arrow tips. I recalled Officer Consodine had located a UPS driver who remembered delivering a package from an archery company to Weldon. I tracked down the UPS man, but he couldn't recall the name of the archery company, nor was he certain of the size or shape of the box he delivered. So I started to call as many sporting goods and hunting supply stores as I could, trying to see if Weldon had bought any broadhead hunting tips for his arrows. The police hadn't had any luck linking Becker to the broadheads; I also had no luck linking his brother to them.

A week or so later Becker had his bail hearing. Over the strenuous objections of the prosecutors, Martin Becker was released on bail—on the condition that he reside with his mother in the nearby town of Rochester until the trial. The trial was scheduled to begin in about ten weeks (because of the freakish nature of the murder—nobody could recall a bow-and-arrow murder in the history of the state—it had attracted a great deal of attention from the media; everybody wanted the trial to begin as soon as possible).

Failing to find John LNU, Sanders and I turned our attention back to Weldon. We began by reinterviewing the people who had occasionally seen a ponytailed and bearded man walking and carrying a bow in the vicinity of Cartman's house. We showed them the photographs I'd taken of Weldon. Most said that it was the same man. Those who couldn't say with certainty that the man they saw was the man in the photographs agreed there was a strong resemblance between the two.

Throughout our investigation we had occasionally encountered witnesses who reported hearing other folks threaten Will Cartman. We reported each of these to the lawyers, who in turn reported the threats to the police. Any response the police detectives made to these reports would work in favor of the defense. If they investigated each of the reported threats it would tie up police resources that otherwise might have been devoted to trying to link Becker to the murder (or, just as important, police resources devoted to discovering the nature of *our* investigation). If they failed to investigate the reported threats, the lawyers could attack the detectives during the trial for not being thorough.

Complications

Around this time, two critical events took place. The first was the discovery that Weldon had gotten rid of his bow. He had apparently traded the bow and his arrows for some trapping equipment. The second, and most alarming, development was that Sanders received information that Weldon had acquired, or was planning to acquire, a modern hunting rifle (in addition to the antique muzzle loader he already owned).

The lawyers, sparked in part by the news that Weldon may have procured a more lethal weapon, decided the investigation of Weldon was becoming too risky. With Becker's permission, they decided to take our information to the prosecutors and lay out the case against Weldon. The hope was that the charge against Becker would be dismissed. Although they felt we had plenty of ammunition for a jury trial, all lawyers know that juries sometimes behave oddly. There was always a chance, even if we could somehow put Weldon on the stand and get him to confess in public, that a jury would still find Becker guilty. A trial should be avoided if possible.

It was a calculated risk, of course. It meant revealing the nature of the defense to the prosecution prior to the trial. If the prosecution refused to drop the charges, it left us in a vulnerable position (actually, it left Becker in a vulnerable position—he'd be the one going to prison for the rest of his life; we'd just be going to a bar to commiserate our loss). Still, it seemed a safe gamble. We thought the case we'd built against Weldon was as strong as, or stronger than, the case the police had built against Becker.

Unfortunately, the prosecution didn't agree. They refused to dismiss the case against Martin Becker. Nor would they initiate an investigation against Weldon Becker. We knew, however, that the police detectives would now begin to do exactly what defense investigators normally do—try to find the weaknesses of our case and rip it apart.

So our investigation of Weldon resumed, made more difficult by the fact that the police would be dogging our movements, by the fact that the trial date was rapidly approaching, by the fact that Weldon was aware we were pointing the finger at him and by the fact that Weldon might now be armed (and had shown no reluctance to kill people in the past). These are not ideal conditions under which to conduct an investigation.

The Murder Weapon

We'd spent enough time in the small town of Riverton by that point that we had a number of contacts in the community. It was relatively easy to discover the name of the person with whom Weldon had swapped his bow for trapping equipment (muskrat and beaver traps, to be specific). He was a distant cousin of the Becker family, a man named Mark Wingate.

Wingate lived in the country, on a road known to the locals as Purdy's Road. The name, of course, didn't appear on any map. It took me most of a day to find the road and Wingate's mobile home. Since Wingate didn't live in Riverton, I made the trip alone. Wingate told me he had, in fact, traded some traps to Weldon in exchange for his bow and half a dozen arrows. They had made the trade a couple of weeks after the murder. He showed me the bow—a mottled green compound bow with an attached quiver. The arrows had aluminum shafts, though not the same color as the two arrows recovered from Cartman's body, and field tips rather than broadheads.

I took the bow and arrows. I gave Wingate a handwritten receipt for them. I had no legal right to seize the bow and arrows, but Wingate never questioned it, and it seemed it might be important to have possession of the murder weapon.

The lawyers were delighted that I had found the bow and taken possession of it. At the same time, however, they were alarmed by the fact. Wingate would almost certainly tell Weldon I had taken the bow. It was the most clear indication to date that we were planning to pin the murder on Weldon. And nobody was quite sure how Weldon would react.

The bow posed a more immediate problem. I kept an evidence locker—a heavy filing cabinet with a lock and a security bar—at my office. It was perfectly adequate for those rare occasions I needed to keep evidence, but it was far too small to contain a bow. I was forced to take the bow home and keep it in a locked closet. I was extremely uncomfortable with the idea of having evidence in my home, but there was nothing else to do.

More Facts About the Killer

In the meantime, Sanders had learned of another incident in which Weldon Becker had allegedly become drunk and attacked a man. Sanders had received the tip from an anonymous telephone caller. The caller had refused to identify himself, saying he didn't want Weldon to find out. The assault, Sanders was told, had taken place not long after Weldon was released from prison. Weldon had been working for a lumbering crew, clearing land for developers. On a Friday afternoon the crew knocked off early and began drinking at the lumber site. One of the crew had apparently made a comment that angered Weldon, who first hit and kicked the man, then grabbed an axe and chased after the man. According to the anonymous caller, the only person who was able to stop Weldon was his brother Theo.

Sanders contacted Weldon's parole officer. Somehow he managed to convince the PO to provide the name of the foreman of the lumber company for whom Weldon worked. Sanders then got in touch with the foreman. The foreman stated he didn't allow people to drink at a work site, so the incident could never have happened. He refused to discuss the matter any further and also refused to give Sanders the names of other workers on the crew.

Together Sanders and I went to Riverton to talk to Theo Becker about the incident. Theo also refused to answer any of our questions, saying he didn't want to get in the middle of a dispute between his two brothers. But while he wouldn't confirm the story, he also did not deny it. We spent two more days tracking down and trying to talk to people who worked for that lumber company. We were never able to confirm the story.

As the trial date approached, all the investigators in the case—the police detectives as well as Sanders and I—began to make the rounds of witnesses once again. For some of the more critical witnesses, this was the fifth or sixth time they had been interviewed. We went over their statements one more time and served subpoenas on the witnesses who were expected to testify.

We waited until the last moment to serve Weldon with a subpoena. There was no point in provoking him any more than necessary. As it was, the defense lawyers were concerned about the rumors that Weldon had acquired a rifle. They thought it was possible that Weldon might try to eliminate his brother, Martin. They were concerned enough that, once jury selection started, I was required to pick up Becker at his door (actually, his mother's door) every morning and escort him to court. At the end of the day, I returned him to his door. Literally, right to the door. I drove up on the lawn, stopped the car as near as possible to the door, rushed Becker from the car into the house, then drove off as quickly as possible. It played hell on Becker's nerves. And mine as well.

The Trial

The trial, from jury selection to verdict, took three weeks. During the opening statement for the defense, the lawyers named Weldon Becker as the real killer. Although the prosecution did the best they could with the evidence, the defense lawyers had all the dramatic moments. By accusing Weldon in the opening statement, the defense lawyers ensured everything the jury heard from the prosecution was evaluated in terms of whether or not it pointed to Weldon. As much as the prosecution tried to keep the focus on Martin Becker, the jury seemed to be waiting for the moment when Weldon would appear in court.

The high point for the prosecution was to be the testimony of Detective Russell. As the primary investigator, his job was to provide testimony linking all the evidentiary strands the police had accumulated pointing to Martin Becker. On the morning he was to testify, the defense lawyers brought in Weldon's bow— the one I had collected from Mark Wingate. They didn't mention the bow, just laid it on the defense table. The jury, instead of paying close attention to Russell's testimony, kept looking at the bow, wondering about it. During cross-examination, one of the defense lawyers got Russell to admit that the bow looked like the one he and two other officers had seen at Weldon's house on the first night of the investigation. He also got Russell to admit the police didn't search Weldon's house for arrows with broadhead tips. Finally, Russell admitted his investigators' failure to find any bow at the defendant's house, nor any arrows—just a few practice tips.

The defense lawyers did a brilliant job of picking away at the prosecution's case, all the while keeping the jury looking more at Weldon Becker than at the man on trial. Only one problem occurred during the prosecution's case. In his statement to the police Becker had claimed that on the night of the murder he had watched a boxing match on television and then later watched an adult movie. I had taken the easiest route to confirm that those programs had aired; I'd consulted the local newspaper's television listings and an issue of *TV Guide*. There were other areas that seemed to demand more investigative time. This demonstrates the advantages of the massive manpower the police can devote to an investigation. They had contacted the network that ran the boxing match and the Canadian cable channel that ran the adult movie. The boxing match had taken place just as Becker had said. The adult movie, however, had been preempted at the last moment by a hockey match. Martin Becker had been caught in a lie.

It was a small lie, but since the momentum of the trial had been controlled almost totally by the defense up to that point, it appeared to be significant. Becker had lied to the police about what he had done at the approximate time of the murder. And the jury knew it.

This damaging bit of evidence was introduced near the end of the prosecution's case. When the defense attorneys began to present their case, they slowly shifted the jury's attention back to Weldon. First they put on witnesses to refute the most important aspects of the prosecution's case against Martin Becker, then they put on witnesses that returned the focus back to Weldon. Then they called Weldon himself to the witness stand.

Extra security precautions had been taken and extra bailiffs were in the courtroom and in the hall outside. Everybody, including the police, saw Weldon, whether he had killed Cartman or not, as a real threat. I understand it was a dramatic day of testimony (as a potential witness I was not allowed to watch the trial). The defense lawyers led Weldon through his early days of spontaneous violence before accusing him of murdering Cartman. Weldon, of course, denied killing Cartman. The defense lawyers pointed out Weldon had also denied setting fire to Garson Cannady's garage and had denied stabbing Walter Brody to death with a bayonet.

On the final day of the trial, Martin Becker took the stand in his own defense. He told his story once again, this time admitting he had lied to the police about three things: He lied about watching the adult movie; he lied about how he learned of Cartman's murder; and he lied when he told the police he knew nothing about the crime.

The jury was only out for two hours. They returned a verdict of not guilty.

Just the Facts, Ma'am?

Exactly what happened on the night Will Cartman was murdered? I don't really know. I suspect it happened largely the way Becker said it did. I suspect Weldon began to drink and found himself brooding over the perceived wrongs Cartman had done to Weldon and to his family. I don't know if he went into town with the intent to kill Cartman (assuming he actually did). But I think he found himself drawn to the light in Cartman's kitchen, to the open kitchen door. And I think he put two arrows into Cartman's chest. I suspect Weldon then went to Martin Becker's apartment and told him what happened. Despite his denial, I believe Martin Becker probably went to Cartman's house—either with Weldon or alone, after Weldon left the apartment—and looked at the body. I think it's unlikely, although entirely possible, that Becker actually helped Weldon kill Cartman. Given the angle of the arrows, it's possible that two bowmen fired at Cartman at approximately the same time.

The fact is, I just don't know the answers. And I'd spent much more time with Martin Becker and the facts of the case than the jury did.

In any event, Martin Becker walked out of court a free man. The police, however, kept a close eye on him—almost, but not quite, to the point of harassment. A couple years later Becker was arrested on a drug charge (which seemed suspicious, since I'd never heard of him being involved with drugs). He was convicted and received a sentence of five years.

Weldon Becker was never formally charged with the murder of Will Cartman. The last I heard of Weldon he was cutting lumber in the summer and trapping in the winter—and staying sober. I won't be surprised if I hear his name in the news again someday.

Bibliography

Ackroyd, James E. 1974. *The Investigator: A Practical Guide to Private Detection*. London. Muller.

Akin, Richard H. 1976. *The Private Investigator's Basic Manual*. Springfield, Illinois. Thomas.

Alpert, Geoffrey P. and Roger G. Dunham. 1988. *Policing Urban America*. Prospect Heights, Illinois. Waveland Press Inc.

Barefoot, J. Kirk. 1995. *Undercover Investigation*. 3rd ed. Boston. Butterworth-Heinemann.

Blackwell, Gene. 1979. *The Private Investigator*. Los Angeles. Security World Publishing Co.

Brady, John. 1977. *The Craft of Interviewing*. New York. Random House.

Brookes, Paul. 1996. *Electronic Surveillance Devices*. Boston. Butterworth-Heinemann.

Brown, Sam and Gini Scott Brown. 1991. *Private Eyes: What Private Investigators Really Do*. Secaucus. Carol Publishing.

Buckwalter, Art. 1983. *Interviews and Interrogations*. Boston. Butterworth-Heinemann.

——— 1983. *Surveillance and Undercover in Investigation*. Boston. Butterworth-Heinemann.

——— 1984. *Search for Evidence*. Boston. Butterworth-Heinemann.

Carroll, John M. 1991. *Confidential Information Sources: Public and Private*. 2nd ed. Boston. Butterworth-Heinemann.

Davies, F. 1974. Relations Between Public Police and Private Security Forces. *Private Policing and Security in Canada: A Workshop*, ed. F. Jeffries. Toronto. University of Toronto.

Fallis, Greg and Ruth Greenberg. 1998. *Be Your Own Detective*. 2nd ed. New York. M. Evans Publishing, Inc.

Fuqua, Paul Q. and Jerry Wilson. 1979. *Security Investigator's Handbook*. Houston. Gulf Publishing Co.

Guarino-Ghezzi, Susan. 1983. A Private Network of Social Control: Insurance Investigation Units. *Social Problems*, Vol 30, No. 5.

Goldfader, Ed. 1970. *Tracer! The Search for Missing Persons.*
Los Angeles. Nash Publishing Co.

Goldsmith, Reginald. 1978. *The Private Detective: The How-
to Book on Becoming a Private Dectective and Owning Your
Own Agency.* Atlanta. Gemini Pub. Co.

Greene, Marilyn and Gary Provost. 1988. *Finder: The True
Story of a Private Investigator.* New York. Crown
Publishing.

Holt, Patricia. 1994. *The Good Detective: True Cases From
the Confidential Files of Hal Lipset, America's Most
Controversial Private Eye.* New York. Pocket Books.

Horan, James. 1967. *The Pinkertons: The Detective Dynasty
That Made History.* New York. Crown Publishing.

Hougan, Jim. 1978. *Spooks: The Haunting of America: The
Private Use of Secret Agents.* New York. Morrow.

Inbau, Fred Edward, John E. Reid and Joseph P. Buckley.
1986. *Criminal Interrogation and Confessions.* 3rd ed.
Williams and Wilkins.

Klockars, Carl B. 1991. Blue Lies and Police Placebos: The
Moralities of Police Lying. *Thinking About Police:
Contemporary Readings.* 2nd ed. Ed. Carl Klockars and
Mastrofski. New York. McGraw-Hill, Inc.

Larsen, Tom. 1996. *The Layman's Guide to Electronic
Eavesdropping: How It's Done and Simple Ways to Prevent
It.* Boulder. Paladin Press.

Linowes, David F. 1989. *Privacy in America: Is Your Private
Life in the Public Eye?* Urbana. University of Illinois Press.

Lyon, David. 1994. *The Electronic Eye: The Rise of
Surveillance Society.* Minneapolis. University of Minnesota
Press.

Marx, Gary. 1987. The Interweaving of Public and Private
Police in Undercover Work. *Private Policing*, ed. Clifford
Shearing and Philip Stenning. Newbury Park. Sage
Publications.

——— 1988. *Undercover: Police Surveillance in America.*
University California Press.

Moenssens, Andre A. and Fred E. Inbau. 1986. *Scientific
Evidence in Criminal Cases.* 3rd ed. Foundation Press.

Morn, Frank. 1982. *The Eye That Never Sleeps: A History of the Pinkerton National Detective Agency.* Bloomington. Indiana University Press.

National Institute of Justice; U.S. Department of Justice. 1991. *Forensic Evidence and the Police.* Washington, DC.

Rush, Donald A. and Raymond P. Siljander. 1984. *Fundamentals of Civil and Private Investigation.* Charles C. Thomas Publishing, Ltd.

Siljander, Raymond P. 1977. *Fundamentals of Physical Surveillance: A Guide for Uniformed and Plainclothes Personnel.* Charles C. Thomas Publishing, Ltd.

Stewart, Charles J. and William B. Cash, Jr. 1996. *Interviewing Principles and Practices.* 8th ed. McGraw-Hill.

Thompson, Josiah. 1988. *Gumshoe: Reflections in a Private Eye.* Boston. Little, Brown and Company.

Wingate, Anne. 1992. *Scene of the Crime: A Writer's Guide to Crime Scene Investigation.* Cincinnati. Writer's Digest Books.

Useful Web Sites

Those of you with access to the World Wide Web have a variety of resources available for research. Below are a few URLs (Uniform Resource Locators, the Internet "address") of sites I've found particularly useful. However, these are only a very small sampling of the information available on the Web; any search engine (such as Yahoo or AltaVista) will reveal many more Web sites.

Law Enforcement

The FBI Law Enforcement Bulletin. Published monthly by the Federal Bureau of Investigation. This site contains articles on crime and the law enforcement response to it. An excellent source of information (http://www.fbi.gov/leb/leb.htm).

Police Dispatch Online. The magazine of the NYPD. Contains articles of interest to street cops (http://www.policedispatch.com).

On Patrol Magazine. A quarterly magazine for line officers. The Web site only allows the reader to read a couple articles from each issue . . . but there is still worthwhile information here (http://www.onpatrol.com).

Law Enforcement Internet Intelligence Report. A digest of information pertaining to various aspects of policing (http://www .lawintelrpt.com).

Private Investigation

The PI Mall. A resource for private investigators, including links to equipment marketers and *PI Magazine* (http://www .pimall.com).

Thomas Investigative Publications, Inc. This is a fine resource for basic PI techniques (http://www.pimall.com/nais/home .html).

Legal Research

FindLaw: Internet Legal Resources. This is a valuable resource on civil and criminal law. It allows searches of legal cases by topic, case name and keywords (http://www.findlaw.com/).

USSC+. A resource for U.S. Supreme Court research. All the Court's decisions handed down during the current term and a searchable database of decisions dating back to 1953. Also information on the Court and its justices (http://www.usscplus .com).

Forensics

Crime Scene Training Update: The Online Journal for Crime Scene Investigators. This site includes articles on crime scene investigation, editorials, schedules of upcoming training events (http://members.aol.com/identtec/training.html).

Zeno's Forensic Page. This contains a wealth of information on forensic science, forensic medicine and forensic psychiatry. There are sections on arson, computer crime, DNA/serology, documents, fingerprints, explosives, firearms, toolmarks, shoeprints, tires, locks—any forensic subject you can imagine. It also provides links to other forensic sites (http://users.bart.nl/~geradts/ forensic.html).

Forensic Entomology. The Web site of Stephen W. Bullington, Ph.D., consulting entomologist. This site includes general information about forensic entomology and case studies (http://ourworld.compuserve.com/homepages/SBullington/).

Equipment

Streicher's Police Supply. Everything from the latest price on a Glock 30 to ribbed shirts to wear beneath body armor to

(I'm not making this up) handcuff keys bearing your department's emblem. Excellent resource (http://www.streichers.com).

MicroVideo Products. This site includes prices and photographs of a variety of surveillance equipment, including miniature and pinhole cameras, wireless video systems and night vision equipment (http://www.interlog.com/%7Emicrovid).

SWS Security. Manufacturers of electronic surveillance, intelligence gathering and radio communications systems. This site includes informative articles on information important to private investigators, including electronic surveillance, night vision devices and vehicle tracking system (http://www.swssec.com/index .html).

In-Sight Police Supplier. Offers a catalog of police equipment ranging from speed loaders to flashlights to badges (http://in-sight.policesupplier.com).

Granite Island Group. Specialists in technical surveillance countermeasures. Contains a wealth of information on wiretappling and bugging, including photos of the equipment used to do it (http://www.tscm.com/threatvid.html).

SpyZone. Basic look at the tools and techniques of surveillance (http://www.spyzone.com/CCS1.html).

Miscellaneous

Florida State University School of Criminology. This impressive page, although it doesn't contain any information itself, may be the most comprehensive site for criminology links. Almost any criminal justice topic imaginable can be researched here. The links range from legal databases (both federal and state), to information on various types of crime (organized crime, domestic violence, vice, even ritual satanic crime), to information on policing resources (http://www.criminology.fsu.edu/cj.html).

The WWW Cop Car Registry. This odd little site lists many of the makes and models of vehicles used by state and municipal police agencies. Also describes the markings of many police cruisers. Want to know what the State Police in Utah drive? Or the local police in Troy, New Hampshire or Ankeny, Iowa? Not terribly useful information, but could help a writer add realism to a story (http://www.speedtrap.com/speedtrap/copcars).

Index